DATE DUE

Women's Roles and Statuses the World Over

Women's Roles and Statuses the World Over

Stephanie Hepburn and Rita J. Simon

LEXINGTON BOOKS

A division of
ROWMAN & LITTLEFIELD PUBLISHERS, INC.
Lanham • Boulder • New York • Toronto • Plymouth, UK

LEXINGTON BOOKS

A division of Rowman & Littlefield Publishers, Inc.
A wholly owned subsidiary of The Rowman & Littlefield Publishing Group, Inc.
4501 Forbes Boulevard, Suite 200
Lanham, MD 20706

Estover Road
Plymouth PL6 7PY
United Kingdom

Copyright © 2006 by Lexington Books
First paperback edition 2007

British Library Cataloguing in Publication Information Available

Library of Congress Cataloging-in-Publication Data
The hardback edition of this book was previously cataloged by the Library of Congress as
follows:

Hepburn, Stephanie, 1977–
    Women's roles and statuses the world over / Stephanie Hepburn and Rita J. Simon.
       p. cm.
    ISBN-13: 978-0-7391-1356-9 (cloth : alk. paper)
    ISBN-10: 0-7391-1356-1 (cloth : alk. paper)
    ISBN-13: 978-0-7391-1357-8 (pbk. : alk. paper)
    ISBN-10: 0-7391-1357-7 (pbk. : alk. paper)
    1. Women's rights. 2. Women—history. I. Simon, Rita James. II. Title.
HQ1236.H46 2006
305.4209—dc22   2005027763

Printed in the United States of America
♾™ The paper used in this publication meets the minimum requirements of American
National Standard for Information Sciences—Permanence of Paper for Printed Library
Materials, ANSI/NISO Z39.48–1992.

Contents

v

Preface

Women's Roles and Statuses the World Over is the ninth in a series of volumes that examines a major social phenomenon using an explicitly comparative approach. This volume describes and analyzes the roles and statuses of women from a comparative perspective. We report data and discuss such issues as the demographic characteristics of women (i.e., age distribution, marital status, and fertility rates), literacy and years of schooling, work force participation, inheritance, citizenship, public office, military service, and health care. When appropriate, we provide a brief history of the major legislative and social changes that have occurred in the status of women in each of the societies over the past half-century.

The countries selected for inclusion in this volume represent a range of geographic locations and variations in their political, economical, ethical, racial, and religious orientations, and characteristics. The countries represented are the United States, Canada, Brazil, Chile, Colombia, the United Kingdom, Ireland, France, Germany, Sweden, Russia, Poland, Romania, Hungary, Israel, Egypt, Iran, Syria, South Africa, Kenya, Ghana, Nigeria, India, China, Japan, and Australia.

In the explicitly comparative section of the volume, we describe the relative freedom and restrictiveness that women enjoy or are limited by in the different societies and how their roles or statuses differ from those of men. Social class and ethnic and racial differences among the women in each of the societies are also considered.

The organizing focus of this series of volumes is the analysis of important social issues about which many societies in the world have enacted laws and statutes, and about which most of its members have opinions that they voice in the public arena. They are issues that receive extensive media coverage as well as judicial attention. Thus far volumes have included the following issues: abortion, euthanasia, marriage and divorce, pornography, capital punishment, education, juvenile justice institutions, and illicit drug policies, trafficking, and usage. Each volume is intended to serve as a handbook containing empirical data and comprehensive references on the social issue, problem, or practice in question.

Rita J. Simon

Chapter One

North America

CANADA

Canada is in North America, north of the United States, and has a population of 32,805,041 (July 2005 est.). The ethnic groups in Canada are those of British Isles origin (28 percent), mixed European background (26 percent), French origin (23 percent), other European (15 percent), Amerindian (2 percent), other, mostly Asian, African, Arab (6 percent). The predominant religions are Roman Catholic (46 percent), Protestant (36 percent), and other (18 percent). The two official languages are English (59.3 percent) and French (23.2 percent).[1] Female life expectancy is 81.8 years compared to a male life expectancy of 76.5 years.[2] Women make up slightly more than half of the Canadian population and a large number of the senior population.[3]

Constitution

Canada became a sovereign authority in 1867 while maintaining strong relations with Britain. It is a confederation with a parliamentary democracy. The Constitution was made effective by the Constitution Act of April 17, 1982. Originally, the government was set up in the British North America Act of 1867 influenced by unwritten and customary laws.[4] The present government is based on English common law, except in Quebec, where the civil law system is based on French law. Citizens, men and women, are eligible to vote at eighteen years of age.[5]

The Constitution expressly prohibits discrimination based on gender under Schedule B of the Constitution Act, 1982, Part I (Canadian Charter of Rights and Freedoms), 15. The Constitution states:

(1) Every individual is equal before and under the law and has the right to the equal protection and equal benefit of the law without discrimination and, in particular,

without discrimination based on race, national or ethnic origin, colour, religion, sex, age or mental or physical disability.[6]

Canada also supports affirmative action programs that benefit women and minorities. The Constitution states:

(2) Subsection (1) does not preclude any law, program or activity that has as its object the amelioration of conditions of disadvantaged individuals or groups including those that are disadvantaged because of race, national or ethnic origin, colour, religion, sex, age or mental or physical disability.[7]

Before January 1, 1915 women automatically became British subjects if their husbands naturalized. From January 1, 1915 to January 14, 1932 there was a provision for the inclusion of a wife's name on a certificate of naturalization granted to the husband. From January 15, 1932 to December 31, 1946, a wife did not automatically become a British subject if her husband became one. Still, she was allowed to file within six months of the date of her husband's naturalization. She would then be considered a British subject and would then be a Canadian citizen under Section 9(1)(a). On April 2, 1946, Paul Martin Senior, the Secretary of State, introduced the First Canadian Citizenship Act which addressed Citizenship, Naturalization and the Status of Aliens. One important provision is that married women would be viewed as individual persons. Consequently, from January 1, 1947 to today a wife does not acquire Canadian citizenship through the naturalization of her husband.[8]

The Canadian Gender Guidelines acknowledge that women face gender-based persecution.[9] Subsequently, as grounds for asylum, the Immigration and Refugee Board considers women's "subordinate status" and "membership of a particular social group," with gender being the particular social group.[10] The Canadian Immigration and Refugee Board stated that original asylum standards were based on the experience of male claimants and ignored the special conditions of women around the world, ranging from genital mutilation and compulsory sterilization to honor killing.[11]

Work Force and Economy

The purchasing power parity of Canada is $1.023 trillion (2004 est.). The labor force is made up of 17.37 million people (2004 est.). Unemployment at 7 percent (2004 est.) is on the rise.[12] However, the unemployment rate is lower for women than for men: 6.8 compared to 7.5 (2004 est.).[13]

Women make up a disproportionate share of the population with low incomes and a larger percentage of single run households.[14]

The number of women in the work force has doubled in the past twenty-five to thirty years.[15] Six out of every ten women are in the paid labor force.[16] Fifty-eight percent of Canadian women work in clerical, sales, or service occupations.[17] Men frequently hold higher paying jobs and are employed in a greater variety of positions.[18] Women make up the majority of jobs such as secretaries, waitresses, and nurses. These jobs receive little autonomy, low wages, and little job mobility. In addition, work is often routine and bureaucratic in female-dominated positions. Women in male-dominated careers often experience social isolation. This limits their chances for social support.[19] Nevertheless, women have increased their representation in managerial positions. Also, there has been an increase of women in professional fields such as medicine, dentistry, business, and finance. In fact, women currently make up almost half the total work force in the recently mentioned groups. Women continue to make up roughly about one in five individuals employed in professional positions in the natural sciences, mathematics, or engineering.[20]

In 2001, the estimated earned income for a woman was $20,990 (U.S.) compared to $33,391 for men. Thus, women earn 63 percent of what their male counterparts earn.[21]

Education

The female to male ratio of student enrollment in secondary schools in 2000 was 101 women to every 100 men. Ninety-eight percent of age eligible females were enrolled in secondary school, putting Canada in the top three countries for female enrollment in secondary education.[22] Women are more likely than men to be high school graduates.[23] Overall women are slightly less likely to have a college degree than men. However, college age women are more likely than men to obtain a college degree.[24]

Women make up the majority of full-time students in most universities. However, they remain concentrated in the humanities and social sciences. These fields have weaker labor market outcomes. Nevertheless, women are entering into traditionally male-dominated fields. Among the twenty-five to twenty-nine year old age group, women are now obtaining higher levels of education than men.[25] In 2000, the female to male ratio of student enrollment in tertiary school was 134 women to every 100 men.[26]

Marriage

Marriage and divorce are the constitutional responsibilities of the federal government. The legal marriage age depends on the province. Usually, males may marry at fifteen. Marriages of girls below the age of twelve can be voided and annulled. The average age for marriage is twenty-nine for men and twenty-seven for women. Fifty-two percent of men are married compared to 46.4 percent for women. The divorce rate is 37 percent.[27] While the marriage rate is dropping the number of couples in unmarried cohabitation or "common law marriage" is rising. Fifty percent of all first unions are common law marriages. Men and women in Quebec tend to cohabitate more than people in other areas of the country. In 1996, 7.9 percent of all children were living with parents in common-law unions. Remarriage is common. In fact, 75 percent of divorced men and 65 percent of women remarry. The majority of those who remarry are people who divorced from their first marriage between the ages of twenty-five and thirty-five.

There are three grounds for divorce in Canada. First, spouses must live separate and apart for twelve months by the time the final application for divorce is made. Also, spouses cannot start a divorce proceeding until they have started to live separately. The second ground for divorce is adultery. The burden of proof is on the accusing party. The third ground for divorce is cruelty. This includes mental and physical cruelty. Hitting one's spouse or excessive shouting, demeaning the spouse, and alcoholism are grounds for divorce. No-fault divorce was introduced in 1985. Religious annulments are not recognized by civil or judicial authorities.

The 1985 Divorce Act gave the court system the ability to mandate spousal support. Spousal support can be awarded to the husband or wife. The court considers the conditions, means, needs, and other circumstances of the spouse who is seeking support. For example, the court will examine the length of time the couple cohabitated, the functions of each spouse during the cohabitation, and any agreements made prior to making the decision to award spousal support.

The legal standard for child custody is "the best interest of the child." Data show that when the mother seeks child custody she is granted custody 90 percent of the time. When the father seeks custody he is granted custody 50 percent of the time. Child support is legally calculated according to the formula contained within the Federal Child Support Guidelines. In 1996, roughly 19 percent of all children lived in a single-parent family, most of which were headed by mothers: 84 percent by mothers, and 16 percent by fathers. Seventy-nine percent of children between the ages of one and eleven live with both parents while 16 percent live with a single parent, and 4 percent live with a parent and a step-parent.[28]

Abortion and Contraceptives

In 1988, the Supreme Court made abortions legal through the case *R. v. Morgentaler.* They may be performed to save the life of the woman, to preserve physical or mental health, on account of rape or incest, because of fetal impairment, or because of economic reasons. A woman does not need to give a reason in order to receive an abortion. Abortions are available upon request with no stipulations as to whom must perform it and where.[29]

Contraceptives are legal. Seventy-six percent of Canadian women use some form of contraception. The contraceptive method most frequently used by Canadian women is male or female sterilization. Twenty-nine percent of women use female sterilization. Canada has one of the highest rates of sterilization in the world. Twenty-seven percent of Canadian women use the pill. Twenty-one percent of women's sexual partners use condoms. Five-percent rely on the withdrawal method. The pill and the condom are most frequently used by young and/or unmarried men and women. Sterilization is primarily used by married couples aged thirty-five or older. Fourteen percent of Canadian women reported that they were currently not using a method of contraception. It is estimated that 40 percent or more of pregnancies in Canada are unplanned. This percentage is higher for teenagers and for women over forty.[30]

In British Columbia and Quebec doctors are allowed to prescribe emergency contraceptives.[31] But Levonorgestrel is the only approved emergency contraceptive in Canada and it is only available by prescription.[32] The Canadian Women's Health Network (CWHN) has been lobbying to get the FDA to move Levonorgestrel from prescription to non-prescription status. The CWHN states that having the drug by prescription only violates a woman's right to privacy and increases costs.[33]

The total fertility rate is 1.6 births per woman (2005 est.).[34]

Health Care

Health care is publicly funded and distributed by each province or territory for its citizens.[35] It was first set up under the 1984 *Canada Health Act*. The plan covers citizens for all hospital and physician procedures that are considered "medically necessary."[36] However, this does not include prescription medications, home care, or dental and vision care.[37] In addition, fewer procedures are covered when the economy is in a recession. Therefore, the general criticism of Medicare is that it does not cover enough procedures.[38] Many employers offer private health care plans that include additional services such as prescription medications, home care, and dental and vision care.[39]

The Canadian Health Act states that people are supposed to have "reasonable access to health care." The term, "reasonable access," is not defined.[40]

The leading cause of death among women is disease of the circulatory system (39.7 percent).[41] Cancer is the second leading cause of death among women (27 percent).[42]

Women in Public Office

Women gained the right to vote in 1917. The first year women were able to run for election was 1920. The first year a woman was elected to parliament was 1921.[43]

Women's entrance into politics was a struggle. Emily Murphy was appointed to the Edmonton Municipal Court in 1916, becoming the first woman police magistrate in Alberta and the British Empire. Her appointment, and consequently her rulings as a magistrate, was challenged on the grounds that women were not persons under the British North American Act ("BNA Act").[44] In 1917, the Alberta Supreme Court rejected the argument that Emily Murphy was ineligible to be a magistrate because she was not a "person."

In response to the questioning of whether she was, in fact, a "person" Emily Murphy allowed her name to be put forward as a candidate for the Senate, a federal level of government.[45] The Canadian Prime Minister, Sir Robert Borden, rejected her candidacy because as a woman she was not considered a person under the BNA Act.[46]

In 1927, Irene Parlby, Emily Murphy, Nellie McClung, Henrietta Muir Edwards, and Louise McKinney, now known as the "famous five," petitioned to the Supreme Court on their interpretation on whether the term *"qualified persons"* in section 24 of the British North America Act of 1867 included women as persons eligible for appointment to the Senate. The court stated that women were not included.[47] The court decision stated that in 1867, when the BNA Act was written, women did not vote, run for office, nor serve as elected officials. Therefore, only male nouns and pronouns were used in the BNA Act. In addition, the Supreme Court stated that since the British House of Lords did not have a female member, Canada should not change the tradition for its Senate.[48]

The "Famous Five" appealed to the Judicial Committee of the Privy Council in England, which was the highest court of appeals at that time. On October 18, 1929, the Committee overturned the decision of the Supreme Court and ruled that "qualified persons" in section 24 did include women.[49] Lord Sankey, Lord Chancellor of the Privy Council, stated that women were persons and subsequently "eligible to become members of the Senate of Canada."[50] In fact, the Privy Council decision stated

> that the exclusion of women from all public offices is a relic of days more barbarous than ours. And to those who would ask why the word "persons" should include females, the obvious answer is, why should it not?[51]

After the 2000 election, women occupied 20.6 percent of the house and 32.4 percent of the seats in the senate.[52] After the 2004 election, women occupied 24.7 percent of the seats in the national parliament.[53]

Women in the Military

The Canadian military is made up of the Canadian Armed Forces (comprising Land Forces Command, Maritime Command, Air Command, and Canada Command [homeland security], 2005). Men and women may join the military at seventeen years of age with parental consent, and at sixteen years of age with parental consent for junior level military college and the reserves. In addition, women and men must be Canadian citizens, have completed grade 10, and have met the physical and medical standards before being accepted into the military.[54]

Women served in the military during World War II. The Canadian Women's Army Corps (CWAC) was created in 1941. Women took on many of the noncombatant support roles. They served as truck drivers, air mechanics, nurses, quartermasters, and provosts (military police).

The CWAC dissolved in 1946.[55] They did not begin to recruit women again until 1951, during the Korean War. In 1989, a Canadian human rights tribunal removed restrictions barring women from all except one job in the Armed Forces. The restriction prohibiting women from serving on submarines was removed in 2001. Women may now serve in all functions and environments including combat.[56] There are presently two women in the General Officer ranks. Women presently make up 11.4 percent (6,558 of 57,441) of the Regular Force and 18.6 percent (5,787 of 31,479) of the Reserve Force. Female representation is very low (1.9 percent) in combat arms such as infantry, artillery, and field engineer.[57]

Women can take up to 119 days paid leave, with an additional 70 days available as parental leave upon application. This is also available to military spouses. It also includes adoptive parents.[58]

UNITED STATES

The United States is in North America. It is bordered by both the North Atlantic Ocean and the North Pacific Ocean and is located between Canada and Mexico. The United States has a population of 295,734,134 (2005 est.). The ethnic groups are White (81.7 percent), Black (12.9 percent), Asian (4.2 percent), Native American and Alaska native (1 percent), native Hawaiian and other Pacific islander (0.2 percent) (2003 est.). Hispanic is not a separate category because

Hispanics may be of any race (Black, Asian, White, etc.). The predominant religions are Protestant (56 percent), Roman Catholic (28 percent), Jewish (2 percent), other (4 percent), and none (10 percent). The main languages spoken are English and Spanish.[59]

Constitution

The American colonies declared their independence from Great Britain on July 4, 1776. The legal system is based on English common law. The Constitution was introduced on September 17, 1787 and became effective on March 4, 1789.[60] The United States is a federal republic based on democratic tradition. There is judicial review of legislative acts.[61]

Suffragists attempted to make a stand for women's rights after the Civil War. They wanted to have the language of the Fourteenth Amendment include women. It did not. Section 1 of the amendment does state:

> All persons born or naturalized in the United States, and subject to the jurisdiction thereof, are citizens of the United States and of the state wherein they reside. No state shall make or enforce any law which shall abridge the privileges or immunities of citizens of the United States; nor shall any state deprive any person of life, liberty, or property, without due process of law; nor deny to any person within its jurisdiction the equal protection of the laws.

In addition, while the language of the second section of the Fourteenth Amendment does explicitly mention "male citizens" the first section (above) does not. In fact, Section 1 refers to "all persons."[62] Many Suffragists interpreted "all persons" to include women and did attempt to vote.[63] In fact, Activist Susan B. Anthony did successfully vote and was arrested and charged with illegal voting.[64] The Fourteenth Amendment did grant citizenship to Blacks but not the right to vote.[65] Susan B. Anthony later used the Fifteenth Amendment, which granted Black men suffrage, when defending herself for voting in the New York election.[66] The Fifteenth Amendment states: "The right of citizens of the United States to vote shall not be denied or abridged by the United States or by any state on account of race, color, or previous condition of servitude."[67] Anthony was tried and fined for voting.[68] In 1920, the Nineteenth Amendment to the Constitution was ratified, giving women the right to vote.[69] Today's citizens, men and women, have the right to vote at eighteen years of age.[70]

The U.S. Constitution does not expressly prohibit discrimination on the basis of gender. In fact, the U.S. Constitution does not forbid Congress from passing laws based in large part on biological differences between the sexes.

In 1839, Mississippi was the first state to pass laws allowing married women to own property separate from their husbands. New York and Massachusetts followed in 1848 and 1854.[71]

In 2001, the Supreme Court confirmed that the U.S. Constitution does not forbid Congress from passing laws based in large part on biological differences between the sexes. In the United States, as well as most nations, courts rule on behalf of what they think is in the best interest of a child. Predominantly it is to be with his mother. In *Nguyen, Tuan, et al. v. Immigration & Naturalization Service* (2001), the U.S. Supreme Court supported federal immigration law, Section 309 of the Immigration and Nationality Act. Under the law, a child born out of wedlock outside of the United States automatically becomes the nationality of his mother regardless if the father is American. In order for the child to acquire his father's nationality, the father must agree, in writing, to financially provide for the child, and legally acknowledge the child before he turns eighteen. Congress, when writing the law, had a presumption that a mother and child's bond was stronger because childbirth is a more involved process for women than for men.[72]

United States immigration law has come a long way since its origin. Nevertheless, an asylum criterion is based almost exclusively on the experience of male claimants. Women are not a classification that would qualify them for asylum. INS is concerned that the percentage of applicants for asylum would dramatically increase if gender became a classification. For example, the number of applicants from particular clans or persecuted religions is relatively small, since they are a minority in their country. Women, on the other hand, are certainly not a minority in the world. INS fears that the creation of women as a classified group could result in opening the floodgates of valid applications. Conservatives fear that applicants would use false domestic violence claims in order to obtain asylum. The chairwoman of the California Coalition for Immigration Reform, Barbara Coe, stated (when describing asylum claims based on gender alone) "You get punched in the mouth and you are home free."[73] Coe is a supporter and sponsor of Proposition 187, that, if passed, would deny illegal aliens public benefits.[74]

Only 1,000 of the 55,000 asylum claims in 1999 were from women claiming gender bias. INS is concerned that these numbers would radically increase if women were created as a classification. However, in Canada women have been granted asylum based on the classification of gender and the number of applications based on gender bias is the same as the United States.[75]

The Bush Administration has put further restrictions and safeguards on immigration as a result of September 11, 2001. One significant change is that INS is now part of homeland security. In addition, the Bush Administration has created the USA PATRIOT Act that restricts civil liberties and further targets immigrant populations by targeting undocumented persons, and providing summary deportations of immigrants who were not charged with a crime.[76] Presently, eight to twelve million undocumented immigrants live in the United States. Despite restrictions of the USA PATRIOT Act, President Bush plans to permit greater numbers of temporary workers to come to the United States legally. Guest-worker status will be given to undocumented aliens who have come to the United States to work.[77] Although the latter will aid some immigrants, the immediate goal of the government is to narrow the entrance of immigrants rather than expand the scope of the asylum law.

Work Force and Economy

In the nineteenth century, large numbers of women began working outside of the home, primarily in textile mills and garment shops. During that time, women worked up to twelve hours a day. In 1910, states passed legislation limiting working hours and improving working conditions for women. However, some labor laws restricted the rights of working women. Labor laws prohibited women from working more than an eight-hour day or from working at night. This prevented women from obtaining certain jobs, that is, supervisory positions, which required overtime. Laws in some states prohibited women from lifting weights above fifteen pounds.[78]

In the 1960s, federal laws were passed in order to improve the economic status of women. The Equal Pay Act of 1963 required that men and women be paid equally for doing equal work.[79] In addition, the Civil Rights Act of 1964 prohibited discrimination based on gender.[80] Yet, equality between men and women, in terms of employment, has not been achieved.

The United States has the largest and most technologically powerful economy in the world. The purchasing power parity is $11.75 trillion (2004 est.). The median household income is $42,409 (2002). The population living below the poverty line is 12.1 percent (2002).[81] The percentage of single mother households that live below the poverty line is 26.5 compared to 12.1 for single father households (2002). Women are more likely than men to live in poverty. In 2001, 12.9 percent of the female population lived in poverty compared to 10.4 percent of the male population.[82] The labor force is made up of 147.4 million people (2004). The unemployment rate is 5.5 percent (2004).[83]

Female workers, who file suit, have relied on Title VII of the Civil Rights Act of 1964, the Equal Pay Act, the Family and Medical Leave Act, and the Americans with Disabilities Act. Title VII prohibits discrimination on the basis of sex. This is the most frequently cited statute used by attorneys in challenging employers' treatment of women. In 1971, the Supreme Court created the "sex-plus" theory to protect female employees. Under the theory, employers cannot treat their female employees differently than their male employees on the basis of their sex *and* having children, and/or race, religion, etc.[84]

The Family and Medical Leave Act requires employers to grant employees up to twelve weeks of unpaid leave per year for the birth (or adoption) of a child and for the care of a seriously ill family member.[85]

The Americans with Disability Act forbids discrimination against a mother (or other caregiver) who takes time off from work to care for a spouse or child with a disability. For example, in *Abdel-Khalek v. Ernst & Young, LLP,* the court found that it is unlawful for an employer to not hire an applicant (with a disabled spouse or child) because they believe the applicant would miss work or often leave early to care for the disabled family member.[86]

The Equal Pay Act prohibits wage discrimination on the basis of sex. In order to succeed using this federal statute, a woman must prove that her employer pays women and men different wages for equal work that requires equal skill, effort, and responsibility, and which is performed under equal working conditions.[87] The case is lost if one of the above elements differs between the woman and her male counterpart. Also, employers do not have to release the earnings of individuals. Therefore, many women do not know that they earn less than their male counterparts.[88] Consequently, women and men are not paid equally for equal work.[89]

State laws may broaden the protection of women. For example, Alaska includes family status in its anti-discrimination law. In addition, many states grant employees with paid maternity/paternity leave to care for a newborn child. Other states like California allow employees to use forty hours per year to attend their children's school activities. However, state laws and federal statutes protecting working women are not often successful. Nevertheless, there has been an increase of success in such cases over the past five years. Therefore, the risk of liability of employers may be increasing.[90]

Women earn less than men. In 2000, women earned 48 percent of the wages in the non-agricultural sector compared to 46 percent in the early 1980s.[91] Presently, the estimated earned income for women is $29,017 compared to $46,456 for men.[92] According to the Human Development Report, women are estimated to earn 62.5 percent of what men earn.[93] Other reports indicate that women earned 75.5 percent of what men earn (2003). The statistical differences between reports may be attributed to other factors such as race, education, etc. For example, White women earn 75.7 percent of what White men earn while Hispanic women earn 54.3 percent of what White men earn.[94]

Female scientists earn roughly one third less than male scientists. The median income for female scientists is $72,000 compared to $94,000 for male scientists.[95] Forty-three percent of employed women earn wages between $25,000 and $49,999. Few women earn over $75,000 (see table 1.1).[96]

Table 1.1.

Wages	Men	Women
Less than $10,000	2.8	4.4
$10,000–$19,999	12.3	20.8
$20,000–$24,999	9.4	13.9
$25,000–$34,999	19.1	23.4
$35,000–49,999	21.4	20.0
$50,000–$74,999	19.2	11.9
$75,000 and over	15.8	5.5

Source: U.S. Census Bureau (2002)

Race does play a factor in wages. The median annual earnings of Black men and women, Hispanic men and women, and White women as a percentage of White men's median annual earnings reveal that White women in the United States have benefited the most over the past twenty-eight years compared to Black and Hispanic men and women. White women's wages increased by 14.7 percent from 1975 to 2000. On the other hand, Black women's wages increased by 9.2 percent and Hispanic women's by 3.5 percent. Black men's wages have only increased 3.9 percent and Hispanic men's wages have decreased by 8.7 percent (see table 1.2 below).[97]

Fifty-seven percent of advertising managers and promotions managers, public relations managers, accountants, and auditors are women.[98] Today, one third of foreign correspondents are women compared to 6 percent in 1970.[99] In the sciences, women are primarily in positions in the fields of psychology and the social sciences.[100] However, women will likely soon equal and then surpass men in the biological sciences (see Education section).

Female science and engineering (S&E) faculty members are less likely than men to be full professors. Women are more likely than men to acquire assistant professor or instructor positions. This can partially be explained by age differences. Nonetheless, differences between men and women remain

Table 1.2. Percentage Minorities Earn Compared to White Males

Race/Gender	1975	2000	Change in Earnings
White Men	100	100	
Black Men	74.3	78.2	3.9 increase
Hispanic Men	72.1	63.4	8.7 decrease
White Women	57.5	72.2	14.7 increase
Black Women	55.4	64.6	9.2 increase
Hispanic Women	49.3	52.8	3.5 increase

Source: National Committee on Pay Equity

even without the age factor. Among S&E, more women obtained full professor positions in psychology and the social sciences than in any other S&E field. Women are least likely to reach full professorship in Engineering than any Science field.[101] Women are employed in many other positions ranging from bus drivers to nuclear engineers; see table 1.3 below.[102]

Minorities make up 27 percent of the work force. According to the Census Bureau, women make up a significant share of doctors and lawyers. The percentages of lawyers and doctors that are female have more than doubled since 1980. Progress has been less rapid for racial minorities (see table 1.4).[103]

Among Black women, 36 percent work in technical, sales, and administrative support jobs. Roughly 27 percent of Black women are in managerial, professional specialty jobs, or service occupations.[104]

Among Hispanic women, 57 percent are in the labor force. Thirty-seven percent are in technical or sales positions. Roughly 28 percent are in the service industry. Eighteen percent are in managerial or professional positions. Twelve percent of Hispanic women are operators or laborers. Three percent are in precision production and 1.7 percent of Hispanic women are in the farming industry. Twenty-eight percent of Hispanic-owned business firms were owned by women in 1997.

Table 1.3.

Occupation	Number of Female Employees
Post-secondary teachers	531,000
Bus drivers	253,000
Chief executives	212,000
Bakers	87,000
Athletes/coaches/umpires	62,000
Musicians/singers	61,000
Clergy	56,000
Producers and directors	52,000
Chefs/head cooks	48,000
News analysts/reporters/correspondents	44,000
Architects	39,000
Dancers and choreographers	23,000
Private detectives/investigators	22,000
Aircraft pilots and flight engineers	5,000
Astronomers and physicists	3,000
Explosive workers	1,000
Ship/boat captain	1,000
Nuclear engineers	700

Source: U.S. Census Bureau

Table 1.4. Civilian Employees by Race and Sex, Percentage of Total Occupation

Occupation	Year	Men	Women	Non-Hispanic White	Non-Hispanic Black	All Other Races	Hispanic (All Races)	Total
Lawyers	1980	86%	14%	95%	3%	1%	2%	468,378
	1990	76	24	93	3	2	2	697,272
	2000	71	29	89	4	4	3	871,115
Doctors	1980	87%	13%	83%	3%	10%	4	421,985
	1990	79	21	81	4	11	5	571,319
	2000	73	27	74	4	17	5	705,960
Firefighters	1980	99%	1%	89%	6%	1%	4%	186,867
	1990	97	3	84	9	2	5	216,914
	2000	96	4	82	8	3	6	242,395
Police Officers	1980	93%	9%	85%	9%	1%	4%	379,758
	1990	87	13	79	12	2	7	492,107
	2000	87	14	76	12	4	9	597,925

Source: Census Bureau (2000)

In 2001, 8 percent of Hispanic women had full-time, year-round positions in which they earned $50,000 or more. Eighty percent of Hispanic women in full time/year round positions make $35,000 or less compared to 70.1 of Hispanic men.[105]

There are fewer female Supreme Court justices, Federal Appellate Court judges, and Federal District Court judges than male. Fewer female attorneys are in private practice, or partners in law firms. Proportionately, more women are in public interest law. Women have recently surpassed men in law school enrollment. This may have a beneficial impact on the future percentages of women in law firms, private practice, and judicial positions.

Total minority participation in the legal profession is approximately 10 percent. Minority women are particularly more likely to enter into government or public interest jobs. Interestingly, the number of minority law graduates entering business has increased substantially. As a result there are more minority graduates entering private practice and business than previously. Nevertheless, the percentage of minorities in the private and business sector is lower than Whites. Accordingly, there is little minority representation among law firm partners and general counsel positions in the Fortune 500.[106]

Minority women leave law firms more than any other group.[107] Twelve percent of female minority attorneys leave their firms within the first year of practice and more than 85 percent leave by their seventh year of practice.[108]

Earnings of women who take leave, that is, maternity leave, for six months or longer never catch up with the earnings of women who never took leave in their careers.[109]

Education

Title IX of the Education Amendments of 1972 made it illegal to discriminate on the basis of sex in education programs or activities that receive federal funding. The legislation states:

> No person in the United States shall, on the basis of sex, be excluded from participation in, be denied the benefits of, or be subjected to discrimination under any education program or activity receiving federal assistance.[110]

Since the passage of this Amendment women's participation in education has dramatically increased.[111]

Oberlin Collegiate Institute (presently called Oberlin College) became the first coeducational college in the United States in 1833.[112] It was at Oberlin where the first black woman was able to obtain a college degree. Mary Jane Patterson graduated in 1862.[113]

In 2000, the female to male ratio of students enrolled in secondary school was 102 women for every 100 men. The female enrollment in secondary school was 88 percent.[114] Women are more likely than men to graduate from high school, to enroll in college, and graduate from college.[115] Still, women are less likely than men to choose science and engineering fields. Interestingly, women earned the majority of bachelor degrees in science and engineering in 2000. Women currently obtain 43 percent of all masters degrees and 36.2 percent of all doctoral degrees in science and engineering (2000).[116] Recently women have begun to surpass male enrollment in many master and doctoral programs. In fact, women earn more degrees than men in the field of education, regardless of whether the degree obtained is a B.A., Masters, or Ph.D. Women have dominated enrollment in Education degrees at the B.A. and Master level for over thirty years and since 1983, for doctorate positions in the field.[117]

Men tend to fair better on standardized exams. In 2005, the average SAT score for men was 513 points on the verbal section compared to 505 for women. The average SAT score for men on the math section was 538 compared to 504 for women (2003).[118]

More women are aspiring to be physicians. In fall 2003, women made up 49.9 percent of the entering class of medical students. In addition, 50.8 percent of the applicants for the 2004 first year class of medical school were women. This is quite a change from forty-four years ago when the 1960 Harvard Medical School class of 150 students had 6 women. Boston University School of Medicine was the country's first all female medical school in 1848. It began accepting men in 1872.[119]

Since 2001, more women apply to law school than men and make up nearly 50 percent of enrollment (49.4 percent).[120] An obstacle that may hinder many women and minorities who desire to enter law school is the Law School Admission Test (LSAT). On average, Whites score higher than Blacks, men score higher than women, and well-to-do students score higher than poor students on the LSAT exam. In fact, questions chosen to appear on the LSAT exams are those in which Whites, men, and the wealthy scored the highest in LSAT pre-testing.

Another reason why many minorities do not score as highly on the exam as Whites may be because many minorities cannot afford expensive preparatory classes. Crucial test-taking strategies taught in preparatory classes give those who are financially able to take the classes a significant advantage.[121]

Minorities

Race, ethnicity, and social status have an impact on education. Seventy-nine percent of Blacks age twenty-five and over have at least a high school diploma. For Blacks ages twenty-five to twenty-nine, 87 percent have at least a high school diploma. Seventeen percent of Blacks, age twenty-five and over, have a bachelor's degree or higher. Roughly 2.6 percent of Blacks, age twenty-five and over, have an advanced degree (e.g., Master's, Ph.D., M.D., or J.D.).[122]

Twenty-eight percent of Hispanics age twenty-five and older have a high school diploma, 10 percent have had some college, and 11.1 percent have a bachelor's degree or more.[123]

The 2003 national SAT scores for Blacks is 426 (math) and 431 (verbal). The 2003 national scores were 459 (math) and 452 (verbal) for Hispanics.[124]

Attacks on Affirmative Action in law school admissions, if successful, will likely decrease minority applications and admission to law school. In fact, minority enrollment dropped 1 percent from 2004 to 2005 according to a survey done at nineteen top law schools.[125] An admission policy based solely on LSAT scores and undergraduate GPAs would most probably result in a drop in minority admissions. Analysis of law school admissions decisions reveal that such a policy would result in a drop of 80 percent in Black admissions, 51 percent in Hispanic admissions, 37 percent in Asian American admissions, and 55 percent in Native American admissions.[126] Though less minority applicants would be accepted to law school under a numbers only policy, studies suggest that under the current admission policies, minority applicants do perform well in law school, pass the bar, and have successful careers. A study performed by the University of Michigan revealed that minority University of Michigan law school graduates are admitted to the bar at roughly the same percentage as Whites. In addition, the study found that minorities have equally successful careers.[127]

Marriage

Marriage in the United States is a civil contract. Both the federal government and the individual states have the authority to pass legislation regarding marriage and matrimonial causes. The legal age for marriage varies by state. The minimum age to marry, with parental consent, ranges from fourteen to eighteen for men and from twelve to eighteen for women. Men or women can only marry without parental consent at eighteen, except in Mississippi (where the minimum age is seventeen for men and fifteen for women), Nebraska (nineteen for both sexes), and Puerto Rico (twenty-one for both sexes). Medical exams and marriage licenses are required by all states. All states restrict marriage between blood relatives. Lastly, common law marriage is recognized by fourteen states.[128]

The percent of men that are married is 48.9 compared to 51.1 for women (2004 est.).[129] Slightly more than 30 percent (30.3) of men, fifteen and older, have never been married compared to 24.1 percent of women. The percentage of women who are divorced is 10.8 compared to 8.6 of men. The U.S. divorce rate is the highest in the world at 54.8 percent. Across most races and ethnicities (with the exception of Asian), fewer women were married in 2000 than men (see table 1.5). Also more women of all races and ethnicities were divorced than men (2000).[130]

In the United States, men and women are given equal legal status and equal marital responsibilities.[131] In *Frontiero v. Richardson* (1973), the U.S. Supreme Court heard a case of a married woman who was an air force officer who wanted increased benefits for her husband as a dependent. Under 37 U.S.C. §§ 1072 and 1076, spouses of male uniformed members are dependents in terms of obtaining quarterly allowances and medical and dental benefits. Husbands of female uniformed members were not considered dependants unless the men were dependant on their wives for over one-half of their support. The court found that this statutory classification was based solely on gender and was unjustifiably discriminatory and in violation of the Fifth Amendment.[132] The holding in this case, and others like it, helped to promote equal treatment and marital benefits for men and women under the law.[133]

Forty-three percent of marriages end up in separation or divorce within fifteen years. Studies reveal that 33 percent of marriages end up in separation or divorce within ten years of marriage, and 20 percent end within five years of marriage. Studies show that the duration of a marriage is influenced by age at the time of marriage. Apparently the older a woman is at the time of her first marriage, the longer the marriage is likely to last.[134]Age not only plays a role in how long a marriage lasts but also whether a woman is apt to remarry. For example, younger women who divorce are more likely to remarry. Eighty-one percent of those divorced before the age of twenty-five remarry within ten years compared to 68 percent of women divorced at twenty-five or older.[135]

Table 1.5.

Race/Ethnicity	Men Married	Women Married	Men Divorced	Women Divorced
Black	41.5	31.2	9.5	12.8
White (non-Hispanic)	60.1	55.5	9.2	11.0
Hispanic or Latino	60.1	50.9	8.5	8.8
American Indian & Alaska Native	45.4	43.5	11.3	13.7
Asian	59.7	60.6	3.3	5.1
Native Hawaiian & Other Pacific Islander	51.5	50.9	6.8	8.4
Two or more races	46.4	44.7	8.5	11.1

Source: U.S. Census Bureau 2000

Race and ethnicity play a role in the divorce rate. After marital separation from their spouse, 97 percent of White women are divorced within five years of that separation compared to 77 percent of Hispanic women and 67 percent of Black women. In fact, Black women are less likely than Hispanics or Whites to remain in first marriages, to make the transition from separation to divorce, and to remarry.[136]

Despite the high divorce rate, unmarried cohabitations, in general, are more unstable than marriages. In fact, the chances of a first marriage ending within the first five years are 20 percent compared to 49 percent in premarital cohabitation relationships. The probability of a marriage dissolving after ten years is 33 percent compared to 62 percent for those in cohabitation. Factors such as age at the time of marriage *or* cohabitation, whether the woman/man was raised by a two-parent family, the role of religion, whether there is high family income and low male unemployment, tends to make both cohabitations and marriages last longer.[137]

Divorce law, like marriage law, varies by state. Sixteen states have adopted "no fault" divorce; Arizona, California, Colorado, Delaware, District of Columbia, Florida, Hawaii, Iowa, Kentucky, Michigan, Minnesota, Montana, Nebraska, Oregon, Washington, and Wisconsin. Thirty-four states have adopted a combination of "no fault" divorce and traditional grounds for divorce. Other states use the concept of "incompatibility" of spouses as ground for divorce; Alaska, Kansas, Montana, Nevada, New Mexico, Ohio, Oklahoma, and Wyoming. Judicial separation is not offered by Delaware, Florida, Georgia, Mississippi, New Hampshire, Ohio, Pennsylvania, Texas, or Vermont. Twenty-four states do not require a specific separation period before divorce.

Nine states have community property division of property. The division of marital property only is applied in thirty states. A majority of states consider non-monetary contributions, such as domestic duties, made to the household in dividing property. The states that do not consider non-monetary contributions are Arizona, Georgia, Idaho, Kansas, Louisiana, New Mexico, Texas, Utah, and Washington.

The U.S. Supreme Court has held that there are equal expectations of the alimony law for men and women. Over half of the states consider marital fault when determining alimony. Most states also consider the spouse's standard of living in determining alimony. Nine states do not: Arkansas, Idaho, Kansas, Louisiana, Maine, Mississippi, Ohio, West Virginia, and Wyoming. Twenty-seven states consider a spouse's status as the custodial parent when deciding alimony, twenty-three states do not.

Children's wishes are considered by the majority of states when determining child custody. However, Arkansas, Massachusetts, Mississippi, and

Vermont do not consider the child's wishes. Joint custody is also widely used; only five states do not allow it. The health of the parent is often considered and so is domestic violence (except in four states).[138]

On average, a woman's standard of living drops 22 percent after divorce, while a man's decreases by 8 percent.[139] In 1990, 15.5 percent of women who had ever been divorced received alimony payments.[140, 141] Thirty-two percent received a property settlement.[142] Roughly forty states use the equitable distribution laws to distribute the marital assets fairly between the spouses upon divorce.[143] This has caused the cost of divorce to increase. For example, in New York, since the equal distribution laws have been put into effect, divorce prices have drastically increased from $6,000 (1980) to $50,000 (1995).[144] The Legal Services Corporation (LSC) was created by Congress in order to provide assistance for those who are unable to afford attorneys.[145] A woman must make $11,100 or less in order to obtain representation for her divorce from the LSC.

The U.S. Census Bureau found that income available for children decreases by 37 percent after a divorce.[146] A study by the Children's Defense Fund (CDF) revealed that after one parent leaves home, almost 50 percent of the families had to move in with friends or family, and 10 percent become homeless. Less than 60 percent of single mother homes have child support awarded to them. Fifty percent of women awarded child support did not receive full payment.[147] The Child Support Recovery Act of 1992 states that it is a federal crime to cross state lines in order to avoid paying child support. In addition, it is illegal, for the non-compliant party, to cross state lines if he or she is a year or $5,000 behind in child support payments. First time offenders may be subject to a six-month prison term, a $5,000 fine, or both. Second time offenders are subject to a two-year prison sentence, a $250,000 fine, or both. However, the majority of offenders have not been prosecuted under the federal law.[148] Many states threaten to take driver's licenses away from fathers who do not pay child support. This has been an effective means of collecting child support.[149]

Minorities

Hispanic households are more likely to be run by a single mother than non-Hispanic White family households. Thirty-seven percent of Hispanic families living below the poverty line are single mother family households.[150]

The percent of Black children living with their married parents was 39 percent in 2000. There are almost as many Black children living with single mothers as with two parents.[151]

Abortion and Contraceptives

Abortions are legal in the United States. They may be performed to save the life of the woman, to preserve physical or mental health, if the woman was raped or the victim of incest, because of fetal impairment, or because of economic reasons. A woman does not need to give a reason in order to receive an abortion.[152] A woman who is under age must obtain parental consent or a judicial waiver of notification from a juvenile court when seeking an abortion in twenty-nine states.[153]

Abortion laws began to appear in the United States around the 1820s forbidding a woman to have an abortion after she has felt the baby move for the first time—roughly four months after gestation. By the early 1960s, all fifty states banned abortions. Some states made exceptions to save the life of the mother, or in cases of rape or incest, or if the fetus was deformed. The Supreme Court in 1973, in the case of *Roe v. Wade,* ruled out any legislative interference in the first trimester of pregnancy and put restrictions on what legislation could be passed on abortions in later stages of pregnancy.[154] In 2001, there were 25 abortions performed for every 100 live births.[155] Age, marital status, and race are all factors in the number of abortions performed. Women under the age of fifteen have 74 abortions performed for every 100 live births compared to 16 for women ages fifteen to forty-four. Black women have 49 abortions for 100 live births compared to 23 for Hispanic women and 17 for White women. Unmarried women have 57 abortions for every 100 live births compared to 7 for married women.[156]

Abortion law changed in 2003. In October of 2003 the Senate passed the partial-birth abortion ban. Partial birth abortions usually take place during the second or third trimester.[157] The passage of the ban limits the scope in which an abortion can take place. How exactly the ban will impact women and procedures is yet to be known.

Teen pregnancy in the United States is the highest in the developed world. In fact, U.S. teens are twice as likely to get pregnant as Canadian teens. In addition, U.S. teens are nine times more likely to become pregnant than teens in Japan or the Netherlands.[158]

In the past decade, women have had access to Depo-Provera. Depo-Provera is an injected contraceptive that is only taken once every three months. In 1995, three percent of women used Depo-Provera. The figures were higher for Blacks (7 percent) and teenagers (9 percent).[159] However, while the number of teenage pregnancies is decreasing, studies have shown that Depo-Provera results in a loss in bone density and is not recommended for long-term use.[160]

The morning after pill can still only be given to those with a prescription. Barr Laboratories filed an application to sell the morning after pill over-the-counter.

On May 6, 2004, the FDA rejected the application. The Scientific Advisory Committee voted 23–4 to approve the drug to be sold over-the-counter. In spite of this, the FDA went against the decision. The FDA states that it may allow for over-the-counter use in the future, if it can be proven that the drug is safe for teens, or that the drug will only be sold to women older than sixteen.[161]

Health Care

Health care programs are publicly and privately funded. Medicaid and Medicare are publicly funded and provide health insurance for the very poor, seniors, and disabled.[162] Medicaid provides health care to women and children who qualify for Aid to Families with Dependent Children (AFDC). The AFDC was replaced in 1997 by the Temporary Assistance for Needy Families (TANF) Program that was created by the Welfare Reform Law of 1996.[163]

Women use more health care services than men.[164] The reason is not known. Women are not often given the same care as men. In fact, women, between forty-six and sixty years old, have half the chance of receiving a kidney transplant as men of the same age. Non-white patients ages twenty-one to forty-five years of age have half the chance of receiving a kidney transplant as White patients of the same sex and age.[165, 166] In instances when smoking habits are similar between men and women, doctors are nearly twice as likely to order lung cancer testing for men than for women, regardless of the fact that women who smoke have twice the risk of lung cancer than their male counterparts.[167, 168] In the case of heart disease, women are more than twice as likely as men to have their symptoms associated with non-cardiac or mental causes.[169] Research has shown that in order to qualify for bypass surgery, a woman has to be sicker than a man. Perhaps this is why twice as many women die during bypass surgery than men. Women are often not diagnosed as early as men for cardiovascular disease and more women than men die during their first heart attack.[170]

Cardiovascular disease is the leading cause of death in women in the United States.[171] Research on cardiovascular disease has focused primarily on men.[172, 173] Women have also been left out of much medical research, including research on AIDS (AIDS is the fourth leading cause of death for women twenty-five to forty-four[174, 175]), depression, and on studies of the aging process (even though there are more elderly women than men[176]). Women of childbearing age have often been left out of critical research because it was thought that women's hormone rhythms could complicate the research results.[177] In addition, the FDA feared the possible impact of experimental drugs on a fetus.[178] Consequently, women often use medication where only men have been tested. However, it is a woman's hormone cycles that may make a drug affect women differently than men. For instance, when looking at antidepressants, women can be overmedicated or undermedicated during different times in their cycle.[179] In addition, women differ than men in body weight, blood flow, organ size, body fat, and kidney function.[180] In 1990, the National Institutes of Health (NIH) spent 13 percent of its budget on studying diseases in women. NIH is the principal source of government-funded research.[181] Congress passed the NIH Revitalization Act (1993), which required that women be included in clinical trials.[182, 183, 184] In 1993, the FDA's guidelines encouraged drug companies to include women in order to evaluate the different ways men and women respond to medication. The FDA also eliminated its 1977 ban that prohibited women of childbearing age from participating in the early stages of clinical trials. The FDA did not require drug companies to include women until 1998.[185]

The two most common surgical procedures in the United States are hysterectomies and cesarean sections.[186, 187] The patients for both procedures are all women. Some doctors believe that hysterectomies should be a last resort.[188] Nevertheless, only 10.7 percent of hysterectomies are performed because of cancerous growths.[189] The remaining hysterectomies are elective surgeries. Some doctors have recommended hysterectomies for backaches or as birth control. In addition, many doctors perform expensive cesarean sections in cases where a child, with no threat to the mother, could have been safely born vaginally. Cesarean sections increased from 5.5 percent (1970) to 23.5 percent (1991).[190, 191] Presently, according to the National Center for Health Statistics (NCHS), one in four pregnant women had a cesarean section in 2002, many of which were unnecessary surgeries. Some doctors believe that the increase is in part due to physician fear of liability in malpractice suits. Other physicians fear that a vaginal birth, when the mother has had a cesarean previously, may place the baby at risk. Other physicians believe that vaginal births are safe, even after a prior caesarian. For many women, especially those who never had a cesarean, the surgery is unnecessary and comes with its own set of risks such as blood clots, increased chances of infection, and a longer recovery period. Some women do elect for the surgery when it is unnecessary, but in many instances, physicians encourage cesarean sections for women who do not want them and who do not need them.[192, 193]

Women in Public Office

The first woman to be elected to the State Senate was Martha Hughes Cannon of Utah in 1896. In 1917, Jeannette Rankin, a Republican from Montana, was the first woman ever elected to Congress. Since 1920, the year women obtained the right to vote nationwide, women have been more involved in the political sphere but have yet to achieve equal representation to men in Congress.

Forty-seven women have succeeded their husbands in Congress. These women have been elected or appointed to fill congressional vacancies created by the deaths of their husbands, eight succeeded their husbands in the U.S. Senate and thirty-nine succeeded their husbands to the U.S. House of Representatives.[194] In U.S. history, a total of 225 (143D, 82R) seats have been held by women in the U.S. Congress. Twenty-six of the women have served in the Senate only, 185 in the House only, and 7 in both. Twenty-nine women have held cabinet or cabinet-level appointments. Thirty-one of the 225 seats have been held by women of color.[195]

Presently, women occupy 81 (15.1 percent) of the 535 seats in the 109th U.S. Congress, 14 percent of the 100 seats in the Senate, and 67 (15.4 percent) of the 435 seats in the House of Representatives. Of the fourteen women in the U.S. Senate, nine are Democrats and five are Republicans.[196]

Of the sixty-seven women in the House of Representatives, forty-three are Democrats and twenty-four are Republicans (2005).[197] There are eighty-one women in statewide elective offices (2005). There are eight female Governors (6D and 2R) and fifteen Lieutenant Governors (6D, 9R). There are five female Attorney Generals (3D, 2R), twelve Secretaries of State (7D, 5R), eight State Treasurers (1D, 7R), and seven State Auditors (2D, 5R). There are three female State Comptrollers/Controllers (1D, 2R), ten Chief Education Officials (5D, 2R, and 3 Non-partisan), two Commissioners of Insurance (1D, 1R), Labor (2R), and Corporation (2R), four Public Service Commissioners (2D, 2R), and two Chief Agricultural Officials (1D, 1R).[198]

Women in the Military

Since the Revolutionary War (1775–1783) women have been nurses on the battlefield.[199]

Women also fought in battles. Prudence Wright commanded a troop of women dressed as men in defense of Pepperell, Massachusetts. The troop captured a British courier carrying military plans that Wright took to Massachusetts military leaders.[200]

Other women fought along side their husbands. Mary Ledwig Hays McCauley, in the Civil War, operated her husband's cannon in his regiment when he was wounded in battle. In appreciation of her actions, she was given a pension of $40 per year by the state of Pennsylvania.

Some women were spies for the Union and others for the Confederacy during the Civil War.[201]

During World War I, women were hired as telephone operators. But when the war was over they were not eligible for honorable discharge or veteran's benefits because they were considered civilian employees, despite having been sworn into the army services.[202]

Also during World War I, Josephus Daniels, former Secretary of the Army, enlisted 11,274 females as Yeomen. "Yeomanettes," as they were commonly referred to, were the first officially recognized enlisted women. Yeomen, made up of both men and women, were put in desk job positions. This allowed men in the Navy to step away from their desk jobs and fight. Female and male Yeomen were paid the same amount, $28.75 per month and $1.25 daily for food. Women were given an additional housing stipend since no housing was provided for them. Female Yeomen had to be between the ages of eighteen and thirty-five. They had to be unmarried, in excellent health, of neat appearance, and good moral character.[203]

All Yeomen received honorable discharges. They could wear the victory metal, and they could qualify for veteran's benefits. After the war, women were not allowed to stay in the Navy. All Yeomen were discharged by July 1919.[204]

Similar clerical positions were available to women in the Marine Corp during World War I.[205]

Women were inducted into the military during and after World War II. Once again, their employment in the military was only temporary and for emergency only. In addition, women were restricted to desk jobs.[206]

In the 1940s, arguments were made against women being inducted into the military under permanent status. Opponents pointed to a woman's physical strength, the impact of menopause and menstruation on a woman's ability to perform her duties, a woman's emotional stability, the possible masculization of a woman as a consequence of participating in the military, and the impact of this on American culture.[207] After much debate, the Armed Forces Women's Integration Act, granting women permanent status, was passed in 1948.[208]

In the 1980s, women began to be included in more military positions such as non-combat flying, missile launch positions, shipboard duty, and combat support positions. Women could not be included in combat positions nor could they be included in the draft.[209] The fact that women were categorized in non-combat positions could have an adverse affect on a woman's career. The limitation on the scope of job opportunities for women in the military often left them in jobs or positions with little mobility.

During the 1990s, women soon began the difficult integration into state military schools such as V.M.I. and the Citadel.[210]

Congress then lifted a ban on female personnel flying fighter and bomber aircrafts.[211]

Presently, men and women may enlist in the military at eighteen.[212] Women make up 15 percent of military personnel.[213] There are few women in high rank positions. The majority of women are in First Lieutenant/Lieutenant Junior Grade, second Lieutenant/Ensign, Corporal/Petty Officer, 3rd Class, or Private.[214]

On February 11, 2003, the chief of U.S. Selective Services System presented to the Pentagon a proposal that will alter the draft. The Chief proposes to include the registration of women. The U.S. Selective System also proposes to expand the age limits from eighteen to thirty-four, as opposed to the existing eighteen to twenty-five for both men and women.[215] The agency has to obtain authorization from Congress before its proposal can be enacted.[216]

Recently, women have participated more in combat than in any previous war in U.S. history. Women have won Purple Hearts for combat wounds. They won medals for valor. Women have been captured and killed by enemy fire.[217]

While, technically, women still can't serve on the front lines in the Army, women can, and do, serve as military police, putting them in combat situations with opposition forces and civilians.[218]

NOTES

1. CIA World Factbook, Canada, <http://www.cia.gov/cia/publications/factbook/geos/ca.html> (5 Oct. 2005).

2. Human Development Reports, United Nations Development Programme, 2003, <http://www.undp.org/hdr2003/indicator/cty_f_CAN.html> (3 Nov. 2004).

3. "Women in Canada 2000," Statistics Canada, <http://www.statcan.ca/english/ads/89-503-XPE/hilites.htm> (June 2003).

4. CIA World Factbook, Canada. This is presently the Constitution Act, 1867; see The Constitution Act, 1867, <http:www.solon.org/Constitutions/Canada/English/ca_1867.html> (Oct. 2005).

5. CIA World Factbook, Canada.

6. The Canadian Constitution, <http://laws.justice.gc.ca/en/const/annex_e.html#I> (June 2003).

7. The Canadian Constitution.

8. "Acquisition of Canadian Citizenship at Birth or by Derivation through a Parent or Spouse," The Ships List, <http://www.theshipslist.com/Forms/CanCitAq_Natz.htm> (June 2003).

9. Association of the Bar of the City of New York, "Gender-Related Asylum Claims and the Social Group Calculus: Recognizing Women as a 'Particular Social Group' *Per Se*," The Committee on Immigration and Nationality Law, 2003, <http://www.abcny.org/pdf/report/FINAL%20%20Gender%20Related%20Asylum%20Claims.pdf> (July 2003).

10. "Guideline 4, Women Refugee Claimants Fearing Gender-Related Persecution, Guidelines Issued by the Chairperson Pursuant to Section 65(3) of the *Immigration Act*, update," Immigration and Refugee Board of Canada, 1996, <http://www.cisr-irb.gc.ca/en/about/guidelines/women_e.html#note5> (June 2003).

11. Caroline O'Conner, "Sexual Violence as 'Persecution' within the 1951 Refugee Convention," *Irish Student Law Review*, <http://www.islr.ie/Reviews/2001/refugee-law.php> (Oct. 2005).

12. CIA World Factbook, Canada; Latest release from the Labour Force Survey, Statistics Canada, September 9, 2005, <http://www.statcan.ca/english/Subjects/Labour/LFS/lfs-en.htm> (Oct. 2005).

13. "Employed and unemployed, numbers and rates, by provinces," Statistics Canada, 2004, <http://www40.statcan.ca/l01/cst01/labor07a.htm?sdi=women> (Oct. 2005).

14. "Women in Canada 2000," Statistics Canada (June 2003).

15. Bonita C. Long, "Women and Work-Place Stress," *Eric Digest*, 1995, <http://www.eric.ed.gov> (June 2003).

16. "Employed and unemployed, numbers and rates, by provinces," Statistics Canada.

17. "Status of Women Canada, for the period ending March 31, 1997, Improved Reporting to Parliament—Pilot Document," Minister of Public Works and Government Services Canada, <http://www.tbs-sct.gc.ca/rma/dpr/96-97/2SWC96e.pdf> (June 2003).

18. "Women and the Economy—UN Platform for Action Committee Manitoba (UNPAC), Men/Women and the 10 Highest/Lowest Paid Occupations in Canada," Statistics Canada, 1996; see nation tables at <http://unpac.ca/economy/wagegap3.html> (June 2003).

19. Long, "Women and Work-Place Stress."

20. "Women in Canada 2000," Statistics Canada.

21. Human Development Reports.

22. Progress of the World's Women, UNESCO Institute of Statistics, 2002, <http://portal.unesco.org/uis> (June 2003).

23. "Canada and the United Nations General Assembly: Special Session: Beijing +5: Factsheets, Women and Education and Training," Statistics Canada, 2003, <http://www.swc-cfc.gc.ca/pubs/b5_factsheets/b5_factsheets_4_e.html> (June 2003).

24. Ibid.

25. Ibid.

26. UNESCO Institute of Statistics, <http://portal.unesco.org/education/> (June 2003).

27. Rita J. Simon and Howard Altstein, *Global Perspectives on Social Issues: Marriage and Divorce* (Lanham: Rowman & Littlefield Publishing Group, Inc., 2003); Gulnar Nugman, World Divorce Rates, Heritage Foundation, 2002, <http://www.divorcereform.org/gul.html> (Sept. 2005).

28. Simon and Altstein, *Global Perspectives on Social Issues.*

29. "Abortion Policies: A Global Review, Canada," United Nations, <www.un.org/esa/population/publications/abortion/profiles.htm> (June 2003).

30. "Contraceptive use in Canada," Childbirth by Choice Trust, <http://www.cbctrust.com> (June 2003).

31. "Food and Drug Regulations, schedule 1272," Health Canada, June 16, 2003, <www.hc-sc.gc.ca/hpfb-dgpsa/tpd-dpt/sch-1272_e.html> (June 2003).

32. Ibid.

33. "CWHN's letter to Health Canada," The Canadian Women's Health Network,<http://www.cwhn.ca/resources/cwhn/ec-letter.html> (June 2003).

34. CIA World Factbook, Canada.

35. Canadian Health Care, <http://www.canadian-healthcare.org/>.

36. Raisa Berline Deber, et al., "Why not private health insurance?" *Canadian Medical Association Journal* 161, no. 5 (7 Sep. 1999): 539–42, <http://collection.nlc-bnc.ca/100/201/300/cdn_medical_association/cmaj/vol-161/issue-5/pdf/pg539.pdf>.

37. Canadian Health Care.

38. Gregory P. Marchildon, "Canadian Health Reform: Financing and Payment Systems," paper prepared for presentation at the 2005 National Health Insurance International Symposium: Toward an Equitable, Efficient, and High Quality National Health Insurance, Taipei, Taiwan, March 2005.

39. Canadian Health Care.

40. "Part I—Equity in Access to Health Care, Access to Health Services for Underserved Populations in Canada," Health Canada, 2003, <http://www.hc-sc.gc.ca/hppb/healthcare/pubs/circumstances/partI/doc1.html> (June 2003).

41. Regional Core Health Data System, Country Health Profile 2001: Canada, Pan American Health Organization, 2001, <http://www.paho.org/english/sha/prflcan.htm> (June 2003).

42. "Bureau of Women's Health and Gender Analysis," Health Canada, 2005, <http://www.hc-sc.gc.ca/english/women/cewh.htm> (5 Oct. 2005).

43. Human Development Reports.

44. "The Governor General's Awards in Commemoration of the Persons Case, The 'Famous Five' and the Persons Case: Early Activists Challenge Conventional Views to Change Canadian History," Status of Women Canada, 2003, <http://www.swc-cfc.gc.ca/dates/persons/case_e.html> (June 2003).

45. "Judges of the Court, Remarks of the Right Honourable Beverley McLachlin, P.C., Famous Five Breakfast," Supreme Court of Canada, October 2000, <http://www.scc-csc.gc.ca/AboutCourt/judges/speeches/famousfive_e.asp> (5 Oct. 2005).

46. "Emily Murphy," The Famous Five Foundation, 2004, <http://www.abheritage.ca/famous5/achievements/emily_murphy.html> (5 Oct. 2005).

47. Mary Bond, "Changing Canadian Women, Changing Canadian History: Women's History Month," *National Library News*, 31 no. 10 (October 1999).

48. "Women's Suffrage," Famous Five Foundation, <http://www.famous5.org/frames/frame_education_issues.htm> (5 Oct. 2005).

49. Ibid.

50. (*Dominion Law Reports,* [1930] 1 DLR); "Women's Suffrage."

51. Susan Munroe, "The Persons Case, A Milestone in the History of Canadian Women," Canada Online, <http://canadaonline.about.com/cs/women/a/personscase.htm>; Famous Five Foundation, Women's Suffrage.

52. "Women in National Parliaments," Inter- Parliamentary Union, 2004, <http://www.ipu.org/wmn-e/classif.htm> (Sept. 2004).

53. Human Development Reports.

54. "Canadian Forces Recruiting," National Defence, 2005, <http://www.recruiting.forces.gc.ca/engraph/howtojoin/eligibility_e.aspx#s2> (3 Oct. 2005).

55. Barbara Dundas and Serge Durflinger, "Military History, Dispatches: Back-grounders in Canadian Military History," The Canadian Women's Army Corps, 1941–1946, Canadian War Museum, 2005, <http://www.civilization.ca/cwm/disp/dis005_e.html> (Oct. 2005).

56. "What is women's work?," CBC Archives, 1945, <http://archives.cbc.ca/IDC-1-71-855-5101/conflict_war/women_ww2/clip11> (June 2003).

57. "Committee on Women in NATO Forces," Canada, NATO, 2002, <http://www.nato.int/ims/2001/win/canada.htm> (June 2003).

58. "Committee on Women in NATO Forces."

59. CIA World Factbook, United States, <http://www.cia.gov/cia/publications/factbook/geos/us.html>.

60. CIA World Factbook, United States.

61. Ibid.

62. The U.S. Constitution, The U.S. Constitution Online, 2005, <http://www.us-constitution.net/const.html#Am14> (Oct. 2005).

63. *Sara J. Spencer vs. The Board of registration*, and *Sarah E. Webster vs. The judges of election*. Votes for Women: Selections from the National American Woman Suffrage Association Collection, 1848–1921, Suffrage conferred by the Fourteenth Amendment. Woman's suffrage in the Supreme Court of the District of Columbia, in general term, October, 1871. Argument of the counsel for the plaintiffs. With the opinions of the court (see page 4), The Library of Congress, 1998, <http://memory.loc.gov/cgi-bin/ampage?collId=rbnawsa&fileName=n3154//rbnawsan3154.db&recNum=4&itemLink=r?ammem/nawbib:@field(NUMBER+@od1(rbnawsa+n3154))&linkText=0> (Oct. 2005).

64. "An Account of the Proceedings on the Trial of Susan B. Anthony on the Charge of Illegal Voting, at the Presidential Election in Nov., 1872, and on the Trial of Beverly W. Jones, Edwin T. Marsh and William B. Hall, The Inspectors of Election by whom her Vote was Received, Rochester, N.Y.," Library of Congress, 1998, <http://memory.loc.gov/cgi-bin/query/r?ammem/naw:@field(DOCID+@lit(rbnawsan2152div1))> (Oct 2005).

65. The U.S. Constitution, Amendment 14.

66. "An Account of the Proceedings on the Trial of Susan B. Anthony."

67. The U.S. Constitution, Amendment 15.

68. "An Account of the Proceedings on the Trial of Susan B. Anthony."

69. The U.S. Constitution, Amendment 19.

70. CIA World Factbook, United States.

71. "Women's History in America," Women's International Center, excerpted from Compton's Interactive Encyclopedia, 1994/1995, <http://www.wic.org/misc/history.htm> (June 2003).

72. See *Nguyen, Tuan, et al. v. Immigration & Naturalization Service*, 533 U.S. 53 (2001).; Debra L. Satinoff, "Sex-Based Discrimination in U.S. Immigration Law: The High Court's Lost Opportunity to Bridge the Gap Between What We Say and What We Do," *The American University Law Review* (May 1999), <http://www.wcl.american.edu/journal/lawrev/47/pdf/satinoff.pdf>.

73. Anna Quindlen, "Torture Based on Sex Alone, Do women have special asylum claims? They do, and they ought to be recognized," *Newsweek* (September 10, 2001): 76; "Union Tribune Exposed Villaraigosa, Now Hides Story," American Patrol, 2001,

<http://www.americanpatrol.com/CALIFORNIA/VILLARAIGOSA/Vil-laraigosaTribStory.html> (July 2003).

74. "Union Tribune Exposed Villaraigosa, Now Hides Story."

75. Quindlen, "Torture Based on Sex Alone."

76. "Domestic Security Enhancement Act of 2003," also known as "PATRIOT Act II," American Civil Liberties Union, February 14, 2003, <http://www.aclu.org/Safe-andFree/SafeandFree.cfm?ID=11835&c=206> (June 2003).

77. "Fact Sheet: Fair and Secure Immigration Reform," The White House, Office of the Press Secretary, January 2004, <http://www.whitehouse.gov/news/re-leases/2004/01/20040107-1.html> (June 2004).

78. "Women's History in America," Women's International Center.

79. Ibid.

80. Civil Rights Act 1964, Department of State, International Information Programs, 1996, <http://usinfo.state.gov/usa/infousa/laws/majorlaw/civilr19.htm> (Oct. 2005).

81. U.S. Census Bureau.

82. U.S. Census Bureau.

83. CIA World Factbook, United States.

84. Joan William and Nancy Segal, "The New Glass Ceiling: Mothers—and Fathers—Sue for Discrimination," Program on WorkLife Law, American University, Washington College of Law (2002), 42 U.S.C. §§ 2000e *et seq.* (1994), <http://www.wcl.american.edu/gender/workfamily/chilly_climate0211.pdf > (July 2003).

85. Ibid.

86. Ibid.

87. Ibid.

88. Ibid.

89. Ibid.

90. Ibid.

91. Progress of the World's Women, UNESCO Institute of Statistics, 2002, <http://portal.unesco.org/uis> (July 2003).

92. Human Development Reports, United Nations Development Programme, 2003, <http://hdr.undp.org/statistics/data/countries.cfm?c=USA> (July 2004).

93. Ibid.

94. "Women's Earnings as a percentage of Men's, 1951–2003," Information Please Database, 2005 Pearson Education, Inc, (2004), U.S. Women's Bureau and the National Committee on Pay Equity, <http://www.infoplease.com/ipa/A0193820.html>.

95. Scott Smallwood, "Prime Numbers, Survey Shows Salary Gap Between Men and Women in the Life Sciences," The Chronicle of Higher Education, <http://chron-icle.com/weekly/v48/i09/09a00803.htm> (July 2004).

96. Reneé E. Spraggins, "Women and Men in the United States," U.S. Census Bureau, (March 2003): 4.

97. "The Wag Gap, by Gender and Race," Information Please Database, 2005 Pearson Education, Inc, 2004, National Committee on Pay Equity, <http://www.infoplease.com/ipa/A0882775.html> (July 2004).

98. "Facts for Features and Special Editions, Women's History Month (March)," U.S. Census Bureau, 2004, <http://www.census.gov/Press-Release/www/releases/archives/facts_for_features_special_editions/001684.html> (July 2004).

99. Heidi Dietrich, "Women Who Cover War," International Women's Media Foundation, <http://www.iwmf.org/features/6831> (Oct. 2005).

100. *Professional Women & Minorities: A Total Human Resources Data Compendium,* 14th Edition (Washington, DC: Commission on Professionals in Science and Technology, 2002), 121.

101. Ibid., 163.

102. "Facts for Features and Special Editions, Women's History Month."

103. D'Vera Cohn and Sarah Cohen, "Minorities, Women Gain Professionally," *Washington Post,* 18 June 2004.

104. "Martin Luther King Jr. Day (Jan. 19) and African-American History Month: February 2004," U.S. Census Bureau, 2004, <http://www.census.gov/Press-Release/www/releases/archives/facts_for_features/001645.html> (July 2004).

105. U.S. Census Bureau, "U.S. Hispanic Population: 2002," Population Division, Ethnicity and Ancestry Branch, 2002, <http://www.census.gov/population/socdemo/hispanic/ppl-165/slideshow/sld001.htm> (July 2003).

106. Williams and Segal, "The New Glass Ceiling."

107. Annemarie Micklo, "Just the Facts: What Demographics Tell Us about the Future of Our Profession and Our Clients," American Bar Association, *GPSolo* 18, no. 1 (January/February 2001), <http://www.abanet.org/genpractice/magazine/janfeb2001/miklo.html> (19 Oct. 2005).

108. Ibid.

109. Frances Cerra Whittelsey and Marcia Carroll, *Women Pay More,* (New York, NY: The New Press, 1995), cited from Julie Connelly, "Divorce, Getting the best Deal," *Fortune,* May 17, 1993, 123.

110. "Title IX of the Education Amendments of 1972, 20 U.S.C.§§1681–1688, Title 20 - Education, Chapter 38, Discrimination Based on Sex or Blindness," U.S. Department of Justice, 2000, <http://www.usdoj.gov/crt/cor/coord/titleixstat.htm> (July 2003).

111. "Impact of the Civil Rights Laws," U.S. Department of Education, 1999, <http://www.ed.gov/about/offices/list/ocr/impact.html> (July 2003), *Digest,* 1997 edition, table 260, page 290, Degrees and Other Awards Conferred by Degree-Granting Institutions: 1995–96, table 1a, 8.

112. "Timeline, 1800–1900," Electronic Oberlin Group, <http://www.oberlin.edu/external/EOG/OberlinTimeline.html> (Oct. 2005).

113. Fletcher, *A History of Oberlin College—From its Foundation through the Civil War,* Vol. II (Oberlin, Ohio: Oberlin College, 1943), 534–535.

114. Progress of the World's Women, UNESCO Institute of Statistics, 2002, <http://portal.unesco.org/uis> (July 2003).

115. *Professional Women & Minorities: A Total Human Resources Data Compendium.* (Washington, DC: Commission on Professionals in Science and Technology, 2002), 1.

116. Ibid., 53.

117. Ibid., 335.

118. "SAT Math Scores for 2005 Highest on Record, College Board Offers Glimpse of New SAT with Writing for Upcoming Class of '06," College Board Office of Public Affairs, 08/30/05, <http://www.collegeboard.com/press/article/0,,46851,00.html> (Oct. 2005).

119. "More Women Aspiring to be Doctors," *CNN* 8 Dec. 2003.

120. Ted Gest, "Law Schools' New Female Face, An influx of women as students has changed courses and attitudes," *U.S. News and World Reports*, 9 April 2001; *Professional Women & Minorities: A Total Human Resources Data Compendium*, 109.

121. Aaron Lamb and Lena Salaymeh, "Artificial Selection: LSAT bias affects us all," *The Record*, Harvard Law School, 19 Sept. 2002.

122. "Martin Luther King Jr. Day (Jan. 19) and African-American History Month: February 2004."

123. U.S. Census Bureau, "U.S. Hispanic Population: 2002," Population Division, Ethnicity and Ancestry Branch, 2002.

124. "2003 SAT Scores for DoDEA Released Strong Gains in SAT Scores Reported for DoDEA's Minority Students," Department of Defense Education Activity, 2003, <http://www.dodea.edu/communications/news/releases/090203.htm> (July 2004).

125. Leigh Jones, "Fewer Students Apply to Top Schools," *The National Law Journal* (22 Aug. 2005).

126. See *Barbara Grutter v. Lee Bollinger*, 539 U.S. 306 (2003), Amicus Brief of Boston Bar Association, Dwyer & Collora, Llp, Day, Berry & Howard, Goulston & Storrs, Krokidas & Bluestein, Llp, Shapiro Haber & Urmy Llp, Sterns Shapiro Weissberg & Garin, Testa, Hurwitz & Thibeault, Llp, And Weisman & Associates In Support Of Respondents, No. 02-241, 18 Feb. 2003.

127. "Executive Summary," American Bar Association, Commission on Racial and Ethnic Diversity in the Profession, <http://www.abanet.org/minorities/publications/milesummary.html> (July 2003).

128. Simon and Altstein, *Global Perspectives on Social Issues*.

129. "2004 American Community Survey, Data Profile Highlights," U.S. Census Bureau, 2004, <http://factfinder.census.gov/servlet/ACSSAFFFacts?_event=&geo_id=01000US&_geoContext=&_street=&_county=&_cityTown=&_state=&_zip=&_lang=en&_sse=on&ActiveGeoDiv=&_useEV= > (Oct. 2005).

130. Gulnar Nugman, World Divorce Rates, Heritage Foundation, 2002, <http://www.divorcereform.org/gul.html> (Sept. 2005); Simon and Altstein, *Global Perspectives on Social Issues*.

131. Ibid.

132. See *Frontiero v. Richardson* 411 US 677 (1973).

133. Centers for Disease Control and Prevention, "First Marriage Dissolution, Divorce, and Remarriage: United States," 1995 National Survey of Family Growth, Advances Data 323, (PHS) 2001–1250, <http://www.cdc.gov/od/oc/media/pressrel/r010524.htm>, <http://fatherhood.hhs.gov/pdf/First-Marriage-Diss-ad323.pdf> (July 2003).

134. Ibid.

135. Ibid.

136. Ibid.

137. Centers for Disease Control and Prevention, "Cohabitation, Marriage, Divorce and Remarriage in the United States," Vital and Health Statistics, Series Report 23, no. 22, 2002, <http://www.cdc.gov/nchs/data/series/sr_23/sr23_022.pdf> (July 2003).

138. Simon and Altstein, *Global Perspectives on Social Issues.*

139. Atlee Stroup and Gene Pollock, "Economic Consequences of Marital Dissolution," *Journal of Divorce and Remarriage*, 22 (1994): 37–54.

140. Judi Bartfeld, "Child Support and the Post-Divorce Economic Well-being of Mothers, Fathers, and Children," University of Wisconsin, Madison Department of Consumer Science Institute for Research on Poverty Cooperative Extension, July 1998: 5, U.S. Bureau of the Census, 1991a.

141. Whittelsey and Carroll, *Women Pay More*, cited from New York City Department of Consumer Affairs, *Women in Divorce* (New York: City of New York, March 1992), 8.

142. Ibid.

143. Whittelsey and Carroll, *Women Pay More*, cited from Frances Leonard, *Women & Money* (New York: Addison-Wesley, 1991), 11.

144. Whittelsey and Carroll, *Women Pay More*, cited from *Women in Divorce,* 39.

145. Ibid., *Women in Divorce*, 9.

146. Ibid., *Women in Divorce*, 8.

147. Whittelsey and Carroll, *Women Pay More*, cited from Nancy Duff Campbell, co-president, National Women's Law Center, testimony on child support assistance, before the Subcommittee on Children, Family, Drugs, and Alcoholism, Committee on Labor and Human Resources, U.S. Senate, August 3, 1993.

148. Ibid., Jeanne L. Reid, "Making Delinquent Dad Pay His Child Support," *Ms.* July/August 1992, 86–87.

149. Ibid., "Maine Targets Deadbeat Parents," *Washington Post*, June 28, 1994, A5.

150. U.S. Census Bureau, "U.S. Hispanic Population: 2002," Population Division, Ethnicity and Ancestry Branch, 2002.

151. "At Last, Good News on the Family (Probably)," *The Economist* 360, no. 8232 (26 July 2001): 29.

152. "Abortion Policies, A Global Review, United States," United Nations, <http://www.un.org/esa/population/publications/abortion/profiles.htm> (July 2003).

153. "Facts in Brief, Teen Sex and Pregnancy," The Alan Guttmacher Institute, 1999, <http://www.agi-usa.org/pubs/fb_teen_sex.html#24> (Oct. 2005); "Abortion Policies, A Global Review, United States," United Nations.

154. "Abortion Policies, A Global Review, United States," United Nations.

155. Lilo T. Strauss, et al., "Abortion Surveillance," Division of Reproductive Health National Center for Chronic Disease Prevention and Health Promotion 53(SS09), (26 Nov. 2004): 1–32.

156. Rita James Simon, *Abortion: Statutes, Policies, and Public Attitudes the World Over* (Westport, CT: Greenwood Publishing Group, 1998).

157. "Senate Passes 'Partial Birth' Abortion Ban, Court Challenge Certain," *CNN*, 21 Oct. 2003.

158. "Facts in Brief, Teen Sex and Pregnancy," The Alan Guttmacher Institute.

159. "At Last, Good News on the Family (Probably)," *The Economist*.

160. Babatunde A. Gbolade, "Depo-Provera and Bone Density," Faculty of Family Planning and Reproductive Health Care of the Royal College of Obstetricians and Gynecologists, 2001, <http://www.ffprhc.org.uk/meetings/factreview.pdf> (Oct. 2005).

161. "Contraception & Family Planning Barr Laboratories Applies for OTC Status for Emergency Contraceptive Plan B for Women Age 16, Older," Henry J. Kaiser Family Foundation, 2004, <http://www.kaisernetwork.org/daily_reports/rep_index.cfm?DR_ID=24916> (July 2004).

162. Citizenship and Immigration Canada, "Looking at Health Care, United States," Cultural Profiles Project, <http://www.cp-pc.ca/english/usa/index.html> (Oct. 2005).

163. U.S. Department of Health and Human Services, "A Profile of Medicaid: 2000 Chartbook, Section 1," Health Care Financing Administration, 2000, <http://www.policyalmanac.org/health/archive/hhs_medicaid.shtml> (July 2003).

164. Dr. Bertakis, et al, "Gender Differences in the Utilization of Health Care Services," *Journal of Family Practice* 49, no. 2 (Feb. 2000): 147–52.

165. C. M. Kjellstrand, "Age, Sex, and Race Inequality in Renal Transplantation," *Archives of Internal Medicine* 148, no. 6 (1 June 1988): 1305–9.

166. Whittelsey and Carroll, *Women Pay More*, cited from Bureau of the Census, "Death, by Age and Leading Causes: 1990," *Statistical Abstract of the United States*, 113th edition (Washington, D.C., 1993) no. 128:93.

167. Amanda Gardner, "Women's Risk of Lung Cancer Double that of Men, 10-year study shows startling susceptibility," HON Foundation, 2003, <http://www.hon.ch/News/HSN/516271.html> (July 2003).

168. Whittelsey and Carroll, *Women Pay More*, cited from Bureau of the Census, "Death, by Age and Leading Causes: 1990," *Statistical Abstract of the United States*.

169. Ibid., Bureau of the Census, "Death, by Age and Leading Causes: 1990," *Statistical Abstract of the United States*.

170. Marianne J. Legato and Carol Colman, "The Female Heart: The Truth about Women and Heart Disease" (New York: HarperCollins, 2000).

171. Ibid.

172. U.S. Food and Drug Administration, "An Interview with a Mayo Clinic Specialist," Mayo Foundation for Medical Education and Research, 2004, <http://www.fda.gov/hearthealth/news/mayo091704.html> (Oct. 2005).

173. Whittelsey and Carroll, *Women Pay More*, cited from American Medical Association, Council on Ethical and Judicial Affairs, "Gender Disparities in Clinical Decision Making," *Journal of the American Medical Association* 266, no. 4 (July 24, 1991): 559.

174. Gena Corea, "The Invisible Epidemic: The Story of Women and AIDS" (New York: HarperCollins, 1992) 356.

175. Whittelsey and Carroll, *Women Pay More*, cited from Laurie Jones, "AIDS Focus Slowly Turning toward Women," *American Medical News* 37, no. 11 (March 21, 1994) 3.

176. Ibid., Michelle Slantalla, "The Lagging War on Breast Cancer," *Newsday*, October 3, 1993, 4.

177. Ibid., Alix Boyle, "Women Gain in Medical Research," *New York Times*, April 26, 1992, sec. 12C, p.14.

178. Martin Sipkoff, "Data Scarce on Women's Reactions to Drugs," Drug Topics Supplements, 2005, <http://www.drugtopics.com/drugtopics/article/articleDetail .jsp?id=157946&pageID=1&sk=&date=> (Oct. 2005).

179. Whittelsey and Carroll, *Women Pay More*, cited from Alix Boyle, "Women Gain in Medical Research," *New York Times*, April 26, 1992, sec. 12C, p.14.

180. Viviana Simon and Eileen Resnick, "Drug Therapy and Gender," *U.S. Pharmacist* 29, no. 9 (2004): 37–38.

181. Whittelsey and Carroll, *Women Pay More*, cited from David Tuller, "Second Class Care Motivates Revolution in Women's Health," *San Francisco Chronicle*, November 22, 1993, A1.

182. Ibid., Robert Herman, "What Doctors Don't Know about Women," *Washington Post*, 8 December 1992.

183. Martin Sipkoff, "Data Scarce on Women's Reactions to Drugs"; Whittelsey and Carroll, *Women Pay More*; cited from "Hysterectomies in the United States, 1965–1984," Center for Disease Control and Prevention, U.S. Department of Health and Human Services 88, no. 1753 (Dec. 1987): 7, National Health Survey 13, no. 92.

184. Whittelsey and Carroll, *Women Pay More*, cited from John Schwartz, "FDA Lifts Restriction on Women; Clinical Trials May Cover Childbearing Age," *Washington Post*, July 22, 1993, A5.

185. U.S. Food and Drug Administration, "FDA Milestones in Women's Health, Looking Back as We Move into the New Millennium," Office of Women's Health, 2001, <http://www.fda.gov/womens/milesbro.html> (July 2003).

186. Ibid.

187. Ibid.; House Committee on Narcotics Abuse and Control, *Women's Dependency of Prescription Drugs: Hearing before the Select Committee on Narcotics Abuse & Control*, September 13, 1979, 46.

188. "If You Absolutely Need a Hysterectomy," edited excerpts from William H. Parker and Rachel L. Parker, *A Gynecologist's Second Opinion*, 1996 <http://www .gynsecondopinion.com/hysterectomy.htm> (July 2003).

189. "Hysterectomies in the United States, 1965–1984," Center for Disease Control and Prevention.

190. Deidre Gifford, "Cesarean Delivery."

191. Whittelsey and Carroll, *Women Pay More*, cited from House Committee on Narcotics Abuse and Control, *Women's Dependency of Prescription Drugs: Hearing before the Select Committee on Narcotics Abuse & Control*, September 13, 1979, 47.

192. Deidre Gifford, "Cesarean Delivery."

193. Whittelsey and Carroll, *Women Pay More*, cited from Public Citizen Health Research Group, Unnecessary Cesarean Sections: Curing a National Epidemic (Washington, D.C.: Public Citizen Health Research Group, May 1994), vii.

194. Rutgers, Eagleton Institute of Politics, "Women Who Succeed Their Husbands in Congress," Center for American Women and Politics (CAWP), 2005, <http://www.cawp.rutgers.edu/Facts/Officeholders/widows.pdf> (Oct. 2005).

195. Rutgers, Eagleton Institute of Politics, "Women in the U.S. Congress 2005," (CAWP), 2005, <http://www.cawp.rutgers.edu/Facts/Officeholders/cong.pdf#page=2> (Oct. 2005).

196. Rutgers, Eagleton Institute of Politics, "Women Serving in the 109th Congress 2005–07," (CAWP), 2005, <http://www.cawp.rutgers.edu/Facts/Officeholders/cong-current.html> (Oct. 2005).

197. Ibid.

198. Ibid., <http://www.cawp.rutgers.edu/Facts/Officeholders/elective.pdf>.

199. "American Women and the Military," Gender Gap, 2001, <http://www.gendergap.com/military/usmil.htm> (July 2003).

200. Ibid.

201. Ibid.

202. Ibid.

203. Ibid.

204. Ibid.

205. Ibid.

206. Lorry M. Fenner, "Either You Need These Women or You Do Not: Informing the Debate on Military Service and Citizenship," *Gender Issues* 16, no. 3 (Summer 1998): 8.

207. Ibid., 9.

208. Ibid., 10.

209. Ibid., 14, 15.

210. Ibid., 18.

211. Ibid., 16, 19.

212. CIA World Factbook, United States.

213. U.S. Census Bureau, "U.S. Armed Forces and Veterans," Facts and Features, 2003, <http://www.census.gov/Press-Release/www/2003/cb03-ff04se.html> (July 2004).

214. "The Military 'Glass Ceiling'," Gender Gap, 1998, <http://gendergap.com/military/glasceil.htm> (July 2003), Information Please Almanac.

215. Eric Rosenberg, "Selective Services Eye Women's Draft," *Seattle Post-Intelligencer*, 1 May 2004.

216. Ibid.

217. Matt Kelley, "G.I. Jane is Taking More Fire Than Ever Before," *Seattle Post-Intelligencer*, 3 January 2004.

218. Ibid.

Chapter Two

Latin America

BRAZIL

Brazil is the largest country in South America. It is slightly smaller than the United States in size and is the only country in South America whose official language is Portuguese not Spanish. Brazil is located in Eastern South America, and is bordered by all of the South American countries except for Ecuador and Chile. It borders the Atlantic Ocean. The population is 186,112,794 and is heavily distributed among the coastal cities and towns. The ethnic groups are White, including Portuguese, German, Italian, Spanish, Polish (55 percent), mixed White and Black (38 percent), Black (6 percent), and other, Japanese, Arab, Amerindian (1 percent). The main religion is Roman Catholic (80 percent). The languages spoken in Brazil are Portuguese (the official language), Spanish, English, and French.[1]

The majority of Brazilians live in the cities such as Sao Paulo, Belo Horizonte, Porto Alegre, and Brazilia. Sixty-eight percent of the population is below the age of fifteen and 6 percent are sixty-five and older. Women make up over 51 percent of the population.[2]

Constitution

Brazil is a federal republic with twenty-six states and the federal district. Brazil officially gained its independence from Portugal on September 7, 1822. The Republic of the United States of Brazil was then formed. In 1967, the country became the Federal Republic of Brazil. Between 1967 and 1985 Brazil was governed by military dictatorships. The first democratic elections were held in 1985. Brazil has had seven constitutions since its Independence. The present constitution was adopted on October, 5, 1988. The new Civil Code was enacted in 2002. The new Civil Code legally altered women's position in Brazil.[3]

Article III of the Constitution states that the country's objective is "to promote the well being of all, without prejudice as to origin, race, sex, color, age, and any other forms of discrimination." In addition, Article 5 states that men and women have equal rights and duties under the Constitution.[4] However, not all genders and races are treated equally. Approximately 30 percent of Brazilian families are headed by women, who by themselves support and care for their children and other relatives. A large percentage of these women are Black. Black women are in the lowest financial position of all Brazilian populations.[5]

Women obtained the right to vote and to run for office in 1932. Voting is compulsory for people over eighteen years of age and optional for the illiterate, people over seventy, and people between sixteen and eighteen years of age.[6]

While the law has changed in favor of women, the Judiciary demonstrates resistance to women's right to equality under the Constitution. There are still many explicitly discriminatory decisions in sexual crime lawsuits. In addition, juries still accept, as a legitimate defense, the defense of honor killing. Under this defense a man may be acquitted for murdering his wife because he was defending his honor. This defense has continued to be successful regardless of the 1991 Supreme Court decision that held that the defense was nonjudicial. In addition, rape is considered a minor crime unless it results in pregnancy.[7]

Work Force and Economy

Brazil is the largest and most populated country in South America. It has many natural resources and is South America's leading economic power and regional leader. Brazil is considered to be the most economically viable country among developing nations. However, a highly unequal income distribution remains a pressing problem.[8] In fact, 2.4 percent of the population have one third of the wealth.[9] Forty percent of households live off of $43.5 per person per month while the top 10 percent live on more than $8,000 per month per person.[10] The minimum wage was raised on May 1, 2004 by 8.33 percent from roughly $80 to $87 per month. The minimum wage barely pays for 69 percent of one's basic living needs. In fact, a worker can end up using all of his/her minimum wage to pay for urban bus trips, getting to and from home and work. The 8.33 percent minimum wage increase is not going to have much of an effect on the present living conditions of workers.[11] Brazil possesses large and well-developed agricultural, mining, manufacturing, and service sectors. Brazil's economy outweighs that of all other South American countries. In addition, it is also expanding its presence in world markets. Brazil has a purchasing power parity of $1.492 trillion (2004 est.).[12] The unemployment rate was 12.8 percent in March 2004.[13] Unemployment is higher for women than men.[14] The current unemployment rate for women is 22.3 percent.[15] The major industries in Brazil are textiles, shoes, chemicals, cement, lumber, iron ore, tin, steel, aircraft, motor vehicles and parts, and other machinery and equipment.[16]

Article 7 of the Brazilian Constitution prohibits gender-based, age-based, color-based, or marital status based discrimination in wages, employment performance of duties, and in hiring criteria. However, wage discrimination is rarely enforced. According to a study performed by the Getulio Vargas Foundation, women have to study 25 percent longer than males in order to receive the same salary. With each additional year of schooling a male received an average of a 10 percent salary increase while women received an 8 percent increase. A study conducted by the Brazilian Institute of Geography and Statistics in 2000 indicated that the median income for women was 67 percent of the median income for men. A 1998 government statistic revealed women with a high-school education or less earned 63 percent of that earned by men of equal education. Afro-Brazilian women earned an average of 26 percent of a White male's salary of equal education.[17] Sixty-seven percent of women employed in the non-agricultural sector work in informal employment, 32 percent of those women are self-employed. Sixty-eight percent of women's wages in informal employment comes from self-employment.[18]

The Maternity Leave Law provides women with 120 days of paid maternity leave and grants men one week of paternity leave. In addition, Article 7 of the Constitution allows for paternity leave. The Constitution also prohibits potential and present employers from requiring applicants or employees to take pregnancy tests or present sterilization certificates. Nevertheless, some employers still seek sterilization certificates and avoid hiring females in their childbearing years. The penalty for violating the Maternity Leave Law is a jail term of one to two years. The company must also pay a penalty, which amounts to ten times the salary of the highest-paid employee. However, there is no record of enforcement of the Maternity Leave Law.[19]

According to a new study by the Brazilian Institute of Public Opinion and Statistics (IBOPE) 74 percent of companies have no Blacks among directors. Additionally, in 58 percent of the five hundred largest companies, women do not figure into the highest executive positions. Of the 6,016 women who hold managerial positions, 372 are Black. Women hold 9 percent of executive positions, 18 percent of managerial positions, and 28 percent of foreman and section head positions in the five hundred largest companies.[20]

Increasing numbers of women are entering the medical profession. In 1996, 31.9 percent of all practicing physicians in the country were women. The health sector accounts for about 8 percent of all jobs in the country.[21]

Women make up 40.4 percent of the work force in Brazil and 43.8 percent in the federal administration. Domestic work makes up 18 percent of female employment. Only 4.5 percent of female domestic workers are legally employed.[22] Few women are in positions of authority. Black and indigenous women make up even fewer of these positions. Black women appear to have little career mobility. Black women make up 80 percent of servants.

In June 2002, a federal government quota system was instituted. The system requires that 20 percent of new federal government hires be Afro-Brazilian, 20 percent women, and 5 percent persons with disabilities. In 2003, the city of Porto Alegre, Grande do Sul required that 12 percent of the slots in competitive exams for public jobs be reserved for Afro-Brazilians.[23]

According to the UN, Brazil is the largest exporter of female sex slaves. The UN and Helsinki International Federation of Human Rights say that 75,000 Brazilian women are forced to work as prostitutes within the boundaries of the European Union. The Special Secretary of Women's policies, Emilia Fernandes, stated that one of Brazil's goals is to confront participation or involvement by the police with this crime.[24]

Adult prostitution is legal. However, operating an establishment of prostitution is illegal. Prostitutes often encounter discrimination when trying to obtain medical care.

Sexual harassment is a criminal offense, punishable by one to two years in prison. The law applies to the work place, between family members, education, and service providers. In the work place sexual harassment can only apply in hierarchical situations, for example, where a boss is harassing her/his employee.[25]

Education

In 2000, the ratio of female to male student enrollment in secondary school was 108 women to every 100 men. Nevertheless, only 71 percent of eligible females are enrolled in secondary school. In 2002, the ratio of female to male youth (ages fifteen to twenty-four) literacy was 104 women to every 100 men. The female youth literacy rate was 94.8 percent compared to 91.7 percent in 1995.[26] Article 208 of the Constitution places a duty on the state to provide compulsory and free elementary education, continual efforts to accommodate free secondary school, special classes for individuals with disabilities, assistance to children up to six years old for day care purposes, access to higher education, regular night courses to fit the needs of working students, assistance to elementary school children so they may have school supplies, transportation, and proper nutrition.[27] In 2000, the female to male ratio of student enrollment in tertiary school was 129 women to every 100 men.[28]

Race also plays a role in access to education. The 1982 Census revealed that 78 percent of White women completed primary education compared to 22 percent of Black women. Only 1 percent of Black women who completed primary school went on to university. Upon graduation most of those who completed university ended up in servant positions because they were unable to find work. In response to the inequality in educational opportunities the Ministry of Education has recently entered into an agreement with the Special Department of Women's Policies, creating the Student Mother Program. The program teaches mothers of students in the Scholarship Program reading and writing classes. This has stimulated school attendance.[29] In addition, in 2003, three state universities instituted race quotas.[30]

Marriage

The minimum age for marriage is twenty-one for both women and men. Sixteen-year-old girls and eighteen-year-old men may marry with parental or guardian consent.[31] A marriage must be registered at the registry office.[32]

In 2002, the Brazilian Congress adopted a law that gave men and women equal authority in the family under the civil code. The former civil code was created in 1917. The former code stated, "every man is capable of rights and obligations."[33] A woman was not capable of rights and obligations. Consequently, under the old code a wife was considered an extension of her husband. The husband had executive power in the family. This power was known as paternal power. From 1916 until 2002 men were able to obtain an annulment up to ten days after marriage if they discovered that their wife was not a virgin before marriage.[34] In addition, a husband had power over joint property.[35] Consequently, a married woman had to obtain her husband's permission to sell or acquire real property. In addition, adulterers (male or female) were not allowed to remarry. Presently, adultery is a ground for divorce, and preventing a parent from obtaining child custody. However, adulterers may remarry.[36]

Since the new civil code, custody is no longer automatically granted to mothers, fathers may obtain custody as well.[37]

Common law marriages are now recognized. Under the new code, the "family entity" is an informal and stable union between spouses. In order to benefit under the law, couples must cohabitate for at least two to three years. Common law marriages have many of the legal respects and issues as registered marriages. In addition, under the new code there are no longer any distinctions between legitimate, illegitimate, incestuous, adopted children, or children that are a result of an adulterous affair. A father cannot dispute paternity within a marriage. Although he may take a paternity test after separation.[38]

Divorce became legal in 1977.[39] Presently, there are 0.28 divorces per 1,000 people. The Brazilian divorce process is time consuming and complicated. The Federal Supreme Court is the only authority that may declare a divorce. After a divorce application is submitted, couples must be separated for one year. After the year passes, the separation may be converted into a divorce. Then the petitioner must go to the Civil Registry Office to have the divorce certified.[40] The divorce process is similar for common law marriages.[41]

Abortion and Contraceptives

There are no statistics on abortions performed in Brazil. In 1991, estimates of the number of abortions performed ranged from 866,003 to 2,020,674.[42] In 1995, the Single Health Care System registered 274,698 hospitalizations for abortion complications.[43] Abortions are illegal and cannot be performed except under prescribed circumstances such as saving the life of the mother or to terminate a pregnancy that resulted from rape or incest. A woman cannot have an abortion to preserve her physical or mental health, or for economic or social reasons.[44] While not legally grounds for abortion, the judiciary permits abortions in cases where the fetus has grave and irreversible abnormalities. Roughly 350 of these type of abortions are performed a year.[45] In addition, if the woman is pregnant as a result of rape, the physician must gain the woman's consent prior to performing an abortion. If she is incompetent, the physician must obtain the consent of her legal representative.[46]

The sentence for rape is eight to ten years. According to a national study, 70 percent of rapes are committed by family members. The Penal Code allows a convict to be exonerated if he offers to marry the victim. Spousal rape is illegal but rarely prosecuted. In 2003, 2 percent of criminal complaints of violence against women led to convictions. When convictions took place the penalties were light.[47]

An abortion is considered a criminal offense. The Penal Code specifies that a pregnant woman who performs an abortion on herself or consents to its performance by another person is subject to one to three years of detention.[48] The abortion law is in the process of being reformed. However, the 2002 Civil Code kept the original 1917 text that states that it "protects the rights of a fetus as of conception."[49]

The Medical Ethics Code contains rules about the doctor-patient relationship concerning reproductive health.[50] For example, a doctor has an obligation to respect a woman's right to choose the contractive method that she desires. The physician must explain the risks of the contraceptive methods.[51] Doctors who do not comply with the Code are tried by their regional Council of Medicine.[52]

Contraceptives are legal in Brazil and are used by 77 percent of married women (ages fifteen to forty-nine; 1996). The majority of women use contraceptive pills or female sterilization. Many women receive tubal ligations during cesarean operations.[53]

There are no legal restrictions on the distribution of information about contraceptives. Under the Family Planning Law, the government must dispense necessary information on contraceptives and promote conditions to assure that all men and women have the right to family planning.[54] In addition, the Ministry of Health has a program to ensure paternal responsibility.[55]

There are legal limitations on sterilization. Men may have vasectomies and women may have tubal ligation. Yet, hysterectomies and ovariectomies are illegal. In addition, the consent of both husband and wife are required for sterilization during a marriage.[56]

In February 2004, Rio de Janeiro began to mail free contraceptive pills to women, including teenagers, in poor neighborhoods. Rio de Janeiro's health secretary, Ronaldo Cezar Coelho, stated that the program was not designed to push contraceptive use on low income women but rather to give poor women the same opportunity to obtain birth control as wealthy women. In addition, all women who subscribe for the free contraceptive pills are given free condoms. The program also distributes free medication for heart problems and diabetes.[57]

Women are 28 percent of the total registered cases of HIV and AIDS. However, HIV and AIDS are spreading rapidly at a high rate among teenage girls. There are six girls, ages thirteen to nineteen, who are infected with the virus for every boy thirteen to nineteen years old. In response to the recent statistic, the Health Ministry began a condom distribution program. Condoms are distributed to schools in 205 municipalities with the highest rate of HIV and AIDS.[58]

The total fertility rate has fallen from 5.8 children per woman in 1970 to 1.9 per woman today.[59] The population growth has been lowered to 1.4 percent a year.[60]

Infant mortality rate is 38 per 1,000 (2002). Maternal mortality was 140 per 100,000 deliveries.[61]

On International Women's Day, March 8, 2004, Health Minister Humberto Costa announced a Health program that will decrease infant mortality and maternal mortality by 15 percent by 2006.[62]

Health Care

The 1988 Constitution put in place the Single Health Care System (Systema Unico de Saude, or SUS). The goal of the SUS was to grant health care coverage to all of Brazil.[63] In reality, the government spends very little money toward health care. And the money that is spent is not given to those most in need. The government claims health as a right to all persons, not just citizens. Much like education, the state has placed a unilateral duty on itself to provide people with medical attention and preventative measures to ensure health and recovery. The public health system provides care to around 70 percent of the population through public health care.[64] Forty-two million Brazilians possess some form of private health care. Those with private insurance may be covered by more than one plan or choose to participate in the public sector as well. Private health care is considered to be supplementary.[65]

For those who can afford it, the gaps in the public health care system can be filled by private healthcare. Private care is expensive and only the middle class and the wealthy can afford the fees. Eighty percent of the hospitals are owned by the private sector. In addition, the majority of doctors are employed by the private sector as opposed to the public as a consequence of its disparity in wages. Lastly, nurses in the public sector do not have adequate training.[66] This leaves the poor without adequate health care.

Since 1994, the Ministry of Health has been carrying out a program of family health as a strategy for reorganizing primary health care. Several programs at the national level are aimed at ensuring comprehensive care for the health of women, children, and adolescents. Since 1995, the project has focused on reducing infant mortality and giving specific maternal and child health care in the areas with the highest levels of poverty.[67]

The main causes of death of women in Brazil are cardiovascular conditions. Such diseases were responsible for 29.9 percent of deaths of men and women. The second leading cause of death of women is cancer, especially breast, lung, and cervical cancer. Women are also often killed by respiratory tract illness such as pneumonia. Maternal deaths are also at high rates. Most maternal deaths are a result of hemorrhage, hypertension, puerperal infections, delivery, puerperium, abortion, and circulatory complications triggered by pregnancy. Maternal death rates have been improving over the past few years. The Ministry of Health is developing a Woman's Health Hot Line to assist women's access to health services.[68]

Brazil has a high HIV/AIDS population. Approximately 0.7 percent of the population has HIV/AIDS. But, they have been successful with their HIV/AIDS policies. Life expectancy of those with HIV/AIDS has increased while death rates have dropped by 80 percent. This is in large part a result of Brazil's accessible and affordable HIV/AIDS treatment.[69]

Brazil has reduced the incidence of AIDS cases resulting from injected drug use from 21.4 percent (1994) to 9.4 percent (2001). However, mortality rates due to AIDs have increased for women from 3.9 per 100,000 people (2001) to 4 (2003).[70]

Since 1997, Brazil began producing its own generic anti-viral AIDS medication. Roughly 125,000 of 610,000 people with HIV/AIDS receive free treatment.[71] Unfortunately the most current and up to date medications are patented. This prevents Brazil's own pharmaceutical companies from producing generic versions of the new medications. This will likely have a negative impact on those who are infected with HIV and cannot afford nongeneric medications.[72]

Married women and youths, particularly females, are the two populations that have recently had the steepest rates of infection. Infections have increased among married women who contracted the virus from their husbands.[73] Women do not request that their husband wear a condom because they have one sexual partner. In addition, there is an increase in the number of women dying from AIDS. Women are not getting diagnosed in the early stages. Consequently, they do not find out that they are HIV positive until much later, when the illness has progressed. As a result they do not obtain treatment early on which would have helped to extend their life.[74]

Violence is also a leading cause of death among women and men. In fact, 40,000 people are killed annually by firearms. Brazil is 2.8 percent of the world's population. Eleven percent of the world's homicides are committed there. In fact, one homicide occurs every twelve minutes in Brazil. In only 1 percent of homicides are the perpetrators successfully found and prosecuted.[75] In response to these statistics President Luiz Inacio Lula da Silva signed into law the toughest gun restrictions in all of Latin America (December 2003). The Act restricts the carrying of guns in public to government agents, such as the police and military. The minimum age a person may own a gun rose from 21 to 25. In addition, the Act requires background checks for all gun buyers.[76]

Another killer of women is maternal deaths. Statistics from the Unified Health System ("SUS") illustrate that 74.5 women die for every 100,000 live births. For every 1000 live births, 18.3 infants die before turning a month old. Brazil's health ministry intends to decrease maternal and infant deaths by 15 percent by the end of 2006 and by 75 percent by 2015.[77]

In 2003, 25 percent of the 2.2 million births were done by cesarean section. The risk of maternal death is seven times higher in cases where cesarean sections are performed. Cesareans are also 32 percent more expensive for the SUS. The SUS pays $86.50 for a normal birth and $127.10 for a cesarean birth. But sometimes cesareans are a necessity to save the life of the mother, child, or both.[78]

Current medical projects, such as cervical cancer screening for 3.5 million women, reveal that the health care system is responding to the needs of women.[79] There are economic benefits to putting more money in to women's health. One third of the boost in the economy resulted from female health care spending. The more money spent on female health care such as family planning and childbirth, the more the fertility rates dropped. This resulted in a decrease in dependant children of the productive working population. As a result there was economic growth.[80]

Women in Public Office

Women gained the right to vote in 1932. Women have the same political rights under the Constitution as men. Women are becoming more and more active in the political sphere. In 1988, 107 cities had female mayors. In 1992, there were 171 with female mayors. Three of these cities were state capitals. In 1994, there were two female candidates for vice-president, there were ten women running for state governor, and there were twelve for the Senate. Forty women won the senate elections; two of them were Black. In 2002, the number of female representatives grew. Women made up 307 mayors in 5,506 municipalities. In addition, two women were elected governor. The first female state governor, Roseana Sarney of Maranhao, was elected in 1994 and reelected in 1998.[81] In the October 2002 elections, 14 percent of the candidates were women (2,647 were female candidates) compared to 12 percent in 1998 (1,778 women candidates). However, before the 2002 elections, women held 6.7 percent of the seats in the national parliament. This placed Brazil in the bottom two positions for women's share of seats in national parliaments in Latin America and the Caribbean. Women presently hold 9 percent of the seats in the national parliament, ten women were elected to the Senate and forty-four women were elected to the Chamber of Deputies. President Lula da Silva nominated four women to his cabinet. One of the newly created cabinet positions was the Secretary of State for Women's Affairs, currently held by a woman, which reports directly to the president.[82]

In 2002 Benedita da Silva became the Governor of Rio de Janeiro.[83] Da Silva has had a remarkable life. She was raised in a Black slum near Copacabana beach. She became a school teacher. She then went to University to obtain a degree in Social Studies and Social Services. In 1982, da Silva was elected Councilwoman by the Worker's Party. During her campaign she used the slogan: "Woman, Black, and from the slums." In 1986, she was elected to the Federal Congress. After two terms as Federal Deputy she was elected to the Federal Senate in 1994. This made her the first Black woman to be in the Federal Senate. In 1998, da Silva was elected to Vice-Governor of the state.[84] At sixty years old she became governor of Rio de Janeiro.[85]

In 1996, Brazil began adopting mandatory quotas for candidates. This means that a certain percentage of candidates must be women. By 1998 mandatory quotas were applied at both the federal and regional levels. Women had to make up 20 percent of candidates in municipal elections in 1996 and 30 percent since 2000. However, the number of female candidates are small and do not come near the 30 percent quota requirement and there are no restrictions or punishments on the political parties that do not fulfill the quota.[86]

There is one woman on the eleven-seat Supreme Court. There are two women in the Federal Court of Justice and thirty-one men. There are no women on the Brazilian Bar Association (OAB). Women make up 7.6 percent of the Bar's membership.[87]

Women in the Military

The Brazilian military is made up of the Army, Navy (includes Naval Air and Marines), Air Force, and the Federal Police (paramilitary).[88] Women and men may join the military the year they turn seventeen. The Brazilian Army was the first army in South America to enlist women into permanent and career ranks. In order to begin a career in the army, a woman must have obtained a bachelor's degree in computer science, law, accounting, or economics.[89] Under the Constitution military service is compulsory for men. Military service is not compulsory for women or clergymen in times of peace but they are subject to other duties that may be attributed to them by law.[90]

CHILE

Chile is located in southern South America. It borders the South Pacific Ocean and is located between Argentina and Peru. Chile has a population of 15,823,957 (July 2004 est.). The ethnic groups are White and White-Amerindian (95 percent), Amerindian (3 percent), and other (2 percent). The predominant religions are Roman Catholic (89 percent), Protestant (11 percent), and Jewish (less than 1 percent). The official language is Spanish. There are 100 women for every 98 males (2004 est.).[91]

Women in Chile have historically pushed for moralizing society and protecting maternity. Historically women have wanted to ban prostitution, alcohol, and tobacco. In addition, women have tried to push for reform of the Civil Code and for equal pay for equal work.[92] Just recently women in Chile are beginning to assert reproductive rights (see Abortion).

Constitution

Chile is a multiparty democratic republic that gained independence from Spain on September 18, 1810. Chile had a three-year-old Marxist government when it was overthrown in 1973 by a dictatorial military regime led by Augusto Pinochet. Pinochet ruled from 1973 until a president was freely elected in 1990. Suits were brought against Pinochet for human rights violations. In July 2002, the Supreme Court ruled that former President Pinochet was mentally unfit to stand trial. Consequently, all legal proceedings against him were terminated and no future proceedings will be allowed to be brought against Pinochet.[93] Under the rule of Pinochet, the existing constitution was introduced on September 11, 1980, and made effective March 11, 1981. It was amended in 1989, 1993, and 1997. The legal system is based on the Code of 1857. The code was derived from Spanish law and subsequent codes were influenced by French and Austrian law. The Supreme Court reviews legislative acts. Official approval for judicial reform occurred in 2000. Consequently, Chile is in the process of completely altering its criminal justice system. Chile's judicial system, like most of Latin America, was based on the inquisitorial legal system of Spain where a judge both investigates and makes a decision on a case without an adversarial trial. Defendants, plaintiffs, and witnesses give their testimony usually without legal representation. The testimony is then entered into private reports. The judge then uses these reports to make his/her decision. Under this system, a person is presumed guilty. This system was greatly abused during the time of Pinochet where secrecy and inquisition left defendants without the right of due process. A new system, based on the U.S. adversarial trial-based system, is being slowly implemented throughout the country. Under the new system, a Public Defenders Program has been created and a defendant is presumed innocent. Consequently, defendants are now granted due process.[94]

Voting is universal and compulsory for men and women once they turn eighteen years of age. Voting is secret.[95] Women were given the right to vote in 1931.[96]

Article I of the Constitution states that "men are born free and equal, in dignity and rights." The interpretation is that men and women are equal under the Constitution. However, the Constitution goes on to say that "the family is the basic core of society."[97]

Women's rights have been undermined by inequality in the Civil and Penal Codes, the labor laws, and the education system.[98] In reaction to this inequality, in 1990, the government created the Servicio Nacional de la Mujer (SERNAM). SERNAM'S mission is to create public policies that are geared towards women. SERNAM has both pushed for equal pay for women and the elimination of discriminatory legislation.[99]

Work Force and Economy

Pinochet introduced strong economic policies that led to economic growth between 1991 and 1997. Chile has a market-oriented economy and a high level of foreign trade. The Chilean economy has continued to develop since 1991. However, growth fell back to 2.8 percent in 2001 and 1.8 percent in 2002, because a global decrease in economic growth and the devaluation of the Argentine peso. In addition, unemployment remains high. Unemployment was roughly 8.5 percent in 2003. The purchasing power parity of Chile is $151 billion (2002 est.). Roughly 20 percent of the population lives below the poverty line (2001).[100] There are slightly more women living in poverty than men.[101] In fact, while poverty has dropped significantly, it is increasing among women. In addition, there is a gap between male and female unemployment. Female unemployment is higher than male unemployment.[102] The labor force is 5.9 million (2000 est.). The main industries in Chile are copper, other minerals, foodstuffs, fish processing, iron and steel, wood and wood products, transport equipment, cement, and textiles.[103]

Women in Chile make up over one third of the labor force.[104] This number is increasing annually. Eighty-two percent of women in the labor force are service workers compared to 49 percent of men.[105] Women are increasingly entering into the professional fields of law and medicine. Nearly one third of all physicians are women and almost half of all judges are women.[106]

Women are more likely than men to be employed on a "temporary basis" even if it is a long-term position that lasts for years. Many of these women do not even have a written employment contract.[107]

Women with no education averaged a salary that was 81.3 percent that of males in the same position. The minimum wage for domestic employees, which are predominantly women, is 75 percent of the minimum wage. There are nearly 300,000 domestic employees. Women who went to college get paid 53.4 percent less than males of the same education level get paid. Overall women get paid 42 percent of what their male counterparts get paid.[108]

The labor code grants recent mothers and pregnant women specific benefits. A woman is not allowed to be fired during that time period. In addition, employers cannot ask a woman to take a pregnancy test prior to hire. Regardless, this practice still occurs in some companies.[109] In addition, while gender discrimination is prohibited, employers may state gender requirements in job descriptions.[110] Lastly, there is no law against sexual harassment.[111]

Adult prostitution is not expressly illegal in Chile. Prostitutes are often detained by police after neighborhood complaints. Prostitutes are arrested on the ground of committing an "offense against morality." Prostitutes may pay a seventy dollar fine or spend five days in prison. Many prostitutes are under age. The Constitution and the Labor Code prohibit forced labor. Underage employment is considered forced labor because a child cannot legally give

consent. Prostitution of children and corruption of minors are prohibited under the Penal Code. The age of consent for sexual relations has recently been
raised from twelve to fourteen.[112] Consequently, a fifteen-year-old prostitute
is not protected under the Labor Code.

Education

The average age that women stop going to school is 13.4 years old, compared to 13.7 old years for men.[113] The ratio of females to males enrolled
in secondary schools in 2000 was 104 women to every 100 men. Female
enrollment in secondary education is 73 percent.[114] In 2000, the female to
male ratio of student enrollment in tertiary school was 92 women to every
100 men.[115] Female to male youth literacy (ages fifteen to twenty-four) in
2002 was equal.[116] The current female literacy rate is 96.1 percent compared to 96.4 percent of men.[117]

Women in Chile are still occasionally expelled from school or college for
being pregnant.[118] Legislation prohibits discrimination against a pregnant student in schools that obtain public finding. But the legislation does not apply
to fully private schools. Under Article 27, a student must make an effort to
reach the best moral goal. According to a holding by the Supreme Court if the
University deems that a student has behaved improperly by becoming pregnant out of wedlock the school may revoke the student's admission to the
University.[119]

Marriage

In Chile, men can legally marry at the age of fourteen and women at twelve.
However, the average age for men to marry is twenty-six and twenty-three for
women. Forty-six percent of men are married compared to 41.2 of women.[120]

Since 1994, only civil marriages are legally valid. Those couples who have
church weddings must also marry at the civil registry.[121] The Chilean Civil
Code grants husbands control over household decisions and their wives property.[122] In addition, the husband manages the family's assets including those
of his underage children (in the absence of a formal agreement). A married
woman cannot enter into a contract without her husband's permission.[123]

Upon a couple's separation, the division of family assets depends on private agreement. The division of assets rests with the discretion of the court if
no such agreement exists.[124]   •

As of March 2004 divorce was made legal. The Roman Catholic Church
disagrees and states that the divorce law is a threat to the family and the sanc-
tity of marriage. Under the divorce law couples may divorce after a year of

separation in a mutual divorce, where both parties want the divorce. If one spouse wants to divorce, and the other does not, then the couple must be separated for three years. The waiting period can be waived by a judge if there were violations of marital duties such as violence, prostitution, homosexuality, criminal conviction, or drug abuse. The law also requires sixty days of counseling for couples seeking divorce. Chile is one of the last countries to legalize divorce. Malta and the Philippines are the only countries that still do not have divorce laws. After a nine-year debate, the new law is supported by most Chileans. Just before the passage of the divorce law there was a significant drop in marriages, and an increase in annulments and separations. Chile had the largest number of separations in South America (8.1 percent). The divorce law will took effect in September of 2004.[125] Prior to March 2004, divorce had been illegal in Chile since 1884. The law did permit separation under certain circumstances. Annulments have been in existence since 1884. Annulments allow the former spouses to remarry. When a couple seeks an annulment, which is normally carried out by an attorney, they must show that there has been some procedural mistake in the civil marriage process. The process often includes calling in witnesses. For example, the witness may attest to the fact that the couple did not reside at the address that they said they did when they were married. Annulments result in high legal fees. Consequently, only those who are wealthy can afford them.[126]

Since 1993, Parliament had debated a draft divorce law. However, the Catholic Church threatened to excommunicate Catholic Parliamentarians if they supported the divorce laws. However, 56 percent of the population favored the legalization of divorce. Men were more likely to favor divorce than women; and young adults favored divorce over middle aged and elderly persons. Higher income respondents were more favorable to legalizing divorce. In fact, 70.1 percent of higher income respondents favored legalizing divorce compared to 15.5 percent of low-income respondents.[127]

The negative affect of the absence of the divorce law was that women who could not afford an annulment and were in abusive relationships could not legally dissolve their marriage.[128]

Another result of the absence of a divorce law was that Chile had a high number of couples who were married to one person and cohabiting with another. The result is that Chile has the largest number of children that are born out of wedlock. An estimated 40–46 percent of all Chilean births are out of wedlock. Although these children have equal rights to those born from married parents there is still discrimination against illegitimate children.[129]

Chilean law is not in favor of same sex unions. In Santiago on June 2, 2004, the Supreme Court denied a woman custody of her children because she is a lesbian. The court held that her open lesbian relationship disqualified her from the right to custody. Mothers are ordinarily automatically granted custody of their children.[130]

Abortion and Contraceptives

Abortion is illegal in Chile, there are no exceptions. Abortion law is ruled by the Chilean Penal Code (12 November 1874, sections 342–345). The Code prohibits all abortions that are performed with malice. However, the historical interpretation was that an abortion could be performed to save the life of the woman. In fact, the Health Code (Decree No. 725 of 11 December 1967, section 119) specifically allowed a therapeutic abortion to save the life of the woman with her permission.[131]

Rape is not a ground for abortion or for emergency contraceptives. The Citizen's Peace Foundation found that there were 1,373 cases of rape reported to the police in 2001, and 1,250 in 2000. It is believed that most cases of rape are not reported.[132]

The government-created group, Servicio Nacional de la Mujer (SERNAM), has not asserted reproductive rights for women because it is a deeply divided issue in Chile.[133]

The Supreme Court recently outlawed emergency contraception (EC). This overturned the Appellate Court's approval of the contraceptive. In addition, the Health Ministry supports the contraceptive. The Health Ministry considers EC a safe method of pregnancy prevention. EC prevents a fertilized egg from implanting onto the uterine wall but EC cannot affect a pregnancy once a fertilized egg has implanted itself onto the uterine wall. EC acts similarly to an inter-uterine device that is a permitted contraceptive in Chile.[134] Health service regulations require that women between fifteen and forty-four have access to contraceptives. However, there are no public family planning programs and little information about contraceptives available to women. In 1996, the Ministries of Education and Health began a national sexual education program. The program was quickly suspended because of the Catholic Church's opposition.[135]

On September 15, 1989, the Government of Chile amended section 119 of the Health Code. It now states, "No action may be executed that has as its goal the inducement of abortion" (Law No. 18,826). The result is that no abortions can now be legally performed in Chile. In fact, under the Penal Code, anyone who performs an abortion with the woman's consent is subject to imprisonment. A woman who induces her own abortion or consents to it is subject to the maximum length of short-term imprisonment. However, few convictions are made for performing abortions because physical proof of abortion, for example, traumatic injury to internal organs, is necessary to obtain a conviction.[136]

Despite these restrictions, Chile has had very high rates of abortion during the last thirty years. Surveys conducted in the early 1960s indicate that one of every four women in Chile had undergone an abortion. The high rates of abortion and the resulting high rates of maternal mortality led the Chilean Government to be one of the first Latin American countries to give official support to family planning activities. After family planning was introduced in the mid-1960s, the deaths from illegal abortion declined from 118 to 24 per 100,000 live births between 1964 and 1979.[137] Current rates are still high. Thirty-five percent of all pregnancies end in abortion.[138] Abortion complications account for up to 40 percent of all maternal deaths.[139]

Eighty percent of women accused of obtaining abortions were reported by public hospitals where they went to obtain aid from complications arising from the abortion. The majority of women accused of obtaining abortions were under the age of twenty-nine, 91 percent had not finished school, and were poor. Contrarily, wealthy women are able to received safe and discrete abortions at private clinics.[140]

Women are recently beginning to push for reproductive rights. In fact, in January 2004, a women's group made a statement in a popular Santiago newspaper to encourage the decriminalization of abortion. The group published the names of 230 women, who voluntarily wanted their names on the list, in the newspaper. The group issued a statement that the country does not make contraceptives available to prevent pregnancy but mistreats women who choose to have a child out of wedlock. The group stated that not only should abortion be decriminalized, but there should also be widespread dispersal of contraceptive information, and more available family planning services for women.[141]

Roughly 30 percent of women of childbearing age use contraceptives. Family planning services in Chile are provided mostly to married women. In addition, the adolescent health program does not include reproductive health services. Contraceptives are easy to obtain for the rich and difficult to obtain for the poor as a result of the privatization of the health care system. Additionally, a woman must receive her spouse's consent before being able to obtain sterilization.[142]

Family planning has resulted in a drop in the total fertility rate. From 1995 to 2000 the fertility rate was 2.4 births per woman.[143]

Health Care

The most frequent cancers among women are cervical cancer (25.6 percent), breast (15.8 percent), and skin (8.7 percent) cancer.[144] Maternal mortality is 23 deaths per 100,000 births. Ninety-six percent of people have been immunized against measles. Ninety-four percent of people have been immunized against tuberculosis. Life expectancy at birth is eighty years for women compared to seventy-four years for men.[145] Domestic violence is still a serious problem. A University of Chile study revealed that over half of women have experienced domestic violence in their relationships, 34 percent were abused physically, and 16.3 percent were abused psychologically.[146]

Women in Public Office

Women first joined the political arena during the military coup. Contrarily men could not rise up against Pinochet without the threat of being jailed or killed. Other men were forced to go underground to preserve their safety. Women had an advantage in the political arena at that time because of their gender. In addition, with the help of the Church, women implemented post-coup survival strategies.[147]

In 2002, women occupied 10 percent of the seats in the national parliament.[148] A nationwide poll revealed that 77 percent of Chileans felt that current female politicians are qualified to become president. Fifty-eight percent of Chileans believe Chile is prepared to accept a female president.[149] In 2003, there were 2 female senators (out of 48), 3 female cabinet members (out of 16), and 15 female deputies (out of 120).[150]

Women in the Military

The military in Chile is made up of the Army, Navy (including Naval Air, Coast Guard, and Marines), Air Force, National Police, and the Investigations Police. Men and women can join the military at nineteen years of age (2003 est.).[151] Chile had its first female general in 1999.[152] Mireya Pérez heads the family protection branch of the military police, which is viewed as a woman's department. Michelle Bachelet became Chile's first female defense minister in 2002. Bachelet, who plans to run for president one day, initiated Chile's first program to recruit women into the military. Female soldiers cannot participate in combat. Women may participate in artillery, communications, logistics, military policing, and other fields of the military.[153] Historically women were primarily nurses.[154]

COLOMBIA

Colombia is located in northern South America.[155] It borders the Caribbean Sea and the North Pacific Ocean and is located between Panama, Ecuador,

Venezuela, Peru, and Brazil. Colombia's population is 44 million (July 2003 est.).[156] The ethnic groups are mixed White-Amerindian (58 percent), White (20 percent), mixed Black-White (14 percent), Black (4 percent), mixed Black-Amerindian (3 percent), and Amerindian (1 percent). The predominant religion is Roman Catholic (90 percent).[157]

In colonial times the hierarchy of society was dictated by bloodline. Those at the top of the hierarchy were the descendants of Spain. At the bottom of the social scale were the indigenous and Afro-Colombians.[158] This hierarchy, to a large degree, still exists today.

The Catholic Church has been a strong influence on Colombian culture.[159] Although over time its power in political matters has lessened.

In 2003, internal conflict caused between 3,000 and 4,000 deaths, many of which were women.[160] In addition, in conflict zones, many women are left as head of household after their spouse is persecuted, disappears, or has been murdered.[161] Many of these women end up forced out of their homes and displaced and/or end up being the target of guerrilla and/or paramilitary groups.[162] As throughout global history, women's position in Colombia has been severely harmed by internal warfare. Women in Colombia often face domestic and political violence. In addition, there is inequality between the sexes in terms of education, employment, and health care. Single women, women in rural areas, indigenous and Afro-Colombian women are most harmed by the present situation.[163]

Constitution

In 1499, Alonso Ojeda stepped onto the Guajira Peninsula. In fact, the famous children's story "El Dorado" was based on the gold-clad Amerindians from the Peninsula that Ojeda saw that day. Soon thereafter the Spaniards conquered New Granada. New Granada was made up of present day Colombia, Venezuela, Ecuador, and Panama, with Santa Fe de Bogotá (known today as Bogotá) as the capital. Colombia did not become independent from Spain until Venezuelan Simon Bolivar and his Colombian army liberated the nation. Together with Venezuela, Ecuador, Peru, and Bolivia, Bolivar created Gran Colombia. Bolivar was soon after elected president.[164] Bolivar, who is often compared to former American President Abraham Lincoln, desired to keep the countries united in order to create one strong nation as opposed to several weaker nations. However, the union dissolved only a decade later. Following the division with its neighbors, Colombia faced many civil wars, due to the conflict between the liberal and conservative parties. Among these civil wars were the bloody war of one thousand days in 1899 in which more than 100,000 people were killed, and la Violencia ("the Violence") in 1948 in which over 200,000 people died.[165]

In addition to the damage to the nation caused by civil war, Colombia was also harmed by losing the Panama Canal. Panama became independent from Colombia in 1903 with the help of the United States. The loss of Panama and the canal was a terrible blow to Colombia. Colombia finally recognized Panama's independence in 1914 in exchange for rights in the Canal Zone and payment of indemnity from the United States.[166]

To resolve the conflict between the two parties as described in the first paragraph, the liberal and conservative parties agreed to support a military coup led by General Gustavo Rojas in 1953. This was short lived. The military reign only lasted four years.[167] In fact, Colombia is one of the few nations in Latin America that has not frequently been run by dictatorships.[168] Liberal and conservative parties returned to sharing power until 1974 when Alfonso López Michelsen was elected president. Left-wing guerrilla groups such as the National Liberation Army (ELN), the April 19 Movement (M19), and the Revolutionary Armed Forces of Colombia (FARC) began to emerge in opposition of the duopoly.[169] ELN, founded in 1963, was inspired by the Cuban revolution. It has roughly 5,000 members. The Communist group FARC, formed in 1964, and declared that it would take arms against the government to seize control.[170]

Illegal drug trafficking began to flourish during the 1970s and 1980s. The drug cartel began to obtain a great deal of money and, consequently, power. Paramilitary groups also began to emerge around this time. Both the paramilitary and guerrilla groups have been tied to the drug cartel and have caused a great deal of violence and disruption to the country.[171] On July 5, 1991 a new constitution was adopted.[172] In fact, a new Criminal Code, enacted in 1992–1993, was modeled after the United States Criminal Code. Under the new code, there is judicial review of executive and legislative acts. Under the code, accused individuals are also presumed innocent until proven guilty. Also in 1991, the head of the Medellín cartel, Pablo Escobar surrendered. Escobar escaped in 1992 and was located and killed while trying to escape officials in 1993.[173] In 1998, former President Pastrana gave the FARC an area of land the size of Switzerland. Former President Pastrana gave the land in hopes that the FARC would be more apt to negotiate with the government. This turned out to be a crucial mistake. Kidnappings and murders by the FARC continued. In 2002, former President Pastrana regained control over the area and FARC retreated into the jungle. This move did not lessen the power of FARC and the disruption that they continue to cause.[174] The current President, Alvaro Uribe, an independent, is strongly opposed to the guerrilla groups. In fact, he survived fifteen assassination attempts before he became president. In addition, his father was killed while fleeing from a kidnapping attempt by the FARC guerrilla group.[175] On August 24, 2004, President Uribe's Peace Commission offered a hostage swap to the guerrilla group.[176] FARC is the largest guerrilla group, with over 17,000 members.[177] Under the proposal, the government offered to release fifty FARC members for sixty-two military officials and politicians including three U.S. citizens and female former presidential candidate Ingrid Betancourt.[178] Roughly two thousand people, including twenty-two citizens of different nations, were kidnapped in 2003.[179] Under the proposal, the released guerrillas would have to leave the country or undergo government-sponsored rehabilitation.[180] FARC rejected the government's proposal while stating that they hope to come to an agreement.[181] In July 2004 President Uribe began peace negotiations with paramilitary commanders of the AUC.[182] In 1987, nineteen merchants were killed because they did not pay taxes for passing through areas under paramilitary control. Colombian Army officials were also implicated in this case pointing to the wide-spread corruption that takes place within the government. Since December 2003, the Colombian armed forces were granted police powers.[183] This means that the military may raid homes, intercept communication, and detain individuals without the need of a warrant.[184] This creates the ability for corrupt officials to further the objectives of paramilitary or guerrilla organizations, leaving civilians with even less protection.[185]

The implication of corruption has even touched the executive office. In fact, former President Ernesto Samper was accused of having received drug money during his presidential campaign. He was cleared of the charge.[186] President Uribe was also allegedly linked with the drug cartel according to a recently released FOIA (Freedom of Information Act) 1991 Defense Intelligence Agency report. The report implicates Uribe as an important narco-trafficker.[187] President Uribe adamantly denies the allegations.[188] The U. S. government has responded to the report by stating that President Uribe has been a strong U.S. ally in reducing the production of cocaine in Colombia under Plan Colombia. Plan Colombia is a U.S. funded drug eradication program developed by former President Pastrana and agreed to by former President Clinton. Under the Plan, the U.S. agreed to give $1.3 billion, in total, in primarily military aid, to Colombia.[189]

Corruption has affected the judiciary branch. The judiciary is often subject to intimidation and corruption by guerilla and paramilitary groups.[190]

The Constitution expressly prohibits gender discrimination and the laws reflect equal rights for men and women. However, discrimination is still prevalent. The age both men and women are eligible to vote is eighteen.[191]

Work Force and Economy

Colombia is in debt (38 billion, 2003), and has internal armed conflict which has deterred investors and travelers alike.[192] The loss of both has been a detriment to

the economy.[193] The two main legal exports of Colombia, oil and coffee, are declining. Oil production and coffee harvests and coffee prices are decreasing.[194]
Columbia makes roughly six to seven billion dollars a year in illegal drug trafficking.[195] The purchasing power parity of Colombia is $262.5 billion (2003
est.).[196] Unfortunately, 55 percent of the population lives under the poverty line
(2003 est.).[197] The labor force is made up of 18.3 million people (1999 est.).[198]
Women make up 48.1 percent of the labor force and 49 percent of professionals.[199] The unemployment rate is 13.6 percent (2003 est.). The major industries
in Colombia are textiles, food processing, oil, clothing and footwear, beverages,
chemicals, cement, gold, coal, and emeralds.[200]

    In 2000, the female share of wages in the non-agricultural sector was 49
percent.[201] Forty-four percent of employed women in the non-agricultural
sector are informally employed; 39 percent of those women are self-
employed. Sixty-four percent of wages women earn in the non-agricultural
sector come from informal employment.[202] The problem with informal employment is that employees do not obtain the same benefits, that is, health
care, a contract, child care, as formal employees.

    No woman may legally be fired for being pregnant or breast-feeding.
Women are entitled to a twelve-week, salary-paid, maternity leave. Adoptive
mothers of children under seven may also exercise maternity leave. Since
1994 employers may not force a woman to take a pregnancy test before hiring her, unless the job is considered a high-risk position. An employer must
transfer a pregnant employee in a high-risk job to one that does not pose a risk
to her pregnancy. Pregnant women may not work more than a five-hour shift.
Women who use their maternity leave prior to giving birth may share their reduced maternity leave with their spouse or companion. Women who have
given birth may take an hour out of their work day to breast feed. A woman's
salary may not be adversely affected by exercising the right to breast feed. If
a woman miscarries she is entitled to two to four weeks of paid leave.[203]

    Companies prefer to hire males over females. Females are considered more
expensive than men because if they become pregnant the above laws apply.
In addition, some employers violate labor laws such as maternity leave.
Women often do not file sex discrimination complaints. Some women do not
file lawsuits because they do not realize that a law has been violated. Other
women fear losing their job. In addition, lawsuits on average take up to two
to three years.[204]

    While the Constitution expressly prohibits discrimination against women
and public administration is required to have female representation in decision-
making, discrimination remains a problem. Women face sexual harassment and
hiring discrimination. Sexual harassment is against the law, yet, is rarely enforced. In addition, in 2003 unemployment for women was 6.4 percent higher

than for men. Women often do not have salaries that match their level of expertise and education. In 2003, women earned 66 percent of what men earned. Rural areas have the biggest differences in wages between men and women.[205]

While prostitution is legal in certain areas called tolerance zones, it is illegal to employ minors as prostitutes. In addition, under the Penal Code it is against the law to have sex with a minor or to introduce any person, minor or not, to prostitution. Nevertheless, there are roughly 35,000 minors working as prostitutes.[206]

Roughly 22 percent of Colombians are in part of African origin.[207] Afro-Colombians suffer great economic and social discrimination. In fact, 74 percent of Afro-Colombians earn less than minimum wage. Afro-Colombians often do not have opportunities to obtain a good education or substantial health care. In addition, Afro-Americans and indigenous populations, especially women, are often the victims of guerilla and paramilitary violence.[208]

Education

Women were first allowed college enrollment in 1933. The average number of years that Colombian adults have attended school is 5.3 (2000 est.).[209] School is compulsory from the ages of five to fifteen. Education is free in public schools. In addition, programs such as the government-sponsored program, Education for Equality, are aiding to bridge the gap of inequality of education between the sexes. Women make up 48.9 percent of primary school students.[210] In 2000, the ratio of female to male students enrolled in secondary school was 111 women to every 100 men. The female enrollment in secondary school was 57 percent.[211] The ratio of female to male youth (ages fifteen to twenty-four) literacy in 2002 was 101 women to every 100 men. Ninety-eight percent of female youths are literate.[212] Ninety-three percent of women, all ages, are literate.[213] In 2000, the female to male ratio of student enrollment in tertiary school was 109 women to every 100 men.[214]

Marriage

Article 116 of the Colombian Civil Code states that the legal age for men and women to marry is eighteen. However, under Article 117, minors may marry, at the age of fourteen for men and twelve for women, with the express written permission of their parents or legal representatives.[215] Any marriage for ages under fourteen for men and twelve for women is void unless the girl is pregnant.[216] According to the Constitution, Articles 5 and 6, a married woman under eighteen years old is denied legal self-representation and must be represented by her husband.[217]

Catholic marriages have legal standing. After the religious ceremony has been performed it must be registered with the civil authorities.[218]

The Constitution states that married women have the same rights and obligations as men under the law.[219] Article 42 guarantees gender equality.[220] Both spouses have a duty to contribute economically.[221] Additionally, if a man and woman live together for two or more years or if they have a child together, their possessions are considered jointly owned. Such property is divided evenly upon the dissolution of the relationship under the Patrimonial Deed between Permanent Partners or Common Law Marriage statute. Women in common-law marriages may claim their partner's pension and have the right of inheritance. Under the labor law, each partner has the right to the health care, retirement, disability, or death benefits of the other.[222]

The Constitution not only states that a marriage is based on equal rights and responsibilities of both parents but also that the spouses share parental responsibility. Either parent can act as the legal representative of their child. Married women have the legal right to manage both her property and the marital property. A woman has the right to enter into contracts and have access to judicial due process. Domestic work is recognized as a contribution to joint property.[223]

Divorce for both civil and Catholic marriages became legal in 1992. Divorce by mutual consent can be performed by a notary. However, divorce for cause must be processed before a judge. Either partner can be eligible for alimony. Catholics who do not want to go through divorce proceedings may have their marriage annulled.[224]

Grounds for divorce are failure to fulfill ones duty as spouse or parent, adultery, cruelty, abuse of drugs or alcohol, a grave or incurable illness that threatens the health of the other spouse, perversion, physical separation of two or more years, or mutual consent before a judge. Alimony, child support, custody, visitation rights, and residence arrangements are all determined in the judicial divorce decree. There are penalties for parents who do not pay alimony or child support.[225]

Abortion and Contraceptives

The only ground on which abortion is permitted is to save the life of the woman with the woman's consent.[226] Rape or incest, fetal impairment, mental or physical health, economic or social requests are not grounds for abortion. Abortion is governed by the Penal Code of 1980. Under the Penal Code, abortion is a crime against life and personal integrity. Under the Constitution, a human life is protected from the moment of conception.[227]

A woman is subject to up to three years in prison for causing her own abortion or allowing another person to abort her fetus. Persons performing the abortion are also subject to one to three years in prison. The penalty is lessened in instances where the woman became pregnant out of incest or rape. In these cases, a woman can be subject to four months to a year in prison. Previous to the Penal Code of 1980 there were reduced penalties for women, including pardons, when the abortion was performed to preserve the honor of the woman. However, prosecution of abortion is rare. Abortions are widely used.[228] There are roughly 450,000 abortions per year.[229] Abortions are the second primary cause of maternal mortality. Sixty percent of all maternal deaths in the late 1980s resulted from induced abortions.[230] The fertility rate is 2.8 children per woman.[231]

The Colombian Basic Health Care Plan contains reproductive health services such as maternal/perinatal care and family planning. In addition, the plan includes a variety of contraceptive methods. Colombia has a sexual and reproductive health policy targeted at reducing maternal mortality as well as the number of deaths due to illegal abortions. In addition, sex education for adolescents was made compulsory in 1993. The government provides twenty percent of family planning services. These services are offered at health centers, clinics, and hospitals. The remainder of family planning services is provided by the private sector. The favored forms of contraceptives are the IUD, the pill, and sterilization. Roughly 72 percent of women use contraceptives.[232]

Health Care

The Constitution grants all citizens access to universal health care. The poorest 30 percent of the population receive vouchers for joining the social insurance system.[233] Citizens obtain their health care via the social security system. This includes disability and retirement benefits. There are two systems within social security, the contributory system and the subsidized system. Workers with salaries receive their benefits through the contributory system. The subsidized system gives coverage to the poor. Under the subsidized system, women receive maternal health care. In addition, pregnant women and mothers with children under a year old receive food subsidy. Under the subsidized plan, women of all ages, especially adolescents and women in rural areas, receive sexual education. The plan also includes reproductive health counseling, breast examinations, pap smear testing, and treatment for STDs. The Ministry of Health has a policy initiative called Health for Women, Women for Health. The focus of the policy is to improve the quality of life for women, strengthen the role of women in decision-making in the health sector, and work to create equality of health care for women.[234]

However, gaining access to health care becomes more difficult each day for the people of Colombia.[235] Health services in the zones most affected by the armed conflict suffer from a lack of infrastructure and personnel. Few medical staff will work in the most dangerous areas where the need is highest. Indigenous populations in the most remote regions are particularly cut off from health care. Hundreds of medical staff have been attacked, and, in many cases, killed because they are working in conflict zones.[236]

Roughly one-fifth of pregnant women do not receive any type of medical care. Many women are affected by illness and diseases of the reproductive system and circulatory system. Cardiovascular disease is the leading cause of death for women forty-five and older. Malignant tumors are the second leading cause of death for women forty-five and older.[237]

Other health issues for women are domestic and sexual violence. While domestic and sexual violence, including sexual violence by a spouse are against the law, they still remain a serious problem. The Institute for Legal Medicine and Forensic Science reported 22,271 cases of domestic violence and 8,666 cases of sexual violence against women. Unfortunately there are not enough safe houses and counseling services available for victims. Abusers may be removed from the home by a judge and sentenced to counseling. Under the Penal Code, a person convicted of crimes against sexual freedom and human dignity, including rape, sex with a minor, and child pornography can face four to forty years in prison. The sentence for violent sexual assault is eight to fifteen years. In instances of spousal violence the sentence is less. The minimum is six months, and the maximum is two years. The law denies probation or bail to convicts that violate restraining orders.[238]

Women in Public Office

Women held 11 percent of the seats in the national parliament in 2002.[239] President Uribe appointed six women (out of thirteen) to his cabinet. Among the women was Marta Lucia Ramirez, an attorney and former ambassador to France. Ramirez is Latin America's second female defense minister.[240]

There are several governmental organizations that are working to foster equality between the sexes through policies. Among them is the National Office for Women's Equality (NOWE) created in 1995 and the Equality and Participation Policy for Women (EPPW). There are also many nongovernmental agencies (NGOs) that focus on women's issues.[241]

In 2000, a quota law was enacted that requires a minimum of 30 percent of public positions be filled by women. Yet, women do not hold over 15 percent of the highest public positions. Women make up 15 percent of the lower houses of congress and 12 percent of the Senate. Women make up 19 percent of cabinet, congressional, and mayoral positions according to the 2001 survey by the Inter-American Dialogue and the International Center for Research on

Women. This places Colombia at the top of female participation in such positions in South America.[242]

Women in politics are in a dangerous position.[243] Paramilitaries target human rights activists, local politicians, and indigenous leaders. In fact, two feminist leaders were murdered in January 2003 by paramilitaries. The paramilitaries suspected the women of collaborating with the guerrilla group FARC. In October 2003, Amaris Miranda of the Women's Popular Organization (OFP) was murdered because she criticized the paramilitary influence in her community.[244] Other female leaders have disappeared while some are seeking political asylum in other nations.[245] The more that women assume leadership positions the more they become a threat to the guerrilla and paramilitary groups. Women in leadership positions have faced threats, intimidation, rape, sexual abuse, torture, and political killings by the guerrilla and paramilitaries and even units of the Colombian military.[246]

Women in the Military

The military branches in Colombia are the Army, Navy (including Marines and Coast Guard), Air Force, and the National Police. A man or woman can join the military at eighteen years of age (2003 est.).[247] Women must voluntarily apply and be selected for the military. Once selected the women are sent to the Military Academy "General Jose Maria Cordova" for Cadets, where they receive military instruction for three months. After three months the women become second lieutenants and are assigned to different military units around the nation's territory, occupying positions related to their specialized fields. In the Colombian Army, women in the officer and enlisted ranks work exclusively in the logistical-administrative field. They are noncombatants.[248]

In 1999, Colombia began to train its first female combat pilots in the Air Force academy. These female soldiers are known as Women of Steel.[249]

Women in Colombia have participated in their military history in various ways. For instance women contributed to the independence movement by participating in combat. In addition, women often performed as informants and nurses. Women also voluntarily took part in the Revolutionary Wars. It has been documented that women played a role in the battle of Boyaca in 1819, at the decisive moment in the battle of New Granada. A woman, Evangelist Tamayo, fought under the command of General Simon Bolivar. She continued serving until her death in 1821, having attained the rank of captain. The most well-known informant of the time was Policarpa Salavarrieta of New Granada. Policarpa, a dressmaker, gained access to the homes of the Realist women of Santa Fe de Bogotá, where she discovered very valuable information that she passed on to the insurgents. She was put before the firing squad in the town square in Santa Fe de Bogotá, Nov. 14, 1817. Policarpa became a national heroine and a symbol of patriotism.[250]

NOTES

1. CIA World Factbook, Brazil, <http://www.cia.gov/cia/publications/factbook/geos/br.html> (Aug. 2003).

2. Ibid.

3. Ibid.

4. Brazilian Constitution, Universität Bern, International Constitutional Law, 1999, <http://www.oefre.unibe.ch/law/icl/br00000_.html> (August 2003).

5. Emilia Fernandes, "Introduction of the National Report Statement," Committee on the Elimination of Discrimination Against Women (CEDAW), 1 July 2003, <http://www.un.int/brazil/speech/03d-ef-cedaw-english-0107.htm> (Aug. 2003).

6. Ibid.

7. Ibid.

8. CIA World Factbook, Brazil.

9. Marc Boucher-Colbert, "Brazil: 2.4 Have 1/3 of Riches," *BrazzilMagazine*, 2004, <http://www.brazzillog.com/2004/html/articles/apr04/p128apr04.htm> (Aug. 2004).

10. Marina Domingos, "Income Gap still huge in Brazil," *BrazzilMagazine*, 2004, <http://www.brazzil.com/2004/html/articles/apr04/p118apr04.htm> (Aug. 2004).

11. Mylena Fiori, "Only Bosses Happy with Brazil's New Minimum Wage," *Brazzil Magazine*, 2004, <http://www.brazzil.com/2004/html/articles/apr04/p140apr04.htm> (Aug. 2004).

12. CIA World Factbook, Brazil.

13. "Brazil unemployment rate up at 12.8 pct in March," *Forbes.com*, 27 April 2004, <http://www.forbes.com/reuters/newswire/2004/04/27/rtr1348610.html> (Aug. 2004).

14. Joanne Blaney, "Women's Blues in Brazil," *Brazzil Magazine*, March 2003, <http://www.brazzil.com/p136mar03.htm> (Aug. 2003).

15. Ibid.

16. CIA World Factbook, Brazil.

17. Country Reports on Human Rights Practices, 2002, Brazil, U.S. Department of State, released by the Bureau of Democracy, Human Rights, and Labor, March 31, 2003, <http://www.state.gov/g/drl/rls/hrrpt/2002/18322.htm> (Aug. 2003).

18. United Nations Educational, Scientific and Cultural Organization (UNESCO), "Progress of the World's Women 2002: Vol. 2: Gender Equality and the Millennium Development Goals," United Nations Development Fund for Women (UNIFEM), 2002, <http://www.unifem.org/www/resources/progressv2/index.html> (Aug. 2003). "Women and Men in the Informal Economy: A Statistical Picture," International Labour Office (ILO), 2002, <http://www.ilo.org/public/english/employment/gems/download/women.pdf> (Aug. 2003).

19. Country Reports on Human Rights Practices, 2002, Brazil, U.S. Department of State.

20. Alana Gandra, "Jobs in Brazil, Exclusion is the Norm," *Brazzil Magazine*, 2004, <http://www.brazzil.com/2004/html/articles/may04/p166may04.htm> (Aug. 2004).

21. Regional Core Health Data System, Country Health Profile 2001: Brazil, Pan American Health Organization, 2001, <http://www.paho.org/english/sha/prflbra .htm> (Aug. 2003).

22. Fernandes, "Introduction of the National Report Statement."

23. Country Reports on Human Rights Practices, 2002, Brazil, U.S. Department of State.

24. Fernandes, "Introduction of the National Report Statement."

25. Country Reports on Human Rights Practices, 2002, Brazil, U.S. Department of State.

26. UNESCO, "Progress of the World's Women 2002."

27. Brazilian Constitution, Article 208, Georgetown University, Political Database of the Americas, <http://www.georgetown.edu/pdba/Constitutions/Brazil/brtitle8 .html> (Aug. 2003).

28. UNESCO, "Progress of the World's Women 2002."

29. Fernandes, "Introduction of the National Report Statement."

30. Country Reports on Human Rights Practices, 2002, Brazil, U.S. Department of State.

31. "Women of the World: Laws and Policies Affecting Their Reproductive Lives, Latin America and the Caribbean," The Center for Reproductive Law and Policy (CRLP), DEMUS, Estudio para la Defensa de los Derechos de la Mujer, <http:// www.crlp.org/pdf/wowlac_brazil.pdf> (Aug. 2003).

32. Rita J. Simon and Howard Altstein, *Global Perspectives on Social Issues: Marriage and Divorce* (Lanham: Rowman & Littlefield Publishing Group, Inc., 2003).

33. Alessandra Dalevi, "Civil Code Remodeled, Brazilian Law-Cover," *Brazzil Magazine*, 1998, <http://www.brazzil.com/cvrjan98.htm> (Aug. 2003).

34. "Women of the World," The Center for Reproductive Law and Policy (CRLP), DEMUS.

35. Ibid.; Dalevi, "Civil Code Remodeled."

36. Dalevi, "Civil Code Remodeled."

37. Ibid.

38. Ibid.

39. The U.S. Library of Congress, "Gender," Country Studies, Brazil, 1985, <http://countrystudies.us/brazil/31.htm> (Aug. 2003).

40. Nationmaster.com, <http://www.nationmaster.com/graph-t/peo_div_rat> (July 2005); "Information Regarding Divorce in Brazil," Embassy of the United States, Brazil, <http://www.embaixada-americana.org.br/index.php?action=materia&id=1942&sub menu=7&itemmenu=58> (Aug. 2004).

41. Ibid.

42. "Women of the World," The Center for Reproductive Law and Policy (CRLP), DEMUS.

43. Ibid.

44. "Abortion Policies, A Global Review, Brazil," United Nations, <http://www.un .org/esa/population/publications/abortion/profiles.htm> (Aug. 2003).

45. "Women of the World," The Center for Reproductive Law and Policy (CRLP), DEMUS.

46. "Abortion Policies, A Global Review, Brazil," United Nations.

47. Country Reports on Human Rights Practices, 2002, Brazil, U.S. Department of State.

48. "Abortion Policies, A Global Review, Brazil," United Nations.

49. Dalevi, "Civil Code Remodeled."

50. "Women of the World," The Center for Reproductive Law and Policy (CRLP), DEMUS.

51. Ibid.

52. Ibid.

53. Ibid.

54. Ibid.

55. Fernandes, "Introduction of the National Report Statement."

56. "Women of the World," The Center for Reproductive Law and Policy (CRLP), DEMUS.

57. Mario Osava, "AIDS spreading six times faster among teenage girls," Inter Press Service News Agency, (10 Mar. 2004), <http://www.aegis.com/news/ips/2004/IP040307.html> (Aug. 2004).

58. Ibid.

59. Fernandes, "Introduction of the National Report Statement"; CIA World Factbook, Brazil.

60. Fernandes, "Introduction of the National Report Statement."

61. The World Bank, Country Brief, Brazil, 2003, <http://wbln0018.worldbank.org/LAC/LAC.nsf/ECADocByUnid/A220784F5BC3A1FB85256DB40070253B?O pendocument> (Aug. 2003).

62. Irene Lôbo, "Being born is still too dangerous in Brazil," *BrazzilMagazine*, 2004, <http://www.brazzil.com/content/view/1783/59/> (Aug. 2004).

63. André Cezar Medici, "Health, Basic indicators and government policies," Ministry of External Relations, <http://www.mre.gov.br/cdbrasil/itamaraty/web/ingles/polsoc/saude/apresent/apresent.htm> (Aug. 2003).

64. "The Two Faces of Brazil: Contrasts between Rich and Poor are a Fact of Life in the Western Hemisphere's Largest Developing Nation," *Medical Post* (6 February 1996): 9–10.

65. Lenaura Lobato, "Reorganizing the Health Care System in Brazil," International Development Research Centre of Canada (15 April 2002), <http://www.idrc.ca/books/focus/923/s2c05htm.> (Aug. 2003).

66. Medici, "Health, Basic indicators and government policies;" Fernandes, "Introduction of the National Report Statement."

67. Regional Core Health Data System, Country Health Profile 2001: Brazil.

68. André Cezar Medici, "Causes of Death in Brazil," Ministry of External Relations, <http://www.mre.gov.br/cdbrasil/itamaraty/web/ingles/polsoc/saude/cmorte/apresent.htm> (Aug. 2003); Fernandes, "Introduction of the National Report Statement."

69. Natalie Haas, "Brazil Receives Accolades for Comprehensive AIDS Program," SIECUS, Policy update, 2003, <http://www.siecus.org/policy/PUpdates/arch03/arch030071.html#BRAZ> (Aug. 2003).

70. United Nations Office on Drugs and Crime, Country Profile, Brazil 2003, prepared by UNODC Regional Office, Brazil, <http://www.unodc.org/pdf/brazil/Country%20Profile%202005.pdf> (Aug. 2003).

71. Haas, "Brazil Receives Accolades for Comprehensive AIDS Program."

72. Ibid.

73. Mariana Timotea de Costa, "Brazil's pioneering AIDS programme," *BBC News*, July 14, 2003.

74. "Brazil faces a condom shortage. The head of Brazil's AIDS programme warns an impending shortage of condoms will have serious implications for AIDS prevention in the country," BBC News-UK edition, May 27, 2004.

75. Angélica Gramático, "Brazil, World's Number 1 Killing Field," *Brazzil-Magazine*, 2004, <http://www.brazzil.com/2004/html/articles/apr04/p138apr04.htm> (Aug. 2004).

76. Jon Jeter, "Brazil passes tough gun-control law," *Washington Post*, December 24, 2003, A12.

77. Lôbo, "Being born is still too dangerous in Brazil."

78. Ibid.

79. Simon Schwartzman, "Health and Health Statistics in Brazil," prepared for the Joint Conference of the International Association of Survey Statisticians and the International Association of Official Statistics (IASS/IAOS), Special Organized Session on "Social welfare: monitoring living conditions by using social and health statistics, and other data sources," Aguascalientes, Mexico, 1–4 Sept. 1998, <http://www.schwartzman.org.br/simon/pdf/health.pdf> (Aug. 2003).

80. Mark Doyle, "UN calls for women's health 'bonus'," *BBC World Affairs*, 3 December 2002.

81. Clara Araújo, "Quotas for Women in the Brazilian Legislation System," "The Implementation of Quotas: Latin American Experiences," International Institute for Democracy and Electoral Assistance, Workshop Report, Lima, Peru, 23–24 Feb. 2003: 72.

82. UNESCO, "Progress of the World's Women 2002."

83. Benedita da Silva, "For the Empowerment of Women," Organization of American States (OAS) speech, 25 Nov. 2002, cited in *Brazzil Magazine*, 1 Dec. 2002, <http://www.brazzil.com/content/view/6228/38/> (Aug. 2003).

84. Ibid.

85. Ibid.

86. Clara Araújo, "Quotas for Women in the Brazilian Legislation System."

87. Fernandes, "Introduction of the National Report Statement."

88. CIA World Factbook, Brazil.

89. The U.S. Library of Congress, "Women in the Armed Forces," Country Studies, Brazil, 1985, <http://www.country-data.com/cgi-bin/query/r-1807.html> (Aug. 2003).

90. The U.S. Library of Congress, "Conscription," Country Studies, Brazil, 1985, <http://www.country-data.com/cgi-bin/query/r-1804.html> (Aug. 2003).

91. CIA World Factbook, Chile <http://www.cia.gov/cia/publications/factbook/geos/ci.html> (Sept. 2003).

92. Asunción Lavrin, *Women, Feminism, and Social Change in Argentina, Chile, and Uruguay, 1890–1940* (Lincoln, Nebraska: University of Nebraska Press, 1995), 480.

93. Country Reports on Human Rights Practices, 2003, Chile, U.S. Department of State, released by the Bureau of Democracy, Human Rights, and Labor, Feb. 25, 2004, <http://www.state.gov/g/drl/rls/hrrpt/2003/27890.htm> (Aug. 2004).

94. David Bosco, "Santiago's aftershocks," *Legal Affairs* (July/August 2002).

95. Constitution of the Republic of Chile, chapter I, Bases of Institutionality, 1980, University of Richmond, <http://confinder.richmond.edu/admin/docs/Chile.pdf> (Sep. 2003).

96. Country Reports on Human Rights Practices, 2003, Chile, U.S. Department of State.

97. Constitution of the Republic of Chile, chapter I, Bases of Institutionality, 1980, University of Richmond.

98. Susan Franceschet and Laura Macdonald, "Hard Times for Citizenship: Women's Movements in Chile and Mexico," *Citizenship Studies* 8, no. 1 (2004): 3–23.

99. Country Reports, Chile, International Women's Rights Action Watch (IWRAW), 1995, <http://iwraw.igc.org/publications/countries/chile.htm> (Sep. 2003).

100. Country Reports on Human Rights Practices, 2003, Chile, U.S. Department of State.

101. Regional Core Health Data System, Country Health Profile 2001: Chile, Pan American Health Organization, 2001, <http://www.paho.org/english/sha/prflchi.htm> (Sep. 2003).

102. Country Reports, Chile, IWRAW.

103. CIA World Factbook, Chile.

104. Regional Core Health Data System, Country Health Profile 2001: Chile.

105. Proportion of Women Engaged in the Service Sector, Nation Master, cited from International Labour Organization (ILO), Estimates and Projections of the Economically Active Population, 1950–2010, 4th ed., rev. 2. Database. Geneva; 2002; Key Indicators of the Labour Market 2001–2002, February 2002; and Laboursta Database, February 2002, <http://www.nationmaster.com/graph-T/lab_ser_wor_fem> (Sep. 2003).

106. The U.S. Library of Congress, "Family Structure and Attitudes Toward Gender Roles," Country Studies, Chile, March 1994, <http://countrystudies.us/chile/54.htm> (Sept. 2005).

107. Kate Raworth, *Trading away Our Rights, Women working in global supply chains*, Oxfam, Make Trade Fair (Boston, Massachusetts: Oxfam International, 2004): 3.

108. Human Development Reports, United Nations Development Programme, 2003, <http://hdr.undp.org/statistics/data/cty/cty_f_CHL.html> (Oct. 2004).

109. Country Reports on Human Rights Practices, 2003, Chile, U.S. Department of State.

110. Country Reports, Chile, IWRAW.

111. Country Reports on Human Rights Practices, 2003, Chile, U.S. Department of State.

112. Ibid.

113. UNESCO, "Progress of the World's Women 2002."

114. United Nations Educational, Scientific and Cultural Organization (UNESCO), "Progress of the World's Women 2002: Vol. 2: Gender Equality and the Mil-

lennium Development Goals," United Nations Development Fund for Women (UNIFEM), 2002, <http://www.unifem.org/www/resources/progressv2/index.html> (Sep. 2003).

115. UNESCO, Education, <http://portal.unesco.org/education/> (Sep. 2003).

116. UNESCO, "Progress of the World's Women 2002."

117. Ibid.

118. Margarita Martinez, "Women's Rights Ignored by Latin American Courts," *Women's E News*, 30 Nov. 2001, <http://www.womensenews.org/article.cfm?aid=738> (Sep. 2003).

119. Country Reports, Chile, IWRAW.

120. Simon and Altstein, *Global Perspectives on Social Issues*.

121. The U.S. Library of Congress, "Attitudes Toward Family and Gender, Divorce, Abortion, and Contraception," Country Studies, Chile, March 1994, <http://countrystudies.us/chile/54.htm> (Sept. 2005).

122. Human Rights Watch, World Report 2002, Women's Human Rights, 2002, <http://www.hrw.org/wr2k2/women.html> (Sep. 2003).

123. Country Reports, Chile, IWRAW.

124. Human Rights Watch, World Report 2002.

125. "Chileans granted right to divorce," *BBC News*, 7 May 2004.

126. Simon and Altstein, *Global Perspectives on Social Issues*.

127. Ibid.

128. Ibid.

129. Ibid.

130. Human Rights Watch, "Chile: High Court Discriminates Against Lesbian Mother," Human Rights News, 6 June 2004, <http://hrw.org/english/docs/2004/06/02/chile8722.htm> (Sep. 2004).

131. "Abortion Policies, A Global Review, Chile," United Nations, <http://www.un.org/esa/population/publications/abortion/profiles.htm> (Sep. 2003).

132. Luisa Cabal, "Chile Endangering Women's Lives by Outlawing Emergency Contraception," Center for Reproductive Rights, Latin American and Caribbean Region of Center's International Program, 10 Sep. 2001, <http://www.crlp.org//pr_01_0910ecchile.html> (Sep. 2003).

133. Franceschet and Macdonald, "Hard Times for Citizenship."

134. Cabal, "Chile Endangering Women's Lives by Outlawing Emergency Contraception."

135. Country Reports, Chile, IWRAW.

136. "Abortion Policies, A Global Review, Chile," United Nations.

137. Ibid.

138. Cabal, "Chile Endangering Women's Lives by Outlawing Emergency Contraception."

139. "Abortion Policies, A Global Review, Chile," United Nations.

140. Ibid.

141. Ipas, "Chilean feminists call for decriminalization of abortion on human-rights grounds," 13 Jan. 2004, <http://www.ipas.org/english/press_room/2004/releases/01132004.asp> (Sep. 2004).

142. The Center for Reproductive Law and Policy (CRLP), "Women's Reproductive Rights in Chile: A Shadow Report," (New York, NY: The Center for Reproductive Law and Policy, 1999) 1–25; Country Reports, Chile, IWRAW.

143. CIA World Factbook, Chile.

144. Regional Core Health Data System, Country Health Profile 2001: Chile.

145. World Health Organization (WHO), Chile, 2003, <http://www.who.int/countries/chl/en/> (Sep. 2004).

146. Country Reports on Human Rights Practices, 2003, Chile, U.S. Department of State.

147. Stanford University News Services, "Women of Chile Redefine Politics and Public Life," Press Release, 1 June 1993, <http://www.stanford.edu/dept/news/pr/93/930601Arc3239.html> (Sep. 2003).

148. UNESCO, "Progress of the World's Women 2002."

149. Kevin G. Hall, "Once tortured outcast, Chile's defense minister a rising political star," *Knight Ridder Newspapers*, 8 July 2004.

150. Country Reports on Human Rights Practices, 2003, Chile, U.S. Department of State.

151. CIA World Factbook, Chile.

152. United Nations, "Women's Anti-Discrimination Committee Concludes Consideration of Chile's Report," Press Release, 22 June 1999, <http://www.un.org/News/Press/docs/1999/19990622.WOM1145.html> (Sep. 2003).

153. Hall, "Once tortured outcast, Chile's defense minister a rising political star."

154. Ibid.

155. CIA World Factbook, Colombia, <http://www.cia.gov/cia/publications/factbook/geos/co.html> (Oct. 2005).

156. Country Reports on Human Rights Practices, 2003, Colombia, U.S. Department of State, released by the Bureau of Democracy, Human Rights, and Labor, March 31, 2003, <http://www.state.gov/g/drl/rls/hrrpt/2003/27891.htm> (Oct. 2004).

157. CIA World Factbook, Colombia.

158. The U.S. Library of Congress, Country Studies, Colombia, 1988, <http://countrystudies.us/colombia/> (Nov. 2003).

159. Ibid.

160. Colombian Women's Organizations, based on a presentation in Bogotá to a witness for Peace delegation in July 2001, notes by Justin Podur, <http://www.zmag.org/crisescurevts/colombia/womencol.htm> (Oct. 2003); Country Reports on Human Rights Practices, 2003, Colombia, U.S. Department of State.

161. Paula Andrea Rossiasco, "Forced Displacement and Women as Heads of Displaced Households in Colombia," *Colombia Journal*, June 2003, <http://www.colombiajournal.org/displacement.htm> (Oct. 2003).

162. Ibid.

163. Colombian Women's Organizations; Country Reports on Human Rights Practices, 2003, Colombia, U.S. Department of State.

164. The U.S. Library of Congress, Country Studies, Colombia.

165. Ibid.

166. Ibid.

167. Ibid.

168. "Women of the World: Laws and Policies Affecting Their Reproductive Lives, Latin America and the Caribbean," The Center for Reproductive Law and Policy (CRLP), DEMUS, Estudio para la Defensa de los Derechos de la Mujer, <http://www.crlp.org/pdf/wowlac_colombia.pdf> (Oct. 2003).

169. The U.S. Library of Congress, Country Studies, Colombia.

170. "Q&A Colombia's Civil Conflict," *BBC News*, 24 May 2005, <http://news.bbc.co.uk/1/hi/world/americas/1738963.stm> (Oct. 2005).

171. The U.S. Library of Congress, Country Studies, Colombia.

172. CIA World Factbook, Colombia.

173. Ibid.

174. "Timeline: Colombia," *BBC News*, 19 Aug. 2004, <http://news.bbc.co.uk/1/hi/world/americas/country_profiles/1212827.stm> (Oct. 2004).

175. This point is debated by the 1991 Defense Intelligence Agency that claims that Uribe's father's murder was related to Uribe's participation in drug trafficking. "Uribe denies drug cartel links," *BBC News*, 2 August 2004, <http://news.bbc.co.uk/2/hi/americas/3527538.stm> (Oct. 2004).

176. "Hopes persist for FARC Swap Deal," *BBC News*, 23 Aug. 2004, <http://news.bbc.co.uk/1/hi/world/americas/3590280.stm> (Oct. 2004).

177. Ibid.

178. Ibid.

179. Ibid.

180. Ibid.

181. Ibid.

182. "Colombia: Paramilitary Commanders Address Congress," by Inter Press Service, 29 July 2004, <http://www.antiwar.com/news/?articleid=3208> (Oct. 2004).

183. Amnesty International Report, Colombia, 2004, <http://web.amnesty.org/report2004/col-summary-eng> (Oct. 2004).

184. Ibid.

185. Ibid.

186. "Timeline: Colombia," *BBC News*.

187. The National Security Archive, "U.S. Intelligence Listed Colombian President Uribe among 'Important Colombian Narco-Traffickers' in 1991," George Washington University, 2 Aug. 2004, <http://www.gwu.edu/~nsarchiv/NSAEBB/NSAEBB131/index.htm> (Oct. 2004).

188. "Colombia Disputes President Uribe's Alleged Drug Ties," USA Today.

189. Uribe denies drug cartel links," *BBC News*, 2 August 2004.

190. Country Reports on Human Rights Practices, 2003, Colombia, U.S. Department of State.

191. CIA World Factbook, Colombia.

192. Ibid.

193. "Q&A Colombia's Civil Conflict," *BBC News*, 24 May 2005.

194. CIA World Factbook, Colombia.

195. Amnesty International Report, Colombia.

196. CIA World Factbook, Colombia.

197. Country Reports on Human Rights Practices, 2003, Colombia, U.S. Department of State.

198. CIA World Factbook, Colombia.

199. "Colombian Profile: Labor," Colombian Labor Stats, 2002, <http://www.nationmaster.com/country/co/Labor> (Oct. 2003).

200. CIA World Factbook, Colombia.

201. United Nations Educational, Scientific and Cultural Organization (UNESCO), "Progress of the World's Women 2002: Volume 2: Gender Equality and the Millennium Development Goals," United Nations Development Fund for Women (UNIFEM), 2002, <http://www.unifem.org/www/resources/progressv2/index.html> (Oct. 2003).

202. UNESCO, "Progress of the World's Women 2002."

203. The Center for Reproductive Law and Policy (CRLP), "Women's Reproductive Rights in Colombia: A Shadow Report," (New York, NY: The Center for Reproductive Law and Policy, 1999) 1–37; "Women of the World," The Center for Reproductive Law and Policy (CRLP), DEMUS.

204. The Center for Reproductive Law and Policy (CRLP), "Women's Reproductive Rights in Colombia: A Shadow Report."

205. Country Reports on Human Rights Practices, 2003, Colombia, U.S. Department of State.

206. Ibid.

207. U.S. Office on Colombia (USOC), "Afro-Colombians under Fire," Understanding Colombia series, June 2004, <http://usofficeoncolombia.org/afrocolombianos.htm> (Oct. 2004).

208. Ibid.

209. Colombian Profile: Education, Nation Master, cited from UNESCO; "Efficiency and Equity in Schools around the World"; World Statistics Pocketbook; World Bank; UNESCO Institute for Statistics; CIA World Factbook; Household survey data, net enrolment data from UNESCO, and data from UNICEF country offices, <http://www.nationmaster.com/country/co/Education&b_define=1> (Oct. 2003).

210. Ibid.

211. UNESCO, "Progress of the World's Women 2002."

212. Ibid.

213. Ibid.

214. UNESCO, Education, <http://portal.unesco.org/education/> (Oct. 2003).

215. "Women of the World," The Center for Reproductive Law and Policy (CRLP), DEMUS.

216. Ibid.

217. Ibid.

218. Ibid.

219. Simon and Altstein, *Global Perspectives on Social Issues*.

220. Ibid.

221. "Women of the World," The Center for Reproductive Law and Policy (CRLP), DEMUS.

222. Ibid.

223. Ibid.

224. Ibid.
225. Ibid.
226. "Abortion Policies, A Global Review, Colombia," United Nations, <http://www.un.org/esa/population/publications/abortion/profiles.htm> (Oct. 2003).
227. "Women of the World," The Center for Reproductive Law and Policy (CRLP), DEMUS.
228. Ibid.
229. Ibid.
230. Ibid.
231. CIA World Factbook, Colombia.
232. "Women of the World," The Center for Reproductive Law and Policy (CRLP), DEMUS.
233. M. Mosquera, "Strengthening user participation through health sector reform in Colombia: a study of institutional change and social representation" *Health Policy and Planning* 16, supp. 2 (2001): 52–60; Jaume Puig-Junoy, "Managing Risk Selection Incentives in Health Sector Reforms," *International Journal of Health Planning and Management* 14, no. 4 (1999): 287–311.
234. "Women of the World," The Center for Reproductive Law and Policy (CRLP), DEMUS.
235. Medecins Sans Frontieres, "The hush of the humanitarian crisis in Colombia," 18 July 2005, <http://www.msf.org/msfinternational/invoke.cfm?objectid=28A1AE6B-E018-0C72-0916631580C685E2&component=toolkit.article&method=full_html> (Oct. 2005).
236. Colombian Women's Organizations.
237. Regional Core Health Data System, Country Health Profile 2001: Brazil, Pan American Health Organization, 2001, <http://www.paho.org/english/sha/prflcol.htm> (Oct. 2003). Regional Core Health Data System, Country Health Profile 2001: Brazil, Pan American Health Organization, 2001, <http://www.paho.org/english/sha/prflbra.htm> (Aug. 2003).
238. Country Reports on Human Rights Practices, 2003, Colombia, U.S. Department of State.
239. UNESCO, "Progress of the World's Women 2002."
240. Juan Pablo Toro, "Colombia president names 6 women to Cabinet," *Laredo Morning Times*, 15 June 2002.
241. Ibid.
242. Carlos Lozada, "Colombia gets's tough with a woman's touch," *The Christian Science Monitor*, 28 Oct. 2002, <http://www.csmonitor.com/2002/1028/p07s01-woam.html> (Oct. 2003).
243. Amnesty International, "Women in Colombia Continue Being Victims of Human Rights Violations and abuses," Hartford Web Publishing, 27 Sep. 1995, <http://www.hartford-hwp.com/archives/42/079.html> (Oct. 2003).
244. Country Reports on Human Rights Practices, 2003, Colombia, U.S. Department of State.
245. USOC Policy Brief, "The Impact of War on Women: Colombian Women's Struggle," Jan. 2004, <http://usofficeoncolombia.org/insidecolombia/women.htm> (Oct. 2004).

246. Country Reports on Human Rights Practices, 2003, Colombia, U.S. Department of State.

247. CIA World Factbook, Colombia.

248. Olga Yolanda Jimenez, "Women in my army," United States Army School of the Americas, <http://carlisle-www.army.mil/usamhi/usarsa/ADELANTE/fall96/jimenez.htm> (Oct. 2003).

249. Stephanie Boyd, "Women prepare for war in Latin America," Dispatch Online, 16 Feb. 1999, <http://www.dispatch.co.za/1999/02/16/features/WAR.HTM> (Oct. 2003).

250. Jimenez, "Women in my army."

Chapter Three

Europe

UNITED KINGDOM

The United Kingdom is located in Western Europe. The U.K. is made up of islands, including the northern portion of the island of Ireland. The U.K. is between the North Atlantic Ocean and the North Sea, and is northwest of France. The population is 60,094,648 (July 2003 est.). The ethnic groups are English (81.5 percent), Scottish (9.6 percent), Irish (2.4 percent), Welsh (1.9 percent), Ulster (1.8 percent), West Indian, Indian, Pakistani, Black Caribbean, Black African, and other (2.8 percent). The religions are Anglican and Roman Catholic (40 million), Muslim (1.5 million), Presbyterian (800,000), Methodist (760,000), Sikh (500,000), Hindu (500,000), and Jewish (350,000). The languages spoken are English, Welsh, and Gaelic.[1]

Constitution

England has existed since the tenth century. In 1284, King Edward passed the Statute of Rhuddlan making Wales part of England. This union was not formalized until 1536. In 1707, Scotland joined England as Great Britain. Ireland joined in 1801. Ireland eventually obtained independence from Great Britain in 1921. Presently, only six counties in Northern Ireland remain part of Great Britain.[2]

The United Kingdom is a constitutional monarchy with a democratic, parliamentary government. The Constitution is unwritten. In fact, it is made up of statutes, common law, practice, and traditional rights.[3]

Wales, Scotland, and Northern Ireland have some central governmental powers.

Under the 1998 Good Friday agreement, Ireland established a local government. The government includes a power-sharing executive and legislative assembly. Under the Agreement, there is a 108-member elected assembly that is overseen by a 12-minister cabinet shared by the unionists and nationalists. In addition, Northern Ireland elects eighteen representatives to the Parliament in London. Under the Good Friday Agreement, a new police force was created and the IRA was supposed to disarm. There are allegations that the IRA has continued paramilitary activity. This has had an adverse affect on the peace process and has resulted in suspension of the assembly.[4]

Northern Ireland had its own Parliament and Prime Minister from 1921 to 1973. In 1973, the British Government imposed direct rule due to Ireland's internal conflict. The Good Friday Agreement was approved by both Northern Ireland and the Republic of Ireland on April 10, 1998. Ireland never renewed its membership of the British Commonwealth once it lapsed. The Republic of Ireland did join the European Union in 1973.[5]

Queen Elizabeth II is the Head of State (the Monarch) and Tony Blair is the Prime Minister (Head of Government). The two major parties are the Tory Party (Conservative) and the Liberal Democrats.[6]

Changes to the existing laws are achieved in a couple of ways. Changes may occur through new acts of Parliament or judiciary precedent, where the result of a case (verdict) sets forth a standard for future cases. The House of Commons is made up of 659 members, 119 of whom are women.[7] The House of Commons has much greater legislative power and has exclusive power over finance. The House of Lords, with 714 members (of whom 125 are women), does not have much power. It may review, amend or delay a bill, except those bills relating to the budget.[8]

The judiciary is independent from the government. Unlike the U.S. Supreme Court, the U.K. judiciary cannot review the constitutionality of legislation.

A resolution in favor of allowing women to vote was first presented in the House of Lords in 1851 by the Earl of Carlyle. In 1881, women were granted the right to vote if they owned property.[9] Female activists such as Emmeline Pankhurst demanded that the United Kingdom grant women the right to vote. Pankhurst, in her speech "Votes for Women" on October 25, 1912, said, "We women have a great mission-the greatest mission the world has ever known. It is to free half the human race, and through that freedom to save the rest."[10] See Women in Public Office for more on Emmeline Pankhurst.

In 1928, women were granted the right to vote and stand for election. Presently, men and women are eligible to vote at eighteen years of age (see Women in Public Office).[11]

Work Force and Economy

The U.K. is a leading global trading and financial power. The U.K. has the fourth largest economy in the world, and second largest economy in the European Union (EU). The purchasing power parity of the U.K. is $1.664 trillion (2003 est.). The U.K. has a strong welfare program that provides most of its citizens with an above average standard of living. Nevertheless, the percentage of people who live under the poverty line is 17 percent. The labor force is made up of 29.8 million people (2003). The unemployment rate is 5.1 percent (2003 est.).[12] Interestingly, the unemployment rate is higher for men than for women. The employment rate, the percentage of persons in the labor force, is 69 percent for women and 79 percent for men.[13] The main industries in the U.K. are machine tools, electric power equipment, automatic equipment, railroad equipment, metals, chemicals, coal, petroleum, paper and paper products, food processing, textiles, clothing, and other consumer goods. Most formerly state owned companies have been privatized.[14]

In 2000, women earned 50 percent of the wages in the non-agricultural sector of employment. Women earned 45 percent of all wages in the early 1980s.[15] In 1998, 44.4 percent of women were employed full time and 44.8 percent were employed half time, and 5.5 percent were unemployed.[16]

The U.K. has a Sex Discrimination Act (1975) and Equal Pay Act (1970) that was implemented by the Equal Opportunities Commission. The Sex Discrimination Act prohibits discrimination against women in employment, training, and education.[17] Although sex discrimination is prohibited in the workplace, it still happens. Discrimination cases against employers must be brought before industrial tribunals and courts. The Equal Opportunities Commission supports those women who bring forward discrimination cases. In addition, the Commission sets guidelines for employers to follow.[18]

The Equal Pay Act prohibits employers to pay women less than men when they are employed for the same or similar position. In order to bring suit the male counterpart must be employed by the same employer as the woman or any associate employer at the same establishment. Difference in pay is legal if it can be proven that the difference is based on something other than gender. The Sex Discrimination Act and The Equal Pay Act are old and need to be updated.[19]

Men earn on average $16.45 per hour while women earn on average $12.70 (dollars), 18 percent less.[20]

The alteration in the national minimum wage gave many women a pay raise in 2002. The wage increased from 4.10 pounds (2001) per hour to 4.20 pounds in (2002).[21]

Women make up 80 percent of the 6.6 million part-time employees. Part-time employees obtain the same wages and rights as their full-time counterparts. Women make up 47 percent of the entire work force (2000).[22]

Parents may obtain parental leave. Single parents may receive aid from the Government for childcare. The Maternity and Parental Leave Regulation (1999) prohibits dismissal of an employee based on maternity leave, parental leave, or time off for dependants, or pregnancy. In July 2002, the Employment Act extended maternity pay from eighteen to twenty-six weeks. Maternity leave was increased to one year.[23]

Sixty percent of women hold jobs in the following occupations: sales, numerical clerks, personal assistants, typists, health related occupations, teaching professionals, childcare, and catering positions. Ninety-nine percent of childcare employees are women.[24]

Women employed full-time in the above occupations earn 78 percent of what their male counterparts earn. Differences in pay historically were in part a result of differences in work experience and educational levels. Female dominated occupations tend to pay little. Women are under-represented in higher pay jobs within occupations, revealing the existence of a glass ceiling. Other factors that contribute to the difference in pay are discrimination, job grading practices, and reward systems.[25]

Minority women (Black, Pakistani, and Indian) tend to earn far less than White women. Among minority women, Black women are most likely to be unemployed.[26]

Education

In 2000, the ratio of female to male enrollment in secondary school was 102 women for every 100 men. Ninety-five percent of eligible females are enrolled in secondary education.[27] The female to male ratio of student enrollment in tertiary school was 127 women for every 100 men.[28] In 1997, 52.6 percent of women had obtained degrees of higher education.[29]

The U.K. has a national curriculum, and men and women must complete twelve years of education. Attendance for both sexes is close to 100 percent.[30, 31]

Marriage

The minimum legal age for men and women to marry is sixteen.[32] The average age at the time of marriage has increased from twenty-six to twenty-eight for men and twenty-five to twenty-seven years for women from 1991 to 2002. Forty-two percent of men are married compared to 34.7 percent of women.[33]

The marriage rate has been decreasing recently while the age of marriage has been increasing. The rate decreased from 7.9 in 1971 to 4.3 in 2001 (out of 1,000 people). The number of divorces in Northern Ireland has significantly increased since the 1960s. In the 1960s, there were roughly 100 divorces per year. In 2001, there were over 2,365 divorces.[34]

In general the United Kingdom has a marriage rate of 5.1 (per 1,000 total population) and a divorce rate of 42.6 percent (per 100 marriages).[35] In England, there were 160,000 divorces in 2002. This was a 1.9 percent increase from 2001. In England and Wales, 70 percent of divorces were made up of couples that were both dissolving their first marriage. The average age of divorce has increased for men and women. For men the average age of divorce rose from thirty-nine to forty-two and from thirty-six to thirty-nine years of age for women. This may reflect the fact that couples are marrying later in life. Women most frequently file for divorce in England and Wales because of negative behavior on the part of their husband. Men most frequently file for divorce from their spouse after a two-year consensual separation.[36]

Marrying at a young age, having previously been married, and/or having a child before marriage are factors that adversely affect a marriage's chances of survival.[37] Ninety-five percent of single parents are mothers.[38]

Abortion and Contraceptives

Abortion is legal to save the mother's life, to preserve the physical or mental health of the mother, if the pregnancy results from rape or incest, if there is fetal impairment, or for economic or social reasons. Abortions are not available upon request. Abortions are legal when certified by two registered medical practitioners. The abortion must be performed in a government-approved location. Abortion is legal during the first twenty-four weeks of gestation.[39]

The first abortion statute, enacted in 1803, sentenced those who performed an abortion after quickening (when the first movements of the fetus are felt) with the death penalty. Those who performed abortions prior to quickening were sentenced up to fourteen years deportation or they received lashing with a whip. In 1861, both the administrators of the abortion or the woman receiving the abortion were subject to fourteen years imprisonment. Under the 1929 Infant Life Preservation Act, an abortion could only be performed to save the life of the mother. As a result of the 1938 *Rex v. Bourne* decision an abortion could be performed for health reasons, both physical and mental, and if the pregnancy resulted from rape or incest. Neither the 1861 Offenses Against the Person Act nor the 1929 Infant Life Preservation Act applied to Scotland. Abortion was a criminal offense in Scottish common law. Nevertheless, prosecutions were not usually brought up when the abortion was performed for "reputable medical reasons." There is no official or judicial definition of "reputable medical reasons." Northern Ireland follows the law of the 1861 Offenses Against the Person Act. In addition, it applies the *Rex v. Bourne* decision whereby an abortion can be performed on serious mental health grounds.

Presently, the abortion law in England, Wales, and Scotland is regulated by the Abortion Act of 1967 that was amended by the 1990 Human Fertilization and Embryology Act of 1990. Abortions are free of charge through the National Health Service. In 1991, the United Kingdom became the second country to approve the use of the RU-486 abortion pill. It can only be used on the National Health Service gynecological units.[40]

The government gives direct support for contraceptive use. Eighty-two percent of married women use modern contraceptives. The rate of male sterilization is 22 percent. It is estimated that 50 percent of women ages sixteen to forty-nine use non-surgical methods of contraceptives, while 12 percent have been sterilized. Forty-two percent of women that use non-surgical contraceptives use the pill and 37 percent are dependent on condoms. The fertility rate is 1.7 births per woman.[41]

Health Care

The National Health Service (NHS) began in 1948. The objective of NHS is "to provide healthcare for all citizens, based on need, not the ability to pay." Presently, more than 10 percent of the population uses private health insurance. Independent Health Care Association (IHA) represents private healthcare insurers and providers. IHA purports that the independent health sector makes up 25 percent of all health care spending. IHA and NHS in 2001 decided to collaborate. For example, NHS members may obtain IHA coverage for expenses not covered by NHS and NHS members can obtain treatment at independent facilities.[42]

While only citizens are guaranteed health care, asylum applicants with prolonged applications may obtain the same NHS coverage as a citizen.[43]

Aside from basic services patients must pay for prescriptions, dental, and optical services. Subsidized aid for such services may be provided for pregnant women, prisoners, pensioners, or children younger than eighteen years of age. Regardless there are still problems with the health care system. The system has funding, staff, and services issues. In fact, patients sometimes end up waiting for more than twelve weeks before a doctor can perform their elective surgery.[44]

Mortality rates are higher for males than females.[45]

The most common cancers affecting women in the U.K. are breast cancer, cervical cancer, ovarian cancer, endometrial cancer, and vulvar cancer. Other illnesses that commonly affect women are anemia, endometriosis, and fibroids. Heart disease and osteoporoses also are illnesses that affect women. Nearly one out of four British women die from heart disease. Women who have a heart attack are less likely to survive than men. Those women who do survive are more likely to die during the year following their heart attack than men. This may be in part because women's symptoms of a heart attack are often different than the symptoms that men display, that is, nausea. Sometimes these signs are ignored or misdiagnosed. In addition, women may respond differently to treatment than men.[46]

Women in Public Office

Female activist Emmeline Pankhurst and her daughters had a monumental hand in the women's suffrage movement. After Emmeline's husband died, she was suddenly a single mother during a time when a woman could not achieve financial independence. She had no means to care for her three children. In 1903, Emmeline and her three daughters formed the Women's Social and Political Union (WSPU). The WSPU did all that they could to gain attention for the cause of women's suffrage. The group disrupted meetings of Parliament, smashed windows, set fire to post boxes, chained themselves to fences outside of Parliament, and organized marches. As a consequence of their actions, members of the WSPU would be arrested. While in prison, members would go on hunger strikes. The police would respond by force-feeding the women. The police would release the women and re-arrest them when they believed the members to be healthy again. In 1914, the Government's Conciliatory Bill granted women the right to vote. Working class women were not included in this group. In 1918, the law was amended to allow all women thirty and over to vote. In 1928, the law was amended to allow all women twenty-one and over to vote.[47] Today, women eighteen years and older may vote.

Another woman who made her stamp on history is Margaret Thatcher. Margaret Thatcher was elected a member of parliament in 1959 and became the United Kingdom's first female prime minister in 1979. She remained in office until 1990.[48]

There are 119 women out of 659 members in the House of Commons and 125 women out of 714 members of the House of Lords. The majority of female members of Parliament are in the Labor Party (ninety-four) and the Conservative Party (fourteen).[49] A Life Peer is an appointed member (such as a baron or a lord) who obtains a seat in the House of Lords.[50] In the House of Lords, there are 120 women who are Life Peers under the Life Peerages Act of 1958, 4 women are Life Peers under the House of Lords Act of 1999, and 1 woman is a Life Peer under the Appellate Jurisdiction Act of 1876. There are four women (out of nineteen) in the cabinet of the House of Commons and one woman (out of two) in the cabinet of the House of Lords. There are eight women (out of twenty-six) who are Ministers of State compared to two (out of three) in the House of Lords. In 1919, Viscountess Nancy Astor became the first woman in Parliament. The first woman to be a member of the House of Lords was the Baroness Wootton of Abinger of The Labor Party. She was a member created under the Life Peerages Act 1958. The first female leader of the House of Lords was Baroness Young (Conservative). She was the leader for three years. The first female chief whip was Baroness Llewelyn-Davies of Hastoe of the Labor party. The first female Law Lord was the Baroness Hale of Richmond who was made a life peer under the Appellate Jurisdiction Act in 2004. The present leader of the House of Lords is Baroness Amos (October 2003–present).[51]

In 1976, the first Ministry to focus on women's issues was the Commission for Equal Opportunities.

There are not as many women in well-paid governmental positions.[52] In 2003, the Government's Women and Equality Unit began a campaign including a regional seminar series. The objective of the campaign is to increase the number of women holding public appointments at the national level.[53]

Women in the Military

The U.K.'s defense expenditure is third out of the North Atlantic Treaty Organization (NATO), of which it was a founding member. There are 42,000 members in the Navy, 110,000 members in the Army (7,600 of which are women), and 54,000 members in the Air Force.[54]

Women may bring sex discrimination suits before the employment tribunal as long as they exhausted the military tribunals.[55]

FRANCE

France is located in Western Europe. It borders the Bay of Biscay and the English Channel and is located between Belgium and Spain and Italy. France has a population of 60,424,213 (July 2004 est.). Ninety-two percent of the population is French (a mix of Celtic, Latin, Germanic, and Slavic origin), 3 percent are North African, and 2 percent are German. The remainder are Slavic, Indochinese, and Basque. Over 85 percent of France's population is Roman Catholic, 2 percent are Protestant, 8 percent are Muslim, four percent are unaffiliated, and 1 percent is Jewish. French is the official and widely spoken language. Some speak regional dialects and languages such as Provencal, Breton, Alsatian, Corsican, Catalan, Basque, and Flemish. There are 100 women for every 95 men (2004 est.).[56]

Not long ago France's laws reflected a patriarchical society. Men were the heads of household, financially and in regards to the children. Inheritance used to pass through the eldest son. Many strides toward equality have occurred since then but things are not yet equal.

Constitution

Since 1958, France has had a presidential democracy. The Head of State is President Jacques Chirac. The Head of Government is Prime Minister Jean-Pierre Raffarin. The Constitution was adopted on September 28, 1958.[57]

Presently, there is a ban against headscarves in public schools. The law was passed by an overwhelming majority and was signed into law by President Chirac. The government argues that the law helps to preserve secularism in public schools. It prohibits all religious apparel, not just head scarves. For example, it prohibits the wearing of large Christian crosses and Yamukah's. The law began to be enforced in September of 2004. The new law has been met by an onslaught of protests from Muslims, including the five million Muslims that live in France. Objectors to the law argue that the law violates a person's right to religious freedom and that the law, in fact, intended to limit Islamic influence on mainstream society.[58]

While rape and spousal abuse are prohibited by the Penal Code, they still remain a problem. Nevertheless, violations of the law most often result in enforcement. There were 25,802 reported rapes and incidents of sexual assaults in 2003. Individuals found guilty of domestic violence face three to twenty years in prison and $56,250 (U.S. dollars) in fines.[59] Anne-Marie Courderc, the Minister of Employment and organizer of the Superior Council of Professional Equality, has instituted many equality and female-based initiatives. Among the initiatives is a national hotline for women affected by domestic violence and rape.[60]

Annually, since 2001, there has been a significant increase in racial threats. In November 2003 a new immigration law took effect. The law provides stricter regulations on preventing illegal immigrants. The law also provides that illegal immigrants be deported. Among the new regulations, the duration that a person may be detained has been extended. While these laws may be bad news for immigrants, other policies have been passed to combat racism. Those found guilty of committing racial acts or acts motivated by prejudice face a prison sentence that is double in duration from what it was prior. In addition, fines for such acts have increased.[61]

Both men and women are eligible to vote at eighteen years of age.[62]

The Constitution guarantees equal rights, in all domains, to men and women.[63] Yet, women are not on equal footing with men in public office and the work force.

Work Force and Economy

France is one of the founding members of the European Union (EU).[64] The purchasing power parity in France is $1.54 trillion (2002 est.). The labor force is 26.6 million (2001 est.).[65]

Women made up 34 percent of the work force in 1954.[66] In the 1980s, women earned 43 percent of the wages in the non-agricultural sector compared to 46 percent in the mid-1990s.[67] France has the highest rate of female employment in the EU; women make up 47 percent of the work force (2003 est.).[68]

In the nineteenth century, women were employed primarily in domestic or factory positions. The number of women employed in law, medicine, and the media are increasing. Yet, female employment predominantly is in the fields of public service, company employees, teachers, health professionals, social occupations, and unskilled industrial workers. Females are still underrepresented in the sciences.[69] In 2003, women made up 29.8 percent of practicing physicians. Interestingly, women made up 90 percent of practicing gynecologists, 62.6 percent of dermatologists, and 66.1 percent of endocrinologists.[70] Women are rarely in upper managerial positions. Despite the fact that women make up 59.6 percent of public service positions, they only make up 5.95 percent of the top tier administrative positions within the field. However, things are changing. Women under twenty-five make up 50 percent of employees in executive and professional positions.[71]

While prostitution is legal, acting as a pimp or madam is not. In addition, it is illegal to assist, aid, or profit from prostitution. However these laws are not consistently enforced. In addition, when enforcement does occur there are varying penalties.[72]

While gender discrimination and sexual harassment in the workplace are prohibited by law, both still exist.[73] Over 2 percent of female employees have reported that they have been subject to sexual harassment or physical aggression in the workplace. Many incidences go unreported. The burden of proof is on the employer not the employee. This means that the employer must show that the harassment did not occur as opposed to the employee having to show that she was harassed.[74]

Women earn less than men in comparable employment positions. In addition, women face 2 percent higher unemployment than men. In 2003, the unemployment rate for women was approximately 10.5 percent.[75]

Employers who fire an employee who is on maternity leave face fines. The minimum penalty is six months salary. In addition, the burden of proof is on the employer to prove that the women had committed gross misconduct as opposed to the burden being on the woman to prove that she was unjustly discharged. Lastly, there is no statute of limitation for women to bring forward a discrimination suit.[76]

The minimum wage is $8.98 (U.S. dollars) per hour. Consequently, this provides a good standard of living. The typical work week is thirty-five hours. However, employers will most likely soon return to the thirty-nine-hour work week.[77]

On average, women make 25 percent less than their male counterparts.[78]

Education

In 1848, the Minister of Education, Hippolyte Carnot, proposed secular, compulsory, and free education for men and women until age fourteen. The parliament opposed the proposal. From 1848 to 1850 all similar proposals were similarly rejected. The Falloux law passed in 1851 required that communities of over 800 residents have an all female school. The classes were solely domestically or clerically focused. In addition, the all-female school received no state funding.[79]

Since 1971, more women than men have been attending university.[80]

In 2000, the ratio of female to male enrollment in secondary school was 102 women for every 100 men. The percentage of female enrollment in secondary school was 94.[81] In 2000, the female to male ratio of student enrollment in tertiary school was 123 women for every 100 men.[82]

Education is compulsory from the ages of six to sixteen and is funded for individuals until they are eighteen years old. This applies to both citizens and non-citizens. Children maintain 100 percent attendance until they are fourteen years old, where the rate drops slightly yearly.[83]

Women are surpassing men in regard to academic success in primary, junior high, senior high, and university.[84]

Marriage

The minimum legal age men can marry is eighteen and fifteen for women.[85] Minors, those under eighteen, may not marry without parental consent.[86] Sons may not marry their mothers or step-mother; daughters may not marry his/her fathers or step-father. In other words a person may not marry another in direct lineage with themselves.[87] In addition, a person may not marry their sister or brother, or aunt or uncle.[88] The average age men marry is 29.2 and 27.2 for women. Thirty percent of men are married compared to 25.2 of women.[89] Only civil marriages are officially recognized. Religious ceremonies may take place only after the civil marriage has been performed.[90] Until 1970 the law stated that men were the legal head of household granting the husband total authority over his children and all financial matters. Today, men and women have equal rights over financial and parental matters.[91]

In 1985, an Act granted married men and women equal rights in regard to the management of property.[92]

Prenuptial agreements must be done no earlier than two months before the marriage. If the parties do not have a prenuptial agreement the parties will be married under the communauté reduite aux acquets. Under "communauté reduite aux acquets" each party keeps property they owned before the marriage and any they inherited during the marriage. Only joint property, property obtained during the marriage, is owned equally by both parties. In addition, both spouses were given the right to work and collect his or her own income.[93] In 1999, the Government granted unmarried couples, homosexual and heterosexual, similar rights as those couples that are married. Unmarried couples enjoy tax, legal, and social welfare benefits. The union may be registered. A union may be dissolved through a letter of separation. The law has been strongly opposed by religious and conservative leaders. In France there are roughly 5 million unmarried cohabitating couples.[94] This number has increased by 900 percent since 1960.[95]

Divorce was legalized in 1792. It was then made illegal in 1816 and was not reinstituted until 1884.[96]

Today, France has no-fault divorce where by couples can obtain a divorce with mutual consent or a spouse can seek a divorce because of lack of compatibility. A person can also be granted a divorce because of a partner's immorality, cruelty, insanity, condemnation for certain crimes, desertion of at least two years, or emigration. In addition, divorce is affordable.[97]

The divorce rate is 38.3 per 100 marriages. The majority of divorces are initiated by women. Seventy-five percent of spouses who have child custody receive child support. Women are usually granted custody of the child(ren).[98]

Under Article 228 a woman must wait three hundred days after her previous divorce is finalized to remarry. The period is ended immediately upon proof that the woman is not pregnant.[99]

Abortion and Contraceptives

Before 1975, legislation prohibited abortion except to save the life of the mother.[100] Abortions have been legal since the Veil Act in 1975.[101] They may be performed to save the life of the woman, to preserve her physical or mental health, on account of rape or incest, because of fetal impairment, or because of economic reasons. A woman does not need to give a reason in order to receive an abortion.[102]

An abortion must be performed before the end of the twelfth week of pregnancy by a physician in an approved hospital.[103] After the twelfth week of pregnancy, an abortion may be performed only if the pregnancy poses a grave danger to the woman's health or there is a strong probability that the child will suffer from severe illness that is incurable.[104] The time in which an abortion could be performed was extended from ten to twelve weeks in 2001. Until 2001, if the woman was an unmarried minor she had to obtain the consent of her parental guardian. However, since 2001 a woman under sixteen may request an abortion without the consent of her parents.[105]

Under the existing Penal Code (section 317), a person who performs or attempts to perform an illegal abortion on a pregnant woman with or without her consent is subject to one to five years' imprisonment and payment of a fine of 1,800 to 100,000 francs.[106]

All public, regional, and general hospitals are required to have the facilities to perform abortions. They must provide patients with information. In 1982, social security was extended to cover 70 percent of the costs of care and hospitalization related to lawful abortions. In addition, the French government approved in 1988 the use of the RU-486 in order to induce legal abortions within forty-nine days of a woman's last period. The drug must be taken in the presence of a physician. Currently, the RU-486 is used to induce 19 percent of all abortions and 46 percent of all abortions performed in the first seven weeks of pregnancy.[107] In 2000, roughly 200,000 abortions were performed.[108]

The fertility rate is 1.7 births per woman.[109] Seventy-nine percent of married women between the ages of twenty and forty-nine use modern contraceptives. Of the 68 percent of women who are using a type of reversible contraceptive, 59 percent use the pill and 23 percent use an IUD. Rarely are IUDs prescribed to women who have not had children. Condoms are not frequently used. Roughly 20 percent of births in 2000 were unplanned.[110]

Health Care

The government provides health care for citizens through social security.[111] France is ranked by the World Health Organization as having the number one health care system out of the 191 countries examined (2000). Nearly 75 percent of health care spending comes from public funding. The remainder is paid by patients (15 percent) and supplemental funding (10 percent). In 2000, France introduced universal health insurance. It provides insurance to all legal residents, employed and unemployed. In addition, supplemental insurance is provided for low-income persons.[112]

Illnesses and deaths related to smoking have increased among French women. Approximately 30.8 percent of French women eighteen to sixty-four years old smoke.[113]

Women in Public Office

Women were granted the right to vote and run for office in 1944.[114]

The Parliament is made up of the National Assembly and the Senate. The National Assembly has 577 members and the Senate has 321 members. In 1993, 6 percent of the National Assembly was made up of women compared to 10.9 percent of the seats in 1997.[115] In 2002, women held 11.8 percent of the seats in the national parliament, putting France in the bottom five in relation to other western European and developed nations.[116] There are 101 women out of 898 members of the legislature. There are ten female ministers out of the thirty-eight-member cabinet. There are 70 women out of 190 members of the Court of Cassation. Out of the eighty-seven members of the EU Parliament, thirty-five are women. Women make up 33 percent of municipal counselors and 10.9 percent of mayoral positions.[117] In 2000, a Constitution Amendment demanded that there are the same number of male and female candidates.[118] The penalty for violation of the amendment is fines.[119] Article 3 of the Constitution states that the law favors equal access for men and women to voting and elected office. Article 4 declares that it is the responsibility of the parties to enforce that there are an equal number of male and female candidates.[120]

Gender-based statistics are published by the Ministerial of Employment during elections in order to make known the status of male and female representation in politics.[121]

Women in the Military

Women have been involved in war for centuries as spies or dressed as male soldiers.

In 1430, Joan of Arc in the Hundred Year War was captured while fighting outside of Paris. She was burned at the stake for heresy, wearing men's clothing, and witchcraft. In 1456, she was pronounced innocent of her crimes. She was canonized as a saint in 1920.[122]

During World War II, French female spies were an asset to the Office of Strategic Services (OSS) after the invasion of Southern France by the Germans. Women appeared less suspicious than men and were able to obtain critical military strategy information from German officers.[123]

Women have been serving in the military on a civilian basis since 1938. In 1972, women were given equal status with men in the military.[124] Presently, any person, male or female, may join the military at eighteen years of age.[133] Women serve in the Army, Gendarmerie, Navy, Medical Service, and Air Force. Men and women train together.[126]

The military complies with governmental laws in regard to sexual harassment and discrimination. The military has parental and maternity leave. This includes adoptive parents.[127]

Women make up 8.55 percent of military personnel and 4.95 percent of the officer corp.[128]

Unlike most other countries, women in France may be employed in combat positions. Women have been employed as fighter pilots since 1995.[129]

IRELAND

Ireland is located in Western Europe. It is bordered by England, Scotland, and Wales. Its population is 3,969,558 (July 2004 est.). The ethnic groups are Celtic and English. The religions are Roman Catholic (91.6 percent), Church of Ireland (2.5 percent), and other (5.9 percent). English is the language most commonly used. However, Irish Gaelic (the official national language) is still spoken in some areas.[130]

Women's position in Ireland is affected by poverty, inequality in the workplace and the political sphere, education, poor health care, and domestic violence. Female minorities and women of the Traveller Community, a nomadic ethnic group, face additional discrimination.

Women make up 51 percent of the population.[131]

Constitution

Ireland obtained independence from the United Kingdom on December 6, 1921. The Constitution was adopted on July 1, 1937. The legal system is based on common law, the Constitution, European Community Law, and legislation. Laws of the European Community take precedent over the Constitution. The Constitution takes precedent over other legislation and common law.[132] There is judicial review of legislative acts by the Supreme Court. All citizens, men or women, have the right to vote at eighteen years of age.

Under the Constitution, men and women are equal. Article 40(1) of the Constitution states that all citizens are equal, regardless of differences "of capacity, physical and moral, and of social function."[133]

Domestic violence and sexual assault remain a problem. There were 10,248 reports of domestic violence in 2002.[134]

Travellers are nomadic persons of Irish origin.[135] There are roughly 23,681 Travellers in Ireland.[136] Traveller women, on account of their lifestyle and the discrimination against them, have difficulty obtaining health care. In addition, they do not have equal access to education. Discrimination against Travellers is widespread among businesses and politicians alike. In fact, upon entrance of a town there are often signs that state that Travellers are not welcome.[137] Despite the ever-present racial discrimination that exists, there are presently not many anti-racism initiatives.[138] Women of the Traveller Community, refugees, or female minorities face social inequality.[139]

Work Force and Economy

Ireland has a trade-dependent economy.[140] Economic growth is primarily based on exports.[141] The purchasing power parity of Ireland is $116.2 billion (2003 est.).[142] Roughly 15.3 percent of the population lives below the poverty line (2004 est.).[143] The majority of those living in poverty are women.[144] The labor force is 1.8 million (2001).[145]

The Constitution states, under Article 45(2)(i), that policy should be geared to aiding women and men, equally, obtain a reasonable standard of living.[146]

In 1999, the female share of wages in non-agricultural employment was 46 percent compared to 45 percent in the mid-1990s and 40 percent in the early 1980s. Women make up 49 percent of the work force.[147]

Under the Employment Equality Act discrimination based on marital status, gender, family status, sexual orientation, age, race, and disability is prohibited. However, discrimination against women in the workplace still exists. Many businesses have not received diversity training.[148] In fact, some employers still ask potential female employees whether they plan to marry or have children, if they are feminists.[149] Inequality in regards to pay and promotion continues. Women make up few of the upper tier managerial positions. Lastly, women earn 85 percent of what their male counterparts earn.[150]

Sexual harassment falls under the Employment Equality Act. Employers must follow the code created by the Equality Authority. The statute of limitations for filing suit against an employer is six months from the last act of sexual harassment.[151]

Minimum wage has recently increased, aiding many women.[152] In 2004, minimum wage increased 5.5 percent over eighteen months. The minimum wage is $8.75 (7 Euros).[153] In addition, the Government has increased the number of Government sponsored childcare facilities. However, only persons who are in employment training may obtain fully sponsored childcare.[154] In addition, childcare in Ireland is not affordable and parental leave is unpaid.[155]

In 1994, there were a total of fourteen female professors in all of the country's seven universities.[156] Women make up 7 percent of professors.[157]

Women make up 5 percent of board members in Ireland's top one hundred companies. Thirty percent of companies with no women on their board state that they do not intend to appoint a woman in the future. Seventeen percent wouldn't state if they do or do not intend to appoint a woman to their board.[158] Seventy-eight percent of companies that responded to a survey have no policy regarding the appointment of women to their boards.[159] Approximately 21.8 percent of male employees are in managerial positions compared to 11.8 percent of women.[160] Nine percent of senior counsel attorneys are women.[161]

Under the Maternity Protection Act, women are given eighteen weeks of paid maternity leave. After maternity leave a woman has the right to return to her previous employment position. In addition, a woman (or a man), under the Parental Leave Act, has the right to fourteen weeks of unpaid parental leave to care for a child who is under five years of age. In 2004, the maternity leave pay increased from 70 to 80 percent of a woman's regular pay.[162]

Households where women are the head of household are vulnerable to poverty.[163] Twenty-three percent of women compared to 19 percent of men are at risk of falling below the poverty line.[164] Thirty percent of female employees are paid below the minimum wage compared to 18 percent of males.[165] More than 50 percent of female employees and 34.8 percent of men earn less than 30,000 pounds per year.[166]

Twenty-five percent of women compared to 67 percent of men receive a state pension based on their own PRSI (Pay Related Social Insurance) contributions. However, 95 percent of individuals claimed as welfare dependants are women. Money is paid directly to the contributor, not to the dependant themselves. Consequently, many women are dependant upon their husband for financial support.[167]

Unemployment benefits do not apply to part-time or seasonal employees, of which many are women.[168]

Women's employment earnings are roughly 30 percent less than their male counterparts. Even recent male graduates receive higher hourly and weekly wages than recent female graduates.[169]

Education

In the nineteenth century, no college would accept a female applicant. By 1965, women made up half of the college student population. In 1995, women made up over half of college students. Female students outnumber men in university.[170]

Under the Child Care Act education is free and compulsory for children from six to fifteen years of age. Ninety-nine percent of children in that age bracket attend school and the majority of them finish secondary school.[171]

The ratio of females to males enrolled in secondary schools is 105 women for every 100 men. The female enrollment in secondary education is 100 percent.[172] The female to male ratio of student enrollment in tertiary school is 127 women for every 100 men.[173]

Seventy-five percent of entering law students are women.[174] And more than 50 percent of medical students are women.[175]

Access to education is less available for poor women.[176] Minorities and Traveller women find it particularly difficult to access education.

Marriage

The minimum legal age of both men and women to marry is eighteen. Twenty-eight percent of men are married compared to 26.5 percent of women.[177]

Couples must give written consent of their intention to marry to the county register at least three months prior to marriage. Marriages can be made official by civil ceremony, by country register, or the church. Prior to marriage, each person must obtain a Certificate of Freedom to Marry, which establishes that the person is not currently married.[178]

The Married Women's Property Act of 1998 gives women the right to hold property in their own name. The Married Women's Status Act of 1957 makes women legally accountable for their own debts and breaches of contract. The Family Home Protection Act of 1976 requires that both spouses give permission before any communal assets are sold. The Family Law Act of 1981 gave the courts the authority to issue protection orders prohibiting contact between abusive spouses and their victims. The Domestic Violence Act of 1996 allows police to arrest individuals without a warrant for the violation of a protective order.[179]

Divorce was legalized by the Family Law Act of 1996. It is based on a no-fault system. The couple must live apart for at least four out of the five years preceding the divorce.[180] There must be no reasonable chance of reconciliation and proper provisions have been put into place for spouses and dependant children. Before the divorce proceedings begin the applicant's petitioner must discuss the options of reconciliation, mediation, and file a written separation agreement. After the divorce is granted, the marriage is dissolved and either spouse may remarry. The court may order either spouse to pay maintenance for the other spouse and dependant children per the Family Act of 1976 and Guardian of Infants Act of 1964. The usual post-divorce arrangement results in the mother remaining in the family home until the youngest child turns eighteen or has left school. Children most often live with their mother. However, under the Children Act of 1997, the court may consider the children's view when granting custody and visitation rights. The working parent makes payment to the custodial parent until the child has turned eighteen or ceased his or her education.[181]

There are approximately 5,000 applications for divorce a year.[182]

Abortion and Contraceptives

Abortions, except to save the life of the mother, have been illegal in Ireland since it separated from England.[183] The abortion law is based on the Offenses Against the Person Act, 1861. In addition, the 1983 Constitution states that "the State acknowledges the right to life of the unborn and, with due regard to the equal right to life of the mother, guarantees in its laws to respect and, as far as practicable, by its laws to defend and vindicate that right."[184] Between 1967 and 1983, women could travel to England to have an abortion. Family planning associations provided counseling and the name and address of facilities in England. Since the 1983 referendum it is illegal for an Irish woman to go to England to get an abortion. While counseling is still allowed, family planning associations no longer make appointments for women at facilities in England. In addition, counselors are further limited in what information they can give to a woman seeking assistance. While the information cannot encourage an abortion it must inform women on all courses of action that are available. Since the amendment more than 100,000 women have gone to Britain for an abortion.[185]

Since 1974 married couples have been able to legally obtain contraceptives.[186] And in 1985 the Health Family Planning Act allowed all persons over eighteen to buy condoms without a prescription. In fact, condoms may be sold in locations where adolescents frequent. All other forms of birth control still require a prescription. Since 2001 emergency contraceptive pills may be sold and used by prescription. While inter-uterine devices (IUDs) have not yet been approved for use, doctors may approve them under an exception basis for individual cases.[187]

The age of consent is fifteen years old for sexual activity between males and females or between females and females. However, the age of consent for two males is seventeen.[188]

The fertility rate is 1.87 births per woman (2004 est.).[189]

Health Care

There are two types of health care, private and public. With the exception of pregnancy, private insurance does not cover reproductive health care. Consequently, contraceptives are not covered by private health care. Contrarily, public health care covers contraceptives including controversial emergency contraceptives.[190]

The most common cancer for women, aside from skin cancer, is breast cancer. One in thirteen women develops breast cancer. Women in Ireland are four times more likely to die from breast cancer than women in other European nations.[191]

Women in Public Office

The Government is made up of two houses of Parliament, the House and the Senate (the Dáil and the Seanad). The members of the Dáil are elected while members of the Seanad are usually appointed. The President is the head of State. However, it is the Prime Minister who is the head of Government. Only Parliament (Oireachtas) may create legislation.[192]

Under the laws of the United Kingdom, women in Ireland were granted restricted suffrage rights in 1918. Women thirty years of age and older, and men twenty-one years of age or older, were allowed to vote. Women in the United Kingdom (including Ireland at the time) were granted equal voting rights to men in 1928.[193] The 1937 Constitution of Ireland allowed every citizen, man or woman, twenty-one years or older, to stand for election and to vote. The age was dropped from twenty-one years of age to eighteen via the Fourth Amendment of the Constitution in 1972.[194]

In 2002, women occupied 14.6 percent of the seats in the national parliament. In 2004, women occupied 13 percent of the seats in the Dáil. This statistic puts Ireland in fifty-ninth place out of 120 Nations in regard to female representation in Parliaments.[195] Women make up 17.5 percent of city and county councillors.[196]

In 1990, Mary Robinson was elected President, making her the first female president of Ireland. After seven years as president, Robinson was appointed High Commissioner for Human Rights in 1997.[197] Mary McAlesse was elected the eighth President and the second female president in 1997.[198] The present Prime Minister is Bertie Ahern.[199] The Deputy Prime Minister is Mary Harney.[200]

The number of women appointed to judicial posts has increased from 28.4 percent (2000/2001) to 34.4 percent (2001/2002).[201]

The Parliamentary Assembly of the Council of Europe is made up of 4 representatives from all participating nations. Ireland is a member of the Assembly. In September 2003 a resolution was passed stating that all national delegations must include at minimum one woman. Despite the decision, Ireland registered all male members. The sanction for violating the resolution is that voting rights are suspended for representatives of the violating nation.[202]

Women in the Military

A male or female can join the army at seventeen years of age. The first female cadet joined the Irish Defense Forces in 1980.[203] Sixteen percent of recruits are women. Women may enlist in the Army, Naval Service, Reserves, or the Air Corp. Women go through the same training and education as men. Women are eligible for the same positions as men. The height requirement for female recruits is five-foot-four-inches and taller.[204]

The Defense Forces prohibit sexual harassment. Recruits receive awareness training on the issue of sexual harassment. Cases of sexual harassment must be brought to the attention of military authorities. In 2001, sexual harassment in the armed forces was widespread.[205] In 2004, the prevalence of sexual harassment in the armed forces is still an issue.[206]

SWEDEN

Sweden is located in northern Europe, between Finland and Norway, bordering the Baltic Sea. Sweden has a population of 8,878,085 (July 2003 est.). The ethnic groups are made up of Swedes, Fins, Yugoslavs, Danes, Norwegians, Greeks, Turks, and the indigenous Sami minority.[207] The Sami, otherwise known as "Sapmelas," are indigenous people who occupied Sweden, Finland, and other parts of Europe before the region was conquered or settled.[208] The Sami people heard and hunt reindeer, as well as fish.[209] The main religious denomination is Lutheran (87 percent). The remaining 13 percent are Roman Catholic, Orthodox, Baptist, Muslim, Jewish, and Buddhist. The language spoken is Swedish. There are a small population of people who speak Sami and Finnish.[210]

Sweden is thought to have been inhabited since 10,000 B.C. Once known as a country of pirates, Vikings, and warriors, Sweden today is a leading nation of social movements and the advancement of women.[211]

Constitution

Sweden has had a written constitution since the fourteenth century.[212]

Sweden is a constitutional monarchy. The Constitution was adopted on January 1, 1975. It is made up of four fundamental laws and consequently, four different writings: The Act of Succession, the Instrument of Government, the Freedom of the Press Act, and the Fundamental Law on Freedom of Expression.[213] The legal system is a civil law system that is influenced by customary law. Sweden became part of the European Union (EU) in 1995.[214] But, Sweden does not enter into certain international alliances in order to maintain political neutrality.[215] Church and State were officially separated in 2000.[216] Women obtained suffrage in the 1920s. Women were also able to obtain access to public office, education, and legal rights within a marriage.[217] Inheritance rights were made equal for men and women in 1845. Prior to 1845, sons inherited twice as much as daughters.[218] The voting age for men and women is eighteen years.

The Prime Minister, Göran Persson, is the head of the Cabinet and has executive authority. The King, Carl XVI Gustaf, is the head of state, though he has few formal powers.[219]

Work Force and Economy

Sweden is a welfare state. It decided to join the EU in 1995. However, they waived the introduction of the Euro in 1995, and again in 2003. The purchasing power parity of Sweden is $227.4 billion (2002 est.). The labor force is made up of 4.4 million people (2000 est.). The unemployment rate is 4 percent (2002 est.). The main industries are iron and steel, precision equipment (bearings, radio and telephone parts), wood pulp and paper products, processed foods, and motor vehicles.[220]

Women make up nearly half of the labor force.[221]

In 1979, the Equal Opportunities Act was passed.[222] Although women in Sweden fare better in regards to wage equality than any other nation, they still earn less than men.[223] In fact, women make roughly 15 to 20 percent less than their male counterparts.[224] However, after factoring education, age and occupation, women make 90 percent of what their male counterparts earn (2001). There were 146 filed cases of gender discrimination in 2003. Fifty percent of the cases were in regard to the individual's salary, 20.5 percent were in regards to discrimination related to pregnancy.[225] In order to make a case that pay discrimination is in effect, a woman must prove that a male counterpart is obtaining more that she. They must have the exact same job description, exact geographical location, responsibility, and educational background. This makes winning a case of pay discrimination a challenge when the jobs are not identical. For example, nurses and midwives make roughly 15 percent less than male medical technicians even though medical technicians usually have less education than midwives or nurses. These cases are often lost because of the differences in job descriptions.[226]

Women's chances of being promoted are less than men. Women have a lower financial return from their education. In fact, women who are employed in upper tier managerial positions have more education than their male counterparts.[227] Regardless, male representation on company boards far outweighs that of female representation.[228]

Women are more often than men employed in part-time or temporary positions than men. In 1996, 35.1 percent of permanent employees with forty or more hours was made up by women. More men than women were also employed in permanent and temporary positions of thirty-five to forty hour work weeks. As the work hours decrease for permanent and temporary employment, significantly more women than men are employed in such positions.[229] Overall, roughly 25 percent of women in the labor force work part-time compared to 7 percent of men. In 2002, 69 percent of those who were underemployed, were women. While the pay gap is partially because many women work part-time, it is also because fewer women than men obtain bonuses and overtime compensation.[230]

Women fare well in regards to government employment. Women make up roughly 54.7 percent of Executive officers, 48.3 percent of advisors and specialists, 56.6 percent of political appointees, 80.1 percent of permanent administrative staff, and 57.4 percent of employees in Government offices. However, women make up only 32.5 percent of heads of administrative units (2003).[231]

Sexual harassment is prohibited under the Equal Opportunities Act. Under the Act, an employer must investigate any case of alleged sexual harassment done to one employee by another.[232] Employers who fail to investigate allegations of sexual harassment may have to pay damages to the harassed individual.[233]

Couples are given 480 days between the two of them for parental leave. These days may be used at anytime before the child's first birthday. Out of the 480 days, 60 are reserved for the father, and 60 are reserved for the mother. Spouses may not transfer theses days to one another. Couples decide between themselves how the remaining 360 days will be divided. Parents earn 80 percent of their wages during the first 390 days of paternity leave. Parents who are unemployed receive a flat daily rate during parental leave. During the remaining days all parents receive a smaller daily rate. Fathers are also given an additional 10 days after the birth of their child. More than 50 percent of fathers use parental leave during the child's first year.[234]

Parents may also take parental leave (sixty days) to care for an ill child. Parents are compensated for lost wages.[235] Men use 43 percent of these days to take care of a sick child, revealing that both mothers and fathers contribute to child-rearing.

Parents who have children less than eight years of age may shorten their work day by two hours. Their pay is reduced accordingly.[236]

Child support goes to all households with minor children.[237] In addition, employed parents are legally entitled to childcare for children ages one to twelve.[238]

Education

In 1861, a training college for teachers, who were primarily women, was established. In 1870, women were allowed to take entrance exams to get into University but were not allowed to enroll in classes in Law or Theology. In 1927, women were granted equal access to secondary school.[239] In 1977, the New Higher Education reform was enacted. The goal of the reform was to create equality of access of education for men, women, and those of different socioeconomic backgrounds. Further reforms were instituted in 1993.[240] Under the Equal Treatment of Students at University Act (2002), discrimination based on gender, ethnic background, disability, or sexual orientation is prohibited at universities. All cases of sexual harassment must be investigated. In addition, universities and colleges are responsible for taking steps to make sure that the harassment does not continue.[241]

The number of female students obtaining higher education degrees has increased significantly over time. Women made up 38 percent of the graduates in 1970, and 60 percent of the graduates in the academic year 1997/1998.[242] Sixty percent of undergraduate students are women. Forty percent of postgraduate students are women.[243] The majority of students in the fields of teaching, health sciences, humanities and theology are women.[244]

The female to male ratio of students enrolled in secondary school in 2000 was 104 women to every 100 men. The female enrollment rate in secondary education was 98 percent, putting Sweden in the top three countries for secondary school enrollment among Western European and other developed countries.[245] The female to male ratio of student enrollment in tertiary school was 152 women for every 100 men.[246]

Sami children are given two weeks off from school during spring and autumn.[247]

Marriage

The legal age for men and women to marry is eighteen. Both men and women may marry under the age of eighteen with permission of the county administrative board. Direct relatives such as fathers and daughters and whole siblings may not marry. Half siblings may marry with permission from the Government. The average age to marry is 33.3 for men and 31 for women. Thirty-six percent of men are married compared to 33 percent of women.[248]

There is a high rate of cohabitation in Sweden. Roughly 30 percent of couples living together are unmarried. The number of marriages has decreased by 75 percent. Consequently, the Cohabitees (Joint Homes) Act was passed in 1997 as well as a new Marriage Code. The reform addressed the division of property upon the dissolution of cohabitation.[249]

Sweden has no-fault divorce. The maximum waiting period for a divorce is six months. Previously, couples had to prove that they had been separated for at least one year. Forty-five percent of marriages dissolve. The law does allow for maintenance of either spouse if needed. This is viewed as a short-term solution until the spouse in need improves his/her income. The court determines child custody by deciding what is in the best interest of the child. Parents are responsible for children until eighteen, or longer if they remain in school.[250] Non-custodial parents must pay maintenance to the custodial parent. If they do not the amount is then paid by the social security system to the custodial parent. 80 percent of divorced couples have joint custody. Most child(ren) live with the mother.[251]

Since 1988 the shared apartment or home is given to the person who is most in need of it upon termination of the relationship.[252] In addition, the couple's common property is divided equally upon death or separation.[253] Children have the right to inherit from both their mother and father. Division of marital property must occur if the deceased person was married. The remainder of the estate passes to the surviving spouse unless the will specifies heirs. If there are no heirs, the surviving spouse may do what he/she wants with the property during his/her life-time, except pass it down to someone in his/her will. When the surviving spouse dies the first spouse's estate goes to the relatives of the first deceased spouse. If the deceased person was not married the surviving cohabitee must request a division of property.[254] Until a child turns sixteen the government pays $94 (U.S.) a month for one child, $188 (U.S.) for two children, $328 (U.S.) for three children, $516 (U.S.) for four children, and $750 (U.S.) for five children.[255]

Abortion and Contraceptives

Abortion is legal in Sweden. An abortion can be performed to save the life of the mother, to preserve her physical or mental health, if the pregnancy results from rape or incest, if there is fetal impairment, or for economic or social reasons. Abortions are available on request. Abortions are legal on these grounds until the eighteenth week of pregnancy, as long as the procedure will not endanger the life of the mother. The woman must speak to a social worker for abortions between the twelfth and eighteenth week. After the eighteenth week, the abortion must be approved by the National Board of Health and Welfare.[256] There are roughly 35,000 abortions per year.[257] All abortions must be performed by a licensed medical practitioner and in an approved health care institution. Abortions are subsidized by the Government. The present maternal mortality ratio is lower than any other developed nation. In Sweden there are 7 deaths for 100,000 live births compared to an average of 27 deaths for 100,000 live births in other developed countries.[258]

Until 1937 abortions were illegal except to save the life of the mother. In addition, dispensing of information and the sale of contraceptives were illegal. The 1938 Abortion Act provided that abortions could legally be performed for reason of health, or eugenic reasons, rape or incest, and in cases of medical or social hardship. An abortion could be performed at any time for medical reasons with the approval of two physicians. Abortions for any other reason had to be performed within the first twenty weeks of pregnancy with the approval of a health authority's board. In 1946, medical-social hardship was broadened to take into consideration living conditions and other socioeconomic circumstances. In addition, the definition was broadened to include the impact the pregnancy or child rearing would have on the mother's physical or mental health. The woman had to have the aid of a social worker who would both investigate the woman's situation and help her prepare the abortion application. The time frame for legal abortions was extended to twenty-four weeks. In 1963, the Act was broadened again to include prenatal injury to the fetus as grounds for abortion.[259]

Between 1935 and 1976 the government committed 60,000 involuntary sterilizations predominantly on women. The majority of these forced sterilizations happened to individuals of mixed race, single mothers with many children, deviants, Gypsies, and those with low I.Q. or even poor eyesight. The government committed the sterilizations in order to prevent inferior persons from multiplying and to preserve the purity and strength of the Nordic population.[260]

The fertility rate is 1.6. births per woman. Family planning services and access to contraceptives is widespread.[261] Seventy-one percent of married women aged twenty to forty-four use modern contraceptives.[262] Contraceptives are readily available. Sterilization is available on request to those over the age of twenty-five. The Government provides direct contraceptive support. Family planning and maternal and child health care are established throughout the country.[263]

Health Care

In 2000, the majority of persons with long-term illness were women (63 percent).[264]

Women are more often diagnosed with mental illness than men.[265]

Since women live longer than men, more money is spent via general pensions on women than men.[266]

Health care has been free for mothers and children since the 1970s.[267]

Women in Public Office

Sweden, after Rwanda, has the greatest number of women in Parliament of any nation.[268] In 1909, women were able to run for municipal council positions. In 1918, universal suffrage was granted to women. Women first voted during the 1921 election.[269] Five women became the first female members of Parliament in 1921. In 1970, women held 13 percent of the seats in Parliament.[270]

In 2002, women occupied 45.3 percent of the seats in its national parliament making Sweden the number one country in the world in regard to seats held by women in a national parliament.[289] Women hold 44 percent of seats in Parliaments standing committees. Thirty-nine percent of state secretaries are women. Women make up over 40 percent of municipal councilors. In 2001, women made up 47 percent of the participants on public boards. However, men still make up the majority of persons on policy-making bodies.[272]

Women in the Military

Women have the legal right to employment in the armed forces. Men and women can join the military at nineteen years of age (2003 est.). National service is mandatory for men and not for women.[273]

Mandatory female military service has been a debated issue in Sweden over the past four or so years. Israel is the sole nation that has mandatory military service for women. In Sweden, it is only mandatory for men to train for the military and participate in the reserves until they are forty-seven years of age.[274]

Women were first allowed into the officer corps in 1980. Females may apply for any military position. However, women make up few, roughly 2 percent, of officers. There are reports of sexual harassment in the military. Some of these women brought attention to officials about the harassment and were told that if they could not handle the situation to go home.[275]

In 2003, women made up three percent of military personnel.[276]

GERMANY

Germany is located in Central Europe. It borders the Baltic Sea and the North Sea and is located between France, the Netherlands, and Poland. The population of Germany is 82,398,326 (July 2003 est.). The population growth rate is 0.04 percent (2003 est.). The ethnic groups in Germany are German 91.5 percent and Turkish 2.4 percent. The remaining 6.1 percent is made up of Serbo-Croatian, Italian, Russian, Greek, Polish, and Spanish. The religions in Germany are Protestant 34 percent, Roman Catholic 34 percent, Muslim 3.7 percent, and unaffiliated or other 28.3 percent. The official language is German.[277]

Constitution

Germany is a Federal Republic. The Constitution of Germany was adopted on October 3, 1990.[278]

The Constitution prohibits discrimination. Denial of access to healthcare, education, or housing may not be based on sex, race, disability, ethnic background, citizenship, or political opinion.[279] The voting age for men and women is eighteen.

Racism and xenophobic crimes continue to be a problem. It is estimated that there are 11,500 members of racist rightwing groups. Individuals of different ethnicities sometimes face harassment and workplace discrimination.[280]

Work Force and Economy

Germany has the purchasing power parity of $2.184 trillion (2002 est.). In addition, Germany is one of the world's largest producers of coal, steel, cement, chemicals, vehicles, machine tools, machinery, electronics, beverages and food, shipbuilding, and textiles.[281]

The labor force in Germany is made up of 41.9 million people (2001). The unemployment rate is 9.8 percent (2002 est.). Germany has a strong social welfare system. The average full-time work week is 35 hours.[282] The average part-time work week is 17.9 hours. The activity rate of women in the workforce is 63.7 compared to 78.8 percent of men.[283]

Although sexual harassment in the workplace is illegal, it still remains a problem.[284] Roughly 2.7 percent of employees have been bullied or harassed. Women are 75 percent more likely to be bullied or harassed than men. Younger individuals, those under twenty-five years of age, have the greatest risk of being bullied or harassed.[285]

While the law states that there must be equal pay for equal work, women earn less than their male counterparts.[286] Women employed in the former East earn 89.9 percent of their male counterparts compared to 76.9 percent earned by women employed in the former West.[287] In addition, there are significantly fewer women in well-paid managerial positions.[288] Eleven percent of women in the work force are employed in higher tier employment positions.[289] Women are primarily employed in the fields of education and health. Women are rarely employed as principals, professors, and physicians.[290]

Women make up 86 percent of part-time employees (2000). Fifty-percent of women in the East said they sought part-time employment because full-time positions were not available. There are twice as many women in the West working part-time than in the East. Part-time employees are entitled to sick pay. Pension is based on the contributions made during the employment period. Consequently, those in part-time employment do not make as much of a contribution to their pension plan as those in full-time employment.[291]

During the Nazi era, women began to lose the progress that had just begun for them in employment. Hitler, during his 1932 election campaign, stated that if he won the election he would take 800,000 women out of employment in four years. Married female civil servants and physicians were fired in 1934. In 1936, women could no longer serve as public prosecutors or as judges. Hitler did not believe that women had the necessary logic for such positions.[292]

Despite the Nazi stance of women in the workplace, women assumed jobs traditionally performed by men during WWII. When East and West Germany were divided the two sides took significantly different directions in regard to women's position in the work force.[293]

In West Germany, a woman could be dismissed from civil service positions because she was married. West Germany held tighter to traditional beliefs that a woman's sole place was at home with the children. Legislation was passed in 1977 allowing women in the West to work outside of the home.[294]

In the East, women continued their participation in the labor force. Roughly 90 percent of women were involved in the workforce. In addition, in the 1950's laws were written to benefit the working mother. Childcare programs were also put into effect.[295]

Presently, under the Parental Leave Act, both men and women may take parental leave. Parents are entitled to a certain income during leave.[296] Women are granted six weeks of paid maternity leave before the birth of the child and eight weeks after the child is born.[297] A certain amount of woman's wages, when she is on maternity leave, is paid by her social insurance. The remainder is usually paid by her employer.[298] It is illegal to fire a new mother or pregnant woman. Between the parents they have three years of unpaid parental leave to care for their children. In addition, parents are given ten paid days per child a year to care for an ill child. The maximum amount of paid days to care for sick children is twenty-five.[299]

Prostitution is legal. Prostitutes may obtain benefits such as health insurance and unemployment. Prostitutes may use the court system in instances of payment disputes. In addition, prostitutes may enter into the social security system. Prostitutes also pay taxes on their earnings.[300] Prostitution is no longer labeled as immoral by the Government. There are roughly 200,000 prostitutes in Germany.[301] Many prostitutes are illegal immigrants and are unable to reap the benefits of these laws.[302]

Education

Women in the East, after WWII, enrolled into higher education institutions in great numbers. They made up roughly half of University students while female enrollment in the West was 41 percent. Women in the East surpassed male enrollment in Universities by 1976. In addition, female students in the East were given childcare and supplemental payments if needed.[303]

In 2000, the female to male ratio for secondary school enrollment was 101 women for every 100 men. Female enrollment in secondary education was 88 percent.[304]

Presently, the number of women enrolled in higher education outnumbers men in both the former East and West.[305]

Marriage

The minimum legal age for both men and women to marry is eighteen. A man or woman can marry at sixteen with parental consent. The average age men marry is 30.3 and 27.5 for women.[306]

The 1977 reform of the Marriage and Family Law gave women and men equal rights in West Germany. Consequently, a woman was allowed to obtain a divorce without the consent of her husband.[307] In 1994, both spouses were granted equal rights in the choice of family name during marriage and divorce and the name of the children. Article 17 provides that all mothers have a claim on society for support and care. Children born out of wedlock have the same rights as those born from a marriage. Marital rape was officially declared a crime in 1996. Nearly one million couples living together are unmarried. In addition, the number of births to unmarried women has increased as well.[308]

Ten out of every one thousand marriages result in divorce.[309] Before 1977 marriages were dissolved under the principal of guilt. Since 1977 divorce is allowed on the grounds of the irretrievable breakdown of the marriage. The breakdown of marriage must be demonstrated by the proof that spouses have lived apart for three years or longer. In 1987, a law was passed that provides maintenance to the divorced parent who cannot obtain gainful employment because of child-rearing obligations, health reasons, or other reasons.[310]

Abortion and Contraceptives

Abortions are legal in Germany.[311] They may be performed to save the life of the woman, to preserve her physical or mental health, on account of rape or incest, because of fetal impairment, or because of economic reasons. A woman does not need to give a reason in order to receive an abortion. They are available upon request with no stipulations as to whom must perform it and where.[312]

Before the unification of the West and East Germany, the countries had very different abortion legislation.[313]

The Federal Republic (West Germany) allowed abortions if there was a threat to the mother's life, if the unborn child was going to be irreparably harmed, on socio-economic grounds, or because of rape or incest. An abortion could be performed during the first twelve weeks of pregnancy. Abortions after twelve weeks could only be performed in order to save the life of the mother or if the unborn child was going to be irreparably harmed. A woman had to prove that she was in distress (socio-economic) and a physician had to approve her request for an abortion.[314]

On the other hand, the communist government of the German Democratic Republic (East Germany) gave easy access to abortions. During the first twelve weeks a woman could obtain an abortion upon request. Similar to the Federal Republic, the German Democratic Republic only allowed abortion after twelve weeks of pregnancy in order to preserve the life of the mother or because the child was going to be irreparably harmed.[315]

The fertility rate is 1.3 births per woman. Seventy-two percent of married women aged twenty to thirty-nine use modern contraceptives.[316] The majority of women use the pill. Few women use sterilization as a form of contraceptive and few males use condoms with their female partners.[317]

Health Care

The majority of people are covered under the state insurance health plans. Both employee and employer contribute to pay for the employee's health care coverage. There are additional subsidies for individuals who are elderly, unemployed, or poor. Students, pensioners, and farmers, are also covered under the state health insurance.[318]

As of January 2004, members of the health care plan have to contribute for the costs of health care. For example, members must pay ten Euros to see a general practitioner. Members also have to contribute for the cost of medicine, and hospital stays. Children under eighteen, people receiving social assistance, the unemployed, students, disabled, and war victims do not have to pay contributions. The reform is extremely unpopular among the members of the state insurance health care plan.[319]

Roughly one-third of German women smoke cigarettes. Twenty-one percent of female smokers smoke while pregnant. Roughly 42,100 women die per year of smoking related illnesses.[320]

Women in Public Office

Women were granted the right to vote and stand for election in 1919.[321]

Women are entitled by law to fully participate in the political arena.[322] Women in Germany hold 31 percent of the seats in the national parliament.[323] Women hold 31.8 percent of seats in the house and 18.8 percent of seats in the senate. This ranks Germany in twelfth place in regard to female representation within Parliament.[324] Women hold seven seats (out of fifteen) of the Federal Cabinet. Five out of sixteen judges on the Federal Constitutional Court are women. One of the female judges is Chief Justice. Some of the parties have instituted a quota system to help increase the number of female representation.[325] The President of Parliament (the Bundestag) in the 1990s was Rita Süssmuth.[326] Women make up roughly 25 percent of public servants.[327]

There are few minorities in the Government. There are two Turkish-German and one German-Indian individuals in the Bundestag.[328]

Women in the Military

In 2000, the European Court of Justice ruled that Germany's Constitution violated European Union rules on sexual discrimination in the military. In response to the ruling, on January 3, 2001 the German military began to open all jobs to women. Two hundred forty-four female recruits immediately entered boot camps.[329] Prior to 2001, German rules on female military personnel were among the most conservative in the NATO alliance, women were primarily restricted to nursing in the German Army. Of the 4, 250 women serving in 1999, only 50 women were not in the medical corp.[330] In 2000, the German Constitution was amended to allow women to perform in combat positions.[331]

Women make up 3.6 percent of persons in the armed forces. Women serve voluntarily.[332] Unlike men, women are not subject to compulsive military service.[333]

HUNGARY

Hungary is located in Central Europe, northwest of Romania. It has a population of 10,032,375 (July 2004 est.). The ethnic groups are Hungarian 89.9 percent, Roma 4 percent, German 2.6 percent, Serb 2 percent, Slovak 0.8 percent, and Romanian 0.7 percent. The religions are Roman Catholic 67.5 percent, Calvinist 20 percent, Lutheran 5 percent, atheist, and other 7.5 percent. Hungarian is the national language.[334]

There are 110 women for every 100 men.[335]

Constitution

Hungary was under Soviet communist rule for forty years. It declared its independence in 1989.[336] Today, Hungary is a parliamentary democracy. The Hungarian Constitution was adopted on August 20, 1949.[337] It was revised on April 19, 1972 and again on October 18, 1989. Hungary became a full member of the European Union (EU) in 2004.[338]

Article 66 of the Constitution grants equal rights to men and women. The Constitution states that the Republic of Hungary assures the equal rights of men and women in every aspect of civilian, political, economic, social and cultural life.[339] It also provides human and civil rights for every person within its territory, without any discrimination as to: race, gender, language, religion, national or social origin, or age (Article 70(A)).[340] Under the Constitution there shall be strict punishment for discrimination (Article 70(A)(2)). Lastly, every person has the right to social security.[341]

Under Article 76 of the Civil Code, discrimination on the basis of gender is a violation of an inherent right. Upon a violation of an inherent right a person may file suit for a remedy and punitive damages.[342]

Spousal rape is against the law. There are criminal penalties for spousal rape and abuse.[343] However, a conviction for spousal rape is only granted if force was involved as opposed to whether the spouse consented to the act.[344] In 2003, there were no prosecutions for domestic violence. In addition, while there are laws against rape, the act often goes unreported. Police have been found to be unsympathetic toward the accuser. In fact, police have often been unwilling to assist the alleged victim.[345]

Women and men have the same rights in regard to property and inheritance.[346]

Despite laws against discrimination, the Roma population faces much discrimination. The Romas are a nomadic people originating from India. They do not have equal access to housing, education, or employment. In fact, the unemployment rate for the Roma is 70 percent. The Roma face police brutality and wide-spread discrimination. Sometimes they are not allowed into restaurants and mistreatment is often over-looked by officials.[347]

While the Constitution and legislation grant equal rights to men and women, equality has not yet been realized in the area of employment.

Work Force and Economy

The purchasing power parity of Hungary is $143.7 billion (2002 est.). The population below the poverty line is 8.6 percent. The labor force is made up 4.2 million (1997). The unemployment rate is 5.8 percent (2002 est.).[348] The unemployment rate is 5.4 for women compared to 6.1 for men.[349] The main industries in Hungary are mining, metallurgy, constructional materials, processed foods, textiles, chemicals, and motor vehicles.[350]

Under Article 70(B) of the Constitution, every person "has the right to work and freely choose his job and profession." In addition, every person has the right to equal pay for equal work. Discrimination is prohibited. Every person has the right to an income that corresponds to the work that they perform. Lastly, every person has the right to free time and a regularly paid vacation.[351]

Women make up 45 percent of the labor force and 46 percent of the economic activity.[352] Women do not receive equal pay for equal work.[353] Women earn roughly 71 percent of the wages of their male counterparts.[354] Women of childbearing years, mothers with small children, and older women face additional discrimination.[355]

Women make up 58 percent of administrative and managerial workers.[356] Few women are in upper tier employment positions. Women are well represented in the fields of medicine, teaching, and in the judiciary.[357]

Employers may not fire a pregnant woman or reduce her salary. Under Article 138 of the Labor Code, an employer must provide unpaid parental leave so that a parent may care for an ill child. It is primarily the mother who takes unpaid leave to care for an ill child. Prospective female employees are often asked by potential employers about their future plans to have children.[358]

Social security fully covers twenty-four weeks of maternity leave.[359] Leave begins four weeks before the child's due date.[360]

Under Article 85(1) a woman may be moved to another employment position temporarily from the time there is knowledge of her pregnancy until the child is one year old if the position is deemed to detrimentally affect the health of the mother or child. The woman's wages must not decrease in the temporary position.[361]

While sexual harassment is not criminalized under the Penal Code, it is prohibited under the Labor Code. An assailant could face up to three years in prison for sexual harassment.[362] Sexual harassment is widespread and in most cases goes unreported. In fact, the first instance of an employee coming forward publicly with allegations of sexual harassment was in July, 2004.[363]

Prostitution is illegal, however, there are designated "tolerance zones" where prostitution takes place.[364]

Education

Discrimination on the basis of gender is prohibited in public education.[365] In 2000, the ratio of female to male enrollment in secondary school was 101 women for every 100 men. The percentage of females that were enrolled in secondary school was 88 percent. The female to male ratio of youth literacy (ages fifteen to twenty-four) in 2002 was 100 percent. The female youth literacy rate is 99.8 percent and that has been constant since 1995.[366] In 2001, the female to male ratio of student enrollment in tertiary school was 127 women for every 100 men.[367]

Marriage

The age of which a man or woman can legally marry is eighteen. With approval from authorities men and women can marry at sixteen. The average age for men is 27.1 years and the average age for women is 23.8 years. Forty-six percent of men are married compared to 35.3 percent of women. The divorce rate is 37.5 percent (per 100 marriages).[368]

The Family Code grants partners equal rights in a marriage. During divorce wives and husbands have equal statutory protection and either can seek a divorce. Courts are mandated to attempt reconciliation prior to issuing a divorce decree. A divorce will be granted if the court holds that the marriage is irreparably damaged or if both spouses agree to an amicable divorce. Divorce is also granted if there is evidence that spouses have been separated for at least three years and they voluntarily agree to all matters relating to children, if they exist. All property, whether acquired before or after the marriage, is considered joint property. Joint property is divided equally in divorce proceedings unless the couple agrees to a different arrangement. Either spouse may be entitled to alimony, however, the granting of alimony is rare.[369]

Child custody, decided by the court, considers the child's best interest. However, the parent who is granted custody must consider the wishes of the other parent in all significant matters relating to the child(ren). Children fourteen years and older may choose which parent with whom they wish to live.[370]

Child support is legislatively mandated but not always enforced.[371]

Abortion and Contraceptives

Abortions may only be performed in situations of emergency (to save the life of the mother) or in the case of "severe crisis" of the pregnant woman. A severe crisis is defined as a situation that causes bodily or psychological shock, or an impossible social situation.

Before 1953 abortions were illegal except if they posed a serious health threat for the mother. In 1953 and in 1956, the abortion law was broadened. Abortions could be performed on health, social and family grounds. Consequently, abortions, in the first twelve weeks of pregnancy, could be performed on request. The law was made more restrictive in 1973. Under the law a woman had to be single, divorced, or widowed. In addition, she had to have been separated from her husband for at least six months. An abortion could be performed if the pregnancy was a result of rape or incest, if the woman did not have available accommodations, the woman was over forty years of age, the woman had three children, her husband was serving in the armed forces, either she or her husband were serving a prison sentence for at least six months, or other special social reasons. In 1982 a woman could get an abortion if she was thirty-five or older. In 1986, fetal abnormality was added as a ground for abortion.

From 1992 to 2002 the abortion law allowed a woman to obtain an abortion on request during the first twelve weeks of gestation. The woman had to obtain counseling and wait three days after the submission of her application for abortion before the abortion can be performed. The law also allowed abortions to be performed later in pregnancy for health reasons, fetal defect, if the pregnancy was a result of rape or incest, when the woman was partially or completely paralyzed, when the woman did not know she was pregnant because of medical error, or if she missed the twelve-week period because of hospital or administrative authority. An abortion could be performed at any time if the pregnancy threatened the life of the mother or if fetal abnormality made postnatal life impossible.[372]

Before 2002, a woman could obtain an abortion in the first twelve weeks of pregnancy by declaring herself to be in a "situation of crisis." In 1998, the term "situation of crisis" was ruled unconstitutional.[373] In 2002, Parliament amended the abortion law.[374] Under the new Amendment Act of LXXIX on the Protection of Foetal Life, an abortion may only be performed in the case of emergency or in the case of "severe crisis" of the pregnant woman. Under Article 9(1), a woman must receive counseling after she requests an abortion, if possible in the presence of the father. Previously abortions cost $40 (U.S.). Women could receive some social security assistance.[375] Presently, abortions are not covered by health insurance unless they are performed for medical reasons.[376] The current cost, $60 (U.S.),[377] may be reduced in accordance with a woman's financial and social situation.[378]

The abortion rate is 35 per 1,000 women (3.5 percent).[379]

Contraceptives are not covered under the National Health Insurance ("NHI"). Consequently, persons must pay for their own contraceptives.[380] Although contraceptives are readily available, they are expensive.[381] In addition, family planning is not covered by NHI. The result is that family planning is not easily accessible.[382] Approximately 69 percent of women use modern contraceptives.[383]

The fertility rate is 1.4 births per woman.[384]

Health Care

Under Article 70(E), each citizen has the right to health care.[385] Health services are funded by the social Health Insurance Fund (HIF). There are three groups within the population: employees, groups who are covered without contribution, and all inhabitants with personal identification cards. Those who are covered without contributions are women on maternity leave, those with low incomes, and their dependants (including the homeless).[386] Children who are school age receive free medical care.[387] Insurance is almost universal. One percent of the population is not covered.[388]

Co-payments are required for medication, medical aids, and long-term chronic care. Certain procedures are not covered by health care, such as abortions (unless done for medical reasons), sterilizations (unless done for medical reasons), and cosmetic surgery.[389]

Those of the Roma population do not have equal access to health care.[390]

Women in Public Office

Women have low representation in Parliament. In 2003, women held 10 percent of the seats in the national parliament. This is significantly less than the 21 percent women held in 1987 (when still under Soviet control).[391]

Women make up 30 percent of representatives in local governments.[392]

Women in the Military

Under Article 70(H), all citizens must complete military service.[393] Although not explicitly stated in the Constitution, only men must perform military service. Discrimination based on gender is prohibited by the Hungarian Constitution. Women are integrated in the military services under the command of the Chief of Defense. They work and train with their male peers, and are subject to the same chains of command, standards of performance and discipline. Starting in 1994, women have been able to apply and compete for entrance into the military academy (university). Female soldiers are covered under maternity/paternity leave policies as stipulated by national law. Combat assignments were introduced for women in 1996. Despite the fact that women can apply for almost all career fields, including combat, the majority of women perform their duties in administrative, medical, and personnel positions. There are only a few women who hold positions at the command level. Hungarian servicewomen make up approximately 6.4 percent (3,017) of the total force (approximately 46,678). Twenty-two percent of women in the military serve in the officer ranks. The highest-ranking female in the Army is currently a Colonel and in the Air Force, a Major. The Hungarian Defense Forces have only two Services: Army and Air Force.[394]

The basic components of the entrance requirements for the military for both men and women are the completion of the eight-year long primary school and an age limit of eighteen to thirty.[395]

The training of women for a military career involves the same provisions of laws and regulations as for men. Women can apply for any of the military occupations and they can be admitted in the same way as men as long as they are physically fit and healthy, and have successfully passed the entrance examinations conducted by the military educational institute.[396]

Female representation in the military has significantly risen over recent years.[397]

POLAND

Poland is located in Central Europe, east of Germany, and west of the Russian Republic. The population is 38,626,349 (July 2004 est.). The ethnic

groups in Poland are Polish (96.7 percent), German (0.4 percent), Ukrainian
(0.1 percent), and Belarusian (0.1 percent). The religions are Roman Catholic
(95 percent), Eastern Orthodox, Protestant, and other (5 percent). The national language is Polish.[398]

There are 106 women for every 100 men.[399]

Constitution

Poland is a multiparty democracy.[400] The Polish Constitution was adopted on
April 2, 1997. The legal system is a mix of Napoleonic civil law and holdover
communist legal theory. Poland has been slowly introducing democracy. All
citizens are eligible to vote at eighteen years of age. Poland is a member of
the Council of Europe (United Nations). Poland joined NATO in 1999 and the
European Union on May 1, 2004.[401]

Under Article 33, Clause 2, men and women are granted equal rights in regards to education, employment and promotion. Men and women are granted
the right to have equal pay for equal work and social security, to hold offices,
and to receive public honors and decorations.[402]

Restraining orders are not provided to protect battered women. Twelve percent of women have been directly affected by domestic violence, according
to a public opinion poll in 2002. According to police statistics 74,000 women
were affected by domestic violence in 2002. There are few shelters for battered women.[403]

Work Force and Economy

The purchasing power parity is $427.1 billion (2004 est.). The population be-
low the poverty line is 18.4 percent (2000 est.). The labor force is 17.6 million (2000 est.).[404] The major industries in Poland are machine building, iron
and steel, coal mining, chemicals, shipbuilding, food processing, glass, beverages, and textiles. The unemployment rate is 18.1 percent (2002).

The employment rate for women is 46.2 percent. This is roughly ten percent less than the employment rate of men.[405] Women make up 65 percent of
employees in part-time positions.[406]

The Government has extended many social benefits in order to increase the
fertility rate, which is 1.3 births per woman. Social security fully covers sixteen to eighteen weeks of maternal leave.[407] Further benefits include a three-
year leave for child rearing, and annual leave for up to sixty days for taking
care of sick children. In addition, the Government supplies birth grants, family allowances for low-income families.

Prostitution is legal, but paying for sex and pimping is illegal.[408]

There are no laws that directly address sexual harassment; however, under the Criminal Code, any person that takes advantage of their position of power to obtain sexual favors may face a prison sentence of up to three years.[409]

Under the Labor Code, gender discrimination is prohibited. If a suit is filed the burden of proof, that the discrimination did not occur, is on the employer. Employers may not hire women for jobs that require heavy lifting or where the employee will be working underground.[410]

Women's wages are less than that of their male counterparts. While women have a higher level of education, they earn 70 percent of what their male counterparts earn, and are less often promoted. Consequently, fewer women are employed in upper tier positions. In fact, men are twice as likely to be placed in a managerial position. Men are more than four times more likely to obtain a senior management position than a woman.[411] Women are more often unemployed than men. In July 2003, 51.2 percent of unemployed individuals were women.[412]

Pension laws require that women retire at age sixty and men at sixty-five.[413] This gives men five additional years to contribute to their pensions.

Education

Education is mandatory for men and women until age eighteen. Under Article 70, clause 4, male and female citizens have the right to universal and equal access to education, including financial and organizational assistance. However, public schools, which are supposed to be free, especially universities, charge expensive fees.[414]

Women, overall, advance further in education than men. More women than men finish secondary school education and graduate from university.[415]

In 2000 the ratio of female to male students enrolled in secondary school was 105 women for every 100 men. The percentage of females enrolled in secondary school was 77 percent. Female and male youth (ages fifteen to twenty-four) literacy in 2002 was 100 percent. The rate of female youth literacy is 99.8 percent, which has been consistent since 1995.[416] In 2000, the female to male ratio of student enrollment in tertiary school was 144 women for every 100 men.[417] Women's enrollment in tertiary school is 57.5.[418]

More women than men study business and management.[419]

Marriage

Marriage and family are focal points of the government. In fact, Article 18 of the Constitution defines marriage to be a union between a man and a woman, the family, motherhood and parenthood. The Article goes on to state that marriage shall be placed under the protection and care of the Republic of Poland.[420]

The legal minimum age for men and women to marry is eighteen. A Family Court can lower this to sixteen for women (not men).[421] Under Article 25 of the Family Code, if a woman wants to keep her maiden name she must state her desire to do so when the marriage is contracted.[422] If this is not done the woman automatically assumes her husband's last name. Under Article 88 of the Family Code, all children must retain their father's last name, regardless if they were born before or after the parents marry and regardless if the child was born out of wedlock. Under Article 89.3, a child can only keep the mother's name if the paternity of the father is unknown.[423]

Polish family law states that men and women are equal. Consequently, both spouses have claim to equal portions of the marital assets and an equal part in decision-making regarding the property. In addition, both spouses have equal part in making decisions regarding marital assets.[424] Article 23 of the Family Code states that:

Spouses shall have equal rights and responsibilities in marriage. They are each obligated to cohabitation (including a physical relationship), mutual help, and faithfulness, as well as to cooperation for the sake of family.

The Polish Supreme Court has ruled that there is an existing legal obligation for a married couple to live together and maintain sexual relations, and any agreement that excludes these elements from a marriage is illegal. In addition, Article 27 states that each spouse must make appropriate contributions to the family according to their earnings. However, traditional family roles still represent the majority of Polish families. Women are predominantly the caregivers and bear the weight of household responsibilities regardless of whether they are employed outside the home.[425] Nevertheless, if a spouse fails to fulfill his/her responsibilities to the family the other spouse may seek assistance from the court. For example, women often seek child support in court before getting a divorce. If a man refuses to pay such support he may face a prison sentence of three years.[426] Many women are unaware of their rights. Consequently, many women do not file suit for any support other than child support.[427]

There has been a 32 percent decrease in marriage since 1980. In 1995, the number of marriages that ended in divorce exceeded the number of new marriages contracted.[428]

The government wants to encourage marriage in order to increase the fertility rate.[429] Consequently, the government supplies loans and scholarships to assist student marriages. The average age for men to marry is 26.3 and 23.1 for women. Fifty-six percent of men are married compared to 45.1 percent of women.[430]

The divorce rate is 17.3 percent (per 100 marriages).[431] Under Article 56 of the Family Code, a couple can only obtain a divorce if the marriage has reached a complete and irretrievable breakdown.[432] The court may refuse to grant a divorce if the minor children's best interest is endangered, if the spouse seeking the divorce is exclusively guilty of the break-up of the marriage, or if the divorce is in conflict with the principles of community life. The court generally assumes that the best interest of the child is to be brought up in a two-parent household, regardless of the relationship between the parents. The majority of divorces are no-fault (67.8 percent). Fault-based divorces usually involve adultery, alcoholism, and physical abuse. Legal separation became an option to couples in May of 1999. Legal separation, an alternative to divorce, cannot be granted if the court holds that it is against to the best interest of the child.[433]

In cases of divorce property is ordinarily equally divided between the spouses. However, under Article 43, Section 2 of the Family Code, a spouse may request that the marital assets be divided based on the contribution each spouse made to the marital assets. In determining the amount, the court examines each spouse's personal involvement in raising the children and household issues and their incomes. However, courts often grant a divorce without issuing a property settlement.[434]

Child custody is determined by the court. Children are ordinarily placed with their mother. The father is granted visitation rights and the right to play a role in important decisions regarding the child. Under Polish family law a parent is required to support their children, a former spouse, and close relatives. A parent is required to support his or her child until the child can support himself or herself. Support includes food, clothing, shelter, and education.[435]

A spouse who is found to be at fault in a divorce is obligated to pay alimony to the other spouse for an indefinite time. However, in a no-fault divorce, a spouse is only obligated to pay alimony to the other party for five years.[436] The Government provides an alimony fund to provide a minimum income to divorced mothers not receiving alimony.[437]

Abortion and Contraceptives

Abortions may be performed in the first twelve weeks of gestation in order to save the life of a woman, to preserve the physical or mental health of the mother, to terminate a pregnancy that resulted out of rape or incest, or where the likelihood of fetal impairment exists. Abortions cannot legally be performed for economic or social reasons. In addition, abortions cannot be performed after the first twelve weeks of pregnancy unless the pregnancy would endanger the health or life of the mother. The abortion must be performed by an obstetrician or gynecologist who has passed the national proficiency test. The abortion must be performed in a hospital or clinic with the consent of the

woman or her parents if she is a minor.[438] It is estimated that somewhere between 80,000 to 200,000 illegal abortions are performed per year.[439]

Until 1932, abortion was illegal in Poland. In 1932, legislation allowed
abortions if the pregnancy endangered the health or life of the mother or if the
pregnancy resulted out of rape or incest. In 1956, the law was expanded to include the permission of abortions on the ground of fetal impairment or social
and economic living conditions. From 1956 until the law's repeal in 1993,
abortions were performed on the grounds of social and economic living conditions.[440]

Legislation guarantees free access to birth control, to provide social, medical, and legal assistance during pregnancy and after childbirth. This includes material and informational support, benefits and services to families
and unmarried mothers. In addition, pregnant students are allowed maternity
leave. Sex education is part of the school curriculum. Forty-nine percent of
married women use contraceptives. The total fertility rate is 1.3 births per
woman.[441]

Health Care

Poland has universal health insurance. While citizens are promised free care,
Poland spends little on health care.[442, 443] Prime Minister Marek Belka has
promised to improve health care.[444]

The majority of health expenditure comes from social security (57.6 percent), out of pocket payments (26.6 percent), the government, excluding social
security (13.6 percent), and corporations (1 percent). Private insurance makes
up 0.4 percent of health expenditure.[445] Due to the large out of pocket expenses, those who are poor have less access to medical aid. More women live
in poverty than men.[446] Consequently, women have less access to health care.

Women in Public Office

Women obtained suffrage in 1918.[447]

In 2002, women occupied 21.0 percent of the seats in the national parliament making it the second highest in eastern European countries for women's
seats in a national parliament.[448] There are 94 women in the Sejm (out of 460
members) and 13 women (out of 100 members) in the Senate (2005 est.).
There is one woman (out of 16 members) in the cabinet.[449]

Women in the Military

Men and women can join the army at nineteen years of age. The military expenditure is $3.5 billion.[450]

In 2003, Parliament granted women access to all military posts and the ability to serve in the private corp. The present retirement age is sixty for both men and women.[451]

Students of military academies may take an unpaid pregnancy leave of one year. If a woman becomes pregnant again—she is dismissed from service.[452]

At present there is no sexual discrimination policy within the military.[453]

In January 2004, there were 346 women in the military of which 213 are officers. Women were first admitted into the military academies in 1999. In January 2004, there were 175 women enrolled in the military academies.[454]

ROMANIA

Romania, the largest of the Balkan countries, is located in Southeastern Europe, bordering the Black Sea, between Bulgaria and the Ukraine.[455] The population is 22,355,551 (July 2004 est.). The ethnic groups are Romanian (89.5 percent), Hungarian (6.6 percent), Roma (2.5 percent), Ukrainian (0.3 percent), German (0.3 percent), Russian (0.02 percent), Turkish (0.2 percent), and other (0.4 percent) (2002 est.). The religions are Eastern Orthodox (87 percent), Protestant (6.8 percent), and Catholic (5.6 percent) (2002 est.). The official language is Romanian.[456] However, English, French, Hungarian, Russian, and German are also spoken.[457]

The life expectancy for women is seventy-four years compared to sixty-seven years for men.[458] There are 105 women per 100 men.[459]

Constitution

Romania is a constitutional democracy.[460] Romania proclaimed independence from Turkey on May 9, 1877. The current constitution was adopted on December 8, 1991. The legal system was formerly a mix of civil law and communist legal theory. Presently, it is based on France's Fifth Republic Constitution.[461] Romania joined Nato in March 2004, and is eligible to join the European Union (EU) in 2007.[462] A citizen, male or female, can vote at eighteen years of age.[463]

The Constitution, under Article 4, prohibits discrimination based on sex, race, nationality, ethnic origin, opinion and political allegiance, wealth, social background, and language.[464] However, members of the Roma population, and other minorities continue to face discrimination.[465] The Roma's are a nomadic people originating from India.

There are no laws that directly address spousal abuse or rape. Prosecution of rape requires a medical certificate and a witness. Consequently, rape, particularly spousal rape, is difficult to prove. In addition, a rapist may avoid punishment if he marries the woman he raped. Since 2003, police may intervene in alleged domestic violence situations.[466]

Work Force and Economy

The purchasing power parity of Romania is $155 billion (2004 est.). The labor force is made up of 9.28 million people (2004 est.).[467] Women make up 46 percent of the labor force.[468] The unemployment rate is 7.2 percent (2004 est.). The percentage of people living below the poverty line is 44.5 percent (2000).[469]

Under the Constitution, women are guaranteed the right to work.[470] Employers may not refuse to hire pregnant or married women. Nor may potential employers request a pregnancy test unless required by working conditions.[471]

Women are offered maternity leave for 126 days (eighteen weeks). The leave may be taken sixty-three days before and sixty-three days after the birth of the child.[472] During maternity leave, women earn 85 percent of the national gross average wage.[473] In addition, pregnant women are granted a maximum of sixteen hours of paid leave per month to attend prenatal medical exams.[474] Men are entitled to five days of paternity leave.[475]

At times working conditions are deemed unsafe for the mother and child. If the employer cannot make alterations to the position to make it safe for mother and fetus, the mother is then put on Maternal Risk Leave. Women take Maternal Risk Leave, if applicable, during pregnancy, for six months post birth of the child, and when breast-feeding. Women earn 75 percent of their normal wages during Maternal Risk Leave.[476]

Parental leave may be taken by either parent. Parental leave is leave taken to care for children under the age of two. Additionally, parents may take fourteen days to care for a sick child. The salary of a person on parental leave is 85 percent of the national gross average wage. In addition to parental leave, mothers may take one year unpaid leave. Those parents who do not take parental leave are given a shorter work day, by two hours. The shortening of the work day does not alter the parent's wages. Lastly, in companies that have at minimum, fifty persons, where women make up at least 20 percent of the employment population, there must be at least one woman on the Work Security and Health Committee of the company.[477]

Sexual harassment is illegal.[478] A copy of the sexual harassment law must be posted, in poster form, in the workplace by employers in order to advise people of their rights.[479] Those found guilty of sexual harassment face fines ranging from $53 to $532 (U.S.).[480] According to a Gallup Poll, 17 percent of women stated that they have faced sexual harassment at work or school. One out of ten women who were sexually harassed filed a complaint. Twelve percent of those harassed resigned from their employment position to avoid the harassment.[481]

Gender discrimination in the workplace is prohibited.[482] Men and women are guaranteed, under the Constitution, the right to freely choose their career, trade, and place of work. In addition, under Article 41 of the Constitution, men and women are to receive equal wages for equal work.[483] Nevertheless, women have a higher rate of unemployment than men. Additionally, women earn lower wages and few are employed in upper tier managerial positions.[484] Women earn roughly 58 percent of what their male counterparts earn.[485] Women make up 54 percent of employees in part-time employment.[486]

Women make up the majority of those employed in the fields of health and social assistance, education, hotels and restaurants, financial intermediations, wholesale and retail trade.[487] In addition, over 50 percent of judges are women.[488] Women make up 56 percent of professional and technical workers, and 31 percent of administrators and managers.[489]

The age of retirement is fifty-seven for women and sixty-two for men.[490] This means that men retire with an additional five years of contributions to their pension than women.

Education

School is compulsory for eight grades. Children, male and female, ordinarily begin school at age seven. School is no longer compulsory when a person turns sixteen years old.[491]

Under Article 32(4) of the Constitution, State education is free. According to the Constitution, scholarships will be granted to disadvantaged individuals.[492]

In 2003, 56.07 percent of those who have gone to primary school were women, and 49.7 percent of people who had completed secondary school were women. Nearly 52 percent of people who completed high school were women, and 46.05 percent of those who completed university were women. The numbers of women participating in university is ever increasing; in fact, 54.5 percent of graduating university students (academic year 2001–2002) were women.[493]

Marriage

The minimum age a person can marry is eighteen for a man and sixteen for a woman.[494] With government approval, a girl may marry at age fifteen.[495] The average age for marriage is 26 for men and 22.4 for women. Sixty-three percent of men are married compared to 53.6 percent of women.[496]

The Romanian Constitution adopted in 1991 gives the state sole authority to pass and regulate marriage laws. The mayor or one of his/her representatives officiates over the ceremony. Religious ceremonies are permitted to take place after the civil service. The Constitution ensures the equality of married men and women. It defines marriage as a relationship of mutual respect, common rights and obligations to each other. It guarantees men and women equal control over marital assets and children. A marriage must be entered into freely. In addition, adultery and bigamy are illegal under the law.[497]

Under the Constitution, women can inherit, own, and pass on property in their own name when married. However, this is not always observed in rural areas.[498]

Unmarried couples do not have the same rights as those who are married. Unmarried couples do not have succession rights. In addition, the woman's contribution in the home or childcare is not considered in the division of property. However, children born out of wedlock are equal under the law.[499]

Divorce is allowed under the Code of Civil Procedure. Both husband and wife are required to appear at a divorce hearing. A marriage may be dissolved if the court holds that the relationship has been irreparably damaged. Romania does not acknowledge no-fault divorce. Fault must be established. However, estranged couples may seek mutual consent divorces. Grounds for which a marriage is often dissolved are illness or non-fulfillment of spousal obligations. Household and sexual duties are considered spousal obligations.[500]

The percentage of divorces is one of the lowest in Europe, 24 percent.[501] Although either spouse can initiate divorce, they are more often initiated by women. Women usually file for divorce on the grounds of infidelity, alcoholism, and physical violence.[502]

The court presides over custody, child support, and the division of marital assets. The Family Code entitles the stay at home spouse one third of the income of the other spouse. This amount plus child support cannot surpass 50 percent of the other spouse's total revenue. Alimony is given if one spouse is unable to work as a result of the marriage. It is not available to non-married partners who separate.[503]

The court must meet with both spouses and the children above the age of ten before awarding custody. The court must also consider the best interest of minor children when making its decision. Although parents have equal right to custody, custody is ordinarily granted to the mother. The parent who does not retain custody is granted visitation rights.[504]

Abortion and Contraceptives

Abortion is legal in Romania.[505] During the first trimester, abortions are allowed to save the life of the woman, to preserve her physical or mental health, if the pregnancy resulted from rape or incest, if there is fetal impairment, and for social or economic reasons. Abortions are available upon request. A legal abortion must be performed by an obstetrician-gynecologist in a hospital or dispensary.[506]

Abortions were first legalized in Romania in 1957.[507] In 1966, the Government became more restrictive with the abortion law in order to boost the fertility rate. Women could get an abortion in order to save the life of the mother, if the fetus was likely to have congenital malformations, if the mother suffered from a serious physical, mental, or sensory disorder, if the pregnancy resulted from rape or incest, if the mother was over the age of forty-five, or if the pregnant woman had given birth to at least four children that were under her care. In 1984, the law became more restrictive. Unmarried persons over twenty-five years of age and childless couples that did not have a medical reason for being childless had to pay special taxes. However, a woman could have an abortion at forty-two instead of forty-five. Investigations were conducted to determine the cause of all miscarriages. In 1985, the law became even more restrictive. The age ground was raised back to forty-five. In addition, having four children was raised to five as grounds for an abortion. As a consequence of the restrictive abortion law Romania's maternal mortality increased from 85 deaths per 100,000 live births in 1965 to 170 in 1983.[508] Illegal and unsafe abortions made up 80 percent of the maternal deaths between 1980 and 1989.[509]

Abortions were made less restrictive in 1996. Consequently, the abortion rate rose from 39 to 199 abortions per 1,000 woman ages fifteen to forty-four years.[510] In fact, in the first nine months of 2003, there were more abortions (170,000) than live births (162,000). However, the number of abortions is decreasing; in fact, there were fewer abortions in 2003 than in 2002.[511] Presently, the abortion rate in Romania is the highest in Europe.

In addition, the maternal mortality rate is the highest in Europe. In 1990, the maternal mortality rate was estimated to be 130 deaths per 100,000 live births.[512]

Although the government gives direct support for contraceptive use,[513] contraceptives are difficult to obtain.[514] Sixty-four percent of married women use contraceptives.[515] The majority of married men and women who use contraceptives also use traditional birth control methods (i.e., periodic abstinence and withdrawal). Condoms are the next most popular birth control (11 percent). Sterilization, IUDs, or injectable forms of birth control are not frequently used.[516] The majority of single persons who use contraceptive methods use condoms or the withdrawal method.[517] The fertility rate is 1.3 births per woman.[518]

Health Care

Under Article 34(1), the right to health care is guaranteed. Medical care and social security was set up to ensure this right.[519] However, there has been an increase of private providers, which are paid out of pocket. In addition, individuals must provide co-payment for drugs.[520] Those with less money are more affected by out-of pocket expenses and co-payments. There are more women who are unemployed and who live below the poverty line than men. Consequently, women have less access to health care and medication.

Women in Public Office

Women were granted the right to vote in 1929 (subject to conditions or restrictions) and 1946 (the year when restrictions or conditions were lifted). The first woman elected or appointed to Parliament was in 1946.[521]

Under Article 16(3) of the Constitution, men and women are guaranteed equal opportunities to obtain public or civil positions.[522]

In 2004, women occupied 10.7 percent of the seats in the lower house of the national parliament.[523] This is significantly less than the 34 percent of seats women held in 1990.[524] In 2004, women occupied 5.7 seats in the upper house or senate of the national parliament.[525] Romania is one of the countries in Europe with the lowest female representation in Parliament.[526]

Women make up 20 percent of government employees at the ministerial level.[527]

Women in the Military

Under Article 16(3) of the Constitution, men and women are guaranteed equal opportunities to obtain military positions.[528]

Men and women can join the military at twenty years of age (2004 est.).[529]

Women were introduced into the military in 1973. At that time, both men and women were required to perform compulsory military service. However, since 1991, the date the present Constitution was adopted, service was made compulsory only for men. Women in the military, at that time, were often placed in secretarial and administrative positions.[530]

Today, 38 percent of women in the military are officers. Sixty-two percent are noncommissioned officers or warrant officers. Women occupy positions in finance, medical service, military law, military engineering, military education, economics, and information management and technology. However, women make up only 3.99 percent of the military.[531]

RUSSIA

Russia is located in Eastern Europe and Northern Asia. It borders the Arctic Ocean and the North Pacific Ocean. The population is 143,782,338 (July

2004 est.). The ethnic groups are Russian (81.5 percent), Tatar (3.8 percent), Ukrainian (3 percent), Chuvash (1.2 percent), Bashkir (0.9 percent), Belarusian (0.8 percent), Moldavian (0.7 percent), other (8.1 percent). The religions are Russian Orthodox, Muslim, and other. The language spoken is Russian.[532] There are 114 women per 100 men.[533]

Constitution

After the Russian Revolution (1917), the Union of Soviet Socialist Republics (USSR) was established. Russia was the dominant force of the union. In 1991, the former USSR splintered into fifteen independent countries.

The present constitution was adopted in 1993. While the Constitution states that men and women have equal rights, in fact, women and ethnic minorities, such as the Roma and Chechen populations, face widespread discrimination.[534]

The voting age for male and female citizens is eighteen.[535]

Work Force and Economy

The purchasing power parity is $1.282 trillion (2004 est.). The population living below the poverty line is 25 percent (January 2003 est.). The labor force is made up of 71.68 million (2004 est.). Unemployment is 8.5 percent. In addition, there is substantial underemployment (2004 est.). The main industries in Russia are coal, oil, gas, chemicals, and metals. Russia also specializes in all forms of machine building ranging from airplanes to scientific instruments.[536]

Women make up 48 percent of the labor force.[537]

The Constitution, under Article 19, states that men and women are equal. It goes on to say that the State will guarantee equality of rights regardless of sex, language, nationality, origin, race, property or employment status, residence, attitude to religion, convictions, membership of public associations or any other circumstance.[538] In addition, the Labor Code (Article 77) states that there will be equal pay for equal work.[539]

While men and women are constitutionally equals, discrimination still happens in the workplace. In fact, job advertisements frequently specify gender and age.[540]

The government, via social security, fully covers 140 days of maternal leave, 70 days prior to and after childbirth.[541] In addition, women are entitled to unpaid parental leave until the child has reached three years of age. This leave may be used by either parent, or guardian of the child.[542]

Employers are prohibited from having female employees work night shifts (except in certain circumstances) or perform underground labor (except in

certain cases) or perform labor-intensive work under harmful working conditions.[543]

Women make up at least 70 percent of the unemployed. Women earn roughly 67 percent of what their male counterparts earn.[544] The estimated annual income is $6,508 (U.S.) for women and $10,189 for men.[545]

Under the Criminal Code, an employer may not refuse to hire a pregnant woman or a woman with small children. Those who are found guilty of the practice are subject to a fine or community service.[546]

Sexual harassment is illegal under the Criminal Code. Those found guilty of such an act face a fine or imprisonment of up to one year.[547]

Women are employed predominantly in education, public health, credit and finance, trade and public catering, and information and accounting services.[548] Women occupy management positions in 89 percent of companies. Women make up 42 percent of senior positions and 69.5 percent of government employees.[549]

The pension age is fifty-five for women and sixty for men.[550] This gives men five additional years to contribute to their pensions.

Education

Under Article 43 every person has the right to a free education, even higher education. Basic general education is mandatory[551] until age fifteen.[552] If a student chooses to pursue higher education, he/she must take an entrance exam. The results of the exam determine whether a student must pay tuition for university. Many seek private classes while in high school to ensure a strong score. These classes are expensive and consequently, inaccessible to most people.[553]

The ratio of female to male youth (ages fifteen to twenty-four) literacy in 2002 was 100 women for every 100 men. The female youth literacy rate is 99.8 percent, which has been consistent since 1995.[554] In 2000, the female to male ratio of student enrollment in tertiary school was 129 women for every 100 men.[555] Gross tertiary school enrollment is 80 percent for women.[556]

Adult literacy is 99.5 percent for women compared to 99.7 percent for men.[557]

Marriage

Article 38 of the Constitution states that motherhood and childhood, and the family are under State protection. The care of children and their upbringing are the right and responsibility of the child's parents. In addition, Articles 38 states that employable children who have reached eighteen years old will care for their non-employable parents.[558]

The legal age for marriage is eighteen for men and women. Individuals, sixteen or older, may be married for acceptable reasons, such as pregnancy, if they obtain a certificate. The average age for marriage is 24.4 for men and 21.8 for women. The percentage of men that are married is 89.8 percent compared to 54.9 percent of women. It is illegal for close relatives to marry. While marriages between cousins are legal, they are uncommon. In addition, it is illegal for adoptive parents to marry their adopted child. A person cannot marry if he/she suffers from mental illness.[559] If one of the spouses is HIV-positive or has a venereal disease, the other party must be informed prior to the marriage.[560]

The divorce rate is 43.3 percent (per 100 marriages).[561] Divorce is not allowed if the wife is pregnant or has a child of less than one year old, and she objects to the divorce. There are two ways to obtain a divorce: with or without court involvement. If both parties agree to the marital dissolution, and do not have a child younger than 18, the couple may register to divorce with no court involvement. In addition, there are three circumstances under which a spouse may receive a divorce without the consent of the other party or litigation: If a party becomes mentally ill during the marriage, or if a party is in jail and is going to remain there for three years or more, or if a party is declared as "an unknown absent" by the court. However, the desiring party must file for divorce in the court when one of the parties wants a divorce and the other does not (and they do not fit the above exceptions), or if they have a child who is under 18. In this case the court must investigate. If the court finds that there is a chance to salvage the relationship they may order a trial separation during which the couple is encouraged to reconcile their differences.[562]

If the parties have a child, the judge decides who will gain custody and the arrangements for support, which is dictated by the number of offspring. Joint custody is not an option. Alimony is unusual and is settled by the court.[563]

Abortion and Contraceptives

Abortions are legal in the Russian Federation.[564] A woman can have an abortion within the first trimester of pregnancy in order to save the life of the mother, to preserve the physical or mental health of the mother, if the pregnancy is a result of incest or rape, if there is fetal impairment, or for economic or social reasons. Abortions are available on request. An abortion requires the consent of the mother. It must be performed by a licensed physician in a hospital or a recognized medical institution.[565] Abortion, with physician authorization on judicial, genetic, vital, medical, personal or social grounds, is available to a woman within the first twenty-eight weeks.[566] Women in urban areas have better access to abortions than women in rural areas.[567]

The Russian Federation used to prohibit abortions except to save the life of the mother or if the fetus could inherit a serious disease from the parents.[568]

However, the law was expanded in 1982 to allow women to have an abortion until the twenty-eighth week for health reasons. The law was further expanded in 1987 to include a broad rage of grounds for abortions performed on request until the twenty-eighth week. These reasons included the death of the husband during pregnancy, imprisonment of the woman or her husband, if the woman already had more than five children, divorce during pregnancy, rape, and heredity of disability in the family. In 1996, social grounds was added to this list. In addition, the list expanded to include the husband's disability, unemployment of either parent, unmarried status of the mother, the mothers financial status, the woman's lack of housing, and if the woman was a refugee. All other reasons would need the consent of a commissioner. In July of 1996, abortions could be performed no later than twenty-two instead of twenty-eight weeks.[569]

There were 3.9 million registered abortions performed in the Russian Federation in 1990. In 2004, the abortion rate was nearly two abortions for every one live birth.[570]

The total fertility rate in the Russian Federation is 1.4 births per woman. Availability and quality of contraceptives is low. According to the United Nations, the only two condom factories closed in 1992 because they could not afford latex. The company manufacturing IUDs was closed down because of the low quality of the product.[571]

Contraceptive use among married women is 73 percent; this includes traditional forms of birth control such as occasional abstinence and withdrawal.[572] IUDs are inserted free of charge. Condoms cost roughly 28 cents (U.S.) and the pill and other hormone-based contraceptives cost 1.8 to 10.8 dollars.[573] This is quite expensive in proportion to the average income.

Health Care

Under Article 41 of the Constitution every person has the right to free, government-financed health care and medical assistance. Many patients, however, pay "under the table" for better service and medicine.[574, 575]

Thirty percent of women, compared to 50 percent of men, who died during their prime, died because of poisoning or accidents.[576]

Rural areas have less access to health care than urban areas. Lacking sufficient funds, many health clinics are old and not renovated and lack modern tools of medicine.[577]

Women in Public Office

Under Article 32 of the Constitution, all citizens have the right to vote and stand for election.[578] Until 1991, under the USSR rule, a quota system guaranteed that women make up one third of Parliament.[579]

In 2002, women occupied 6.4 percent of the seats in the national parliament leaving Russia at the bottom of the four eastern European counties in regard to women's share of seats in a national parliament.[580]

In 2003, women made up 9.8 percent of the lower or single house and 3.4 of the upper house or senate.[581]

Women in the Military

Women served in regiments as captains and pilots during both world wars. In fact, the first female military pilot was a Russian, Eugenie Shakhovskaya, who flew in World War I. During World War II, the USSR drafted women to fight in combat units.[582]

The age men and women can join the military is eighteen years.[583]

Under Article 59 of the Constitution, all citizens must serve in the military.[584] In actuality, only men must fulfill service requirements.[585]

Women currently represent roughly 10 percent of military personnel. Although a few women serve in conflict situations, most function in medical, clerical, and administrative capacities. Few women are officers.[586]

Maternity leave is the same as in civilian life.[587]

NOTES

1. CIA World Factbook, United Kingdom, <www.cia.gov/cia/publications/factbook/geos/uk.html>.

2. England, Infoplease, The Columbia Electronic Encyclopedia, 6th ed., copyright 2004, Columbia University Press, <http://www.infoplease.com/ce6/world/A0817363.html> (Nov. 2005).

3. Country Reports on Human Rights Practices, 2003, United Kingdom, U.S. Department of State, released by the Bureau of Democracy, Human Rights, and Labor, Feb. 25, 2004, <http://www.state.gov/g/drl/rls/hrrpt/2003/27872.htm> (Aug. 2004).

4. England, Infoplease.

5. Ibid.

6. U.S. Department of State, Background note: United Kingdom, Bureau of European and Eurasian Affairs, August 2004, <http://www.state.gov/r/pa/ei/bgn/3846.htm> (Aug. 2004).

7. The United Kingdom Parliament, "Members of Parliament by Gender: Numbers," 1 July 2004, <http://www.parliament.uk/directories/hciolists/gender.cfm> (July 2004).

8. The United Kingdom Parliament, "House of Lords, Analysis of Composition," 1 July 2004, <http://www.parliament.uk/directories/house_of_lords_information_office/analysis_by_compostition.cfm> (July 2004).

9. England InfoPlease.

10. Marina Warner, "Emmeline Pankhurst: The Victorian Englishwoman Marshaled the Suffragist Movement," *Time* 100, 1999, <http://www.time.com/time/time100/heroes/profile/pankhurst01.html> (July 2004).

11. Country Reports on Human Rights Practices, 2003, United Kingdom, U.S. Department of State.

12. CIA World Factbook, United Kingdom.

13. Hilary Metcalf and Aphrodite Korou, "Towards a Closing of the Gender Pay Gap," United Kingdom Country Report, Women and Equality Unit, Department of Trade and Industry, Feb. 2003, <http://www.womenandequalityunit.gov.uk/pay/eu/tow_clo_pay_gap_ukr.pdf> (March 2004).

14. CIA World Factbook, United Kingdom.

15. United Nations Educational, Scientific and Cultural Organization (UNESCO), "Progress of the World's Women 2002: Volume 2: Gender Equality and the Millennium Development Goals," United Nations Development Fund for Women (UNIFEM), 2002, <http://www.unifem.org/www/resources/progressv2/index.html> (July 2004).

16. Penny Spelling and Liz Bavidge, "Women in Decision-making," European Database, Country Report United Kingdom, Women's Computer Centre Berlin, <http://www.fczb.de/projekte/wid_db/CoRe/UK.htm> (Aug 2003).

17. Metcalf and Korou, "Towards a Closing of the Gender Pay Gap."

18. Country Reports on Human Rights Practices, 2003, United Kingdom, U.S. Department of State.

19. Metcalf and Korou, "Towards a Closing of the Gender Pay Gap."

20. Country Reports on Human Rights Practices, 2003, United Kingdom, U.S. Department of State.

21. Metcalf and Korou, "Towards a Closing of the Gender Pay Gap."

22. Ibid.

23. Ibid.

24. Ibid.

25. Ibid.

26. Ibid.

27. UNESCO, "Progress of the World's Women 2002."

28. Ibid.

29. Spelling and Bavidge, "Women in Decision-making."

30. U.S. Department of State, Background note: United Kingdom, Bureau of European and Eurasian Affairs.

31. "The National Curriculum for England: Chosing the Right Curriculum," GEMS Education, <http://www.gemseducation.com/server.php?show=nav.001004006001> (May 2004).

32. Rita J. Simon and Howard Altstein, *Global Perspectives on Social Issues: Marriage and Divorce* (Lanham: Rowman & Littlefield Publishing Group, Inc., 2003).

33. The Northern Ireland Statistics and Research Agency (NISRA), Statistical Press Notice, "Eightieth Annual Report of the Register General, 2001," A National Statistical Publication, 2002, <http://www.nisra.gov.uk/whatsnew/RG%202001%20 Statistical%20Press%20Notice.pdf> (July 2004); Simon and Altstein, *Global Perspectives on Social Issues*.

34. Ibid.

35. Crude Marriage Rates for Selected Countries, Infoplease, Cited from United Nations, Monthly Bulletin of Statistics, April 2001, <http://www.infoplease.com/ipa/ A0004385.html> (March 2004); Gulnar Nugman, World Divorce Rates, Heritage Foundation, 2002, <http://www.divorcereform.org/gul.html> (Sept. 2005).

36. Divorce Rates in England, Queensland Government, cited from Statistics New Zealand, <http://www.aldridgeshs.qld.edu.au/sose/modrespq> (Nov. 2004).

37. Ibid.

38. Metcalf and Korou, "Towards a Closing of the Gender Pay Gap."

39. "Abortion Policies, A Global Review, United Kingdom," United Nations, <http:// www.un.org/esa/population/publications/abortion/profiles.htm> (July 2004).

40. Ibid.

41. Ibid.

42. "Healthcare in the United Kingdom," National Coalition on Healthcare, <http:// www.nchc.org/facts/UnitedKingdom.pdf> (July 2004).

43. Ibid.

44. Ibid.

45. Alison Macfarlane, "Health and the gender agenda: What do official statistics tell us?" *Radical Statistics*, no. 74 (Spring 2000), <http://www.radstats.org.uk/no074/ article4.htm> (July 2004).

46. Women's Health, BBC, <www.bbc.co.uk/health/womens/index.shtml> (March 2004).

47. Warner, "Emmeline Pankhurst: The Victorian Englishwoman Marshaled the Suffragist Movement."

48. Margaret Thatcher, biography, <http://www.margaretthatcher.net/biography/> (July 2004).

49. The United Kingdom Parliament, "House of Lords, Analysis of Composition."

50. Encyclopedia: Life Peer, Wikipedia, Nationmaster.com, <http://www.nation-master.com/encyclopedia/Life-peer> (July 2004).

51. The United Kingdom Parliament, "House of Lords, Analysis of Composition."

52. Sex Discrimination and Equal Pay Acts, Equal Opportunities Commission, <http://www.eoc.org.uk/Default.aspx?page=15501> (July 2004).

53. Spelling and Bavidge, "Women in Decision-making sources;" Country Reports on Human Rights Practices, 2003, United Kingdom, U.S. Department of State.

54. U.S. Department of State, Background Note: United Kingdom, Bureau of European and Eurasian Affairs.

55. Metcalf and Korou, "Towards a Closing of the Gender Pay Gap;" Women and Equality Unit. "Towards a Closing of the Gender Pay Gap."

56. CIA World Factbook, France, <http://www.cia.gov/cia/publications/factbook/ geos/fr.html>.

57. Ibid.

58. Elaine Granley, "France Bans Head Scarves in School," *CBS News*, 3 March 2004.

59. Country Reports on Human Rights Practices, 2003, France, U.S. Department of State, released by the Bureau of Democracy, Human Rights, and Labor, Feb. 25, 2004, <http://www.state.gov/g/drl/rls/hrrpt/2003/27837.htm> (June 2004).

60. "Women's rights in the Spotlight," *News From France* Vol. 96.5, Embassy of France in the United States, 12 March 1996, <http://www.info-france-usa.org/publi/nff/96nff5/societe1.htm> (June 2004).

61. Country Reports on Human Rights Practices, 2003, France, U.S. Department of State.

62. CIA World Factbook, France.

63. "Excerpts from the French Constitution," Left Justified Publiks, <http://www.leftjustified.com/leftjust/lib/sc/ht/wtp/france.html> (June 2004).

64. France Country Analysis Brief, Energy Information Administration, Official Energy Statistics from the U.S.Government, April 2003, <http://www.eia.doe.gov/emeu/cabs/france.html>.

65. CIA World Factbook, France.

66. Janine Mossuz-Lavau, "French women seek to conquer politics," Minister of Justice, Ministry of Foreign Affairs, *Label France* Magazine, no. 37, Oct. 1999, <http://www.diplomatie.gouv.fr/label_france/ENGLISH/DOSSIER/femmes/05conquete.html> (Nov. 2004).

67. United Nations Educational, Scientific and Cultural Organization (UNESCO), "Progress of the World's Women 2002: Volume 2: Gender Equality and the Millennium Development Goals," United Nations Development Fund for Women (UNIFEM), 2002, <http://www.unifem.org/www/resources/progressv2/index.html> (July 2004).

68. "Violence Against Women in France," report Prepared for the Committee on the Elimination of Discrimination Against Women, The World Organization Against Torture (OMCT) operating the SOS- Torture Network.

69. Mossuz-Lavau, "French women seek to conquer politics."

70. The French Healthcare Sector, UK Trade and Investment, Medical report, 20 May 2004, <www.fco.gov.uk> (June 2004).

71. Mossuz-Lavau, "French women seek to conquer politics."

72. Country Reports on Human Rights Practices, 2003, France, U.S. Department of State.

73. Ibid.

74. "Violence against Women in France," CEDAW.

75. Country Reports on Human Rights Practices, 2003, France, U.S. Department of State.

76. Equal Opportunities Commission, "Pregnant and Productive, An update on our investigation," Scotland, EOC February 2004.

77. Country Reports on Human Rights Practices, 2003, France, U.S. Department of State.

78. Mossuz-Lavau, "French women seek to conquer politics."

79. S. Joan Moon, "Women's Rights in France," <http://www.cats.ohiou.edu. ~Chastain/rz/womrgt.htm>.

80. Mossuz-Lavau, "French women seek to conquer politics."

81. UNESCO, "Progress of the World's Women: 2002."

82. UNESCO, Education, <http://portal.unesco.org/education/> (Sep. 2003).

83. Country Reports on Human Rights Practices, 2003, France, U.S. Department of State.

84. Mossuz-Lavau, "French women seek to conquer politics."

85. France's Civil Code, Art. 144, International Development Law Organization (IDLO), <http://www.idlo.int/texts/leg6505.pdf> (March 2005).

86. Ibid., Art 148.

87. Ibid., Art 161.

88. Ibid., Art 162, 163.

89. Simon and Altstein, *Global Perspectives on Social Issues.*

90. France Marriage Laws—License Requirements, <http://usmarriageslaws .com/search/europe/france/> (June 2003).

91. Simon and Altstein, *Global Perspectives on Social Issues.*

92. Ibid.

93. France Marriage Laws—License Requirements.

94. "French 'gay marriage' law passed," *BBC News*, 13 October 1999.

95. Simon and Altstein, *Global Perspectives on Social Issues.*

96. Michèlle Plott, "Divorce and Women in France," <http://cscwww.cats.ohiou .edu/~Chastain/dh/divorce.htm>.

97. Simon and Altstein, *Global Perspectives on Social Issues.*

98. Ibid; Gulnar Nugman, World Divorce Rates, Heritage Foundation, 2002; http://www.divorceform.org/gul.html (Sept. 2005).

99. France's Civil Code, Art. 228.

100. Rita J. Simon, *Abortion: Statutes, Policies, and Public Attitudes the World Over* (Greenwood Publishing Group, 1998).

101. Françoise Laurant, "Is abortion a right? France reforms the Veil Act," *International Planned Parenthood Federation* Vol. 28, no. 2 (2000).

102. Simon, *Abortion: Statutes, Policies, and Public Attitudes the World Over.*

103. "France approves new abortion period," *BBC News*, 31 May 2001, <http:// news.bbc.co.uk/1/hi/world/europe/1360960.stm> (June 2004); Simon, *Abortion: Statutes, Policies, and Public Attitudes the World Over.*

104. Simon, *Abortion: Statutes, Policies, and Public Attitudes the World Over.*

105. "France approves new abortion period," *BBC News.*

106. Simon, *Abortion: Statutes, Policies, and Public Attitudes the World Over.*

107. Ibid.

108. Nathalie Bajos, et al., "Contraception: from accessibility to efficiency," *Human Reproduction* Vol. 18, no. 5 (2003): 994–99, 2003.

109. Simon, *Abortion: Statutes, Policies, and Public Attitudes the World Over.*

110. Bajos, et al., "Contraception: from accessibility to efficiency."

111. Country Reports on Human Rights Practices, 2003, France, U.S. Department of State.

112. Patrick Lenain, "Santé to the French health system," *OECD Observer* no. 223, Oct. 2000, <http://www.oecdobserver.org/news/fullstory.php/aid/356/Sant%E9 _to_the_French_health_system_.html> (June 2003).

113. "Smoking-Related Deaths on the Rise among American, French Women," *Science Daily*, 20 Nov. 1998, <http://www.sciencedaily.com/releases/1998/11/ 981120080005.htm> (June 2004).

114. Mossuz-Lavau, "French women seek to conquer politics."

115. Ibid.

116. UNESCO, "Progress of the World's Women 2002."

117. Country Reports on Human Rights Practices, 2003, France, U.S. Department of State.

118. Archives Premier Ministre, "Parity: Removing Obstacles to the participation of Women in Public Life," Modernizing Politics, 28 Nov. 2001, <http://www.archives .premier-ministre.gouv.fr/jospin_version3/en/ie4/contenu/29964.htm> (June 2004).

119. Country Reports on Human Rights Practices, 2003, France, U.S. Department of State.

120. Archives Premier Ministre, "Removing Obstacles to the participation of Women in Public Life."

121. "Women's rights in the Spotlight," *News From France* 96, no. 5, Embassy of France in the United States, 12 March 1996, <http://www.info-france-usa.org/publi/ nff/96nff5/societe1.htm> (June 2004).

122. Mrs. Margaret Oliphant, *Jeanne D'Arc: Her Life and Death* (New York: G. P. Putnam's Sons, 1896).

123. Wayne Nelson, "Women of the OSS, France spies rendered valuable services to the OSS in the days following the invasion of Southern France," *World War II Magazine* July 1997, <http://www.historynet.com/wwii/blundercoverwomen/> (June 2004).

124. International Military Staff, Committee on Women in NATO Forces, France, Introduction, updated: 26 March 2002, <http://www.nato.int/ims/2001/win/france.htm> (June 2004).

125. Military of France, Wikipedia.org, Fact-index. com, <http://www.fact-index .com/m/mi/military_of_france.html> (June 2004).

126. International Military Staff, Committee on Women in NATO Forces, France, Introduction.

127. Ibid.

128. Ibid.

129. Ibid.

130. CIA World Factbook, Ireland, <http://www.cia.gov/cia/publications/factbook/geos/ei.html>.

131. "Women in an Ireland of Equals 2004," Sinn Féin, Building an Ireland of Equals, June 2004, <http://sinnfein.ie/policies/document/187> (June 2004).

132. Julie Kay, "Ireland, Irish Judicial System," Women's Link Worldwide, September 2002, <http://womenslinkworldwide.org/co_eur_ireland.html> (June 2004).

133. Bunreacht Na Héireann Constitution of Ireland, Enacted By The People 1st July, 1937, In Operation As From 29th December, 1937, Department of the Taoiseach, <http://www.taoiseach.gov.ie/upload/publications/297.htm> (June 2004).

134. Country Reports on Human Rights Practices, 2003, Ireland, U.S. Department of State, released by the Bureau of Democracy, Human Rights, and Labor, Feb. 25, 2004, <http://www.state.gov/g/drl/rls/hrrpt/2003/27843.htm> (Aug. 2004).

135. Encyclopedia: Irish Traveller, Wikipedia, Nationmaster.com, <http://www.nationmaster.com/encyclopedia/Irish-Traveller> (March 2004).

136. The Equality Authority, "Minority Ethnic People with Disabilities in Ireland," Central Statistics Office, 2002a, <www.equality.ie/stored-files/PDF/Minority_Ethnic_People_With_Disabilities.pdf> (June 2004).

137. Vicky Donnelly, "Women's Rights as Human Rights, A Case Study on Domestic Violence," Galway Traveller Support Group, Ireland, *Education Action*, issue 11, Aug. 1999, <http://217.206.205.24/resources/publications/EA11Eng/womens rights.htm> (June 2004).

138. National Women's Council of Ireland reacts to the outcome of the Citizenship Referendum, 15 June 2004, National Women's Council of Ireland, <http://www.nwci.ie/documents/pr_150604.doc> (June 2004).

139. Donnelly, "Women's Rights as Human Rights."

140. CIA World Factbook, Ireland.

141. UN Human Development Report 2004, "Irish Richer Than Americans; Second in Poverty Index," Finfacts Ireland, <http://www.finfacts.com/comment/unhuman developmentreportirelandcomment18.htm> (June 2004).

142. CIA World Factbook, Ireland.

143. "Irish Richer Than Americans; Second in Poverty Index," UN Human Development Report.

144. "Ireland gets Richer, as Women Lose Out," National Women's Council of Ireland, 16 July 2004, <http://www.nwci.ie/documents/pr_160704.doc> (June 2004).

145. CIA World Factbook, Ireland.

146. Bunreacht Na Héireann, Constitution of Ireland.

147. United Nations Educational, Scientific and Cultural Organization (UNESCO), "Progress of the World's Women 2002: Volume 2: Gender Equality and the Millennium Development Goals," United Nations Development Fund for Women (UNIFEM), 2002, <http://www.unifem.org/www/resources/progressv2/index.html> (July 2004); Human Development Reports, United Nations Development Programme, 2003, <http://www.undp.org/hdr2003/indicator/cty_f_IRL.html> (Jan. 2005).

148. Country Reports on Human Rights Practices, 2003, Ireland, U.S. Department of State.

149. Carol Coulter, "Old, Rich and Male? Must be a Lawyer," *The Irish Times*, 25 October 2003.

150. Country Reports on Human Rights Practices, 2003, Ireland, U.S. Department of State.

151. Sexual Harassment at Work, Oasis, Information on Public Services, An Irish Government Resource, <http://www.oasis.gov.ie/employment/employment_rights/sexual_harassment_at _work.html> (July 2004).

152. Country Reports on Human Rights Practices, 2003, Ireland, U.S. Department of State.

153. Irish National Pay Agreement 2004, Finfacts Ireland, Business & Personal Finance Portal, <http://www.finfacts.com/private/personel/nationalpayagreement.htm> (July 2004).

154. Sexual Harassment at Work, Oasis.

155. Kitty Holland, "Constitution 'impedes women's rights,'" *The Irish Times*, 8 April 2003.

156. Yvonne Healy, "Few Women Reach Top Jobs at Third Level," *The Irish Times*, 4 March 1997.

157. "NL: Lowest number of female professors within the EU," Tilburg University, 20 June 2002, <http://www.tilburguniversity.nl/univers/foreignaffairs/2002/2006/female.html> (June 2004).

158. Kathy Sheridan, "It Pays to Get Women on Board," *The Irish Times*, 24 Jan. 2004, <http://www.ireland.com/newspaper/newsfeatures/2004/0124/70141290WK24WOMEN.html> (June 2004).

159. Yvonne Galligan, "Ireland Needs More Women Directors," *The Irish Times*, 23 Jan. 2004.

160. Carol Coulter, "Women's Earnings Remain 30 Percent below Men's," *The Irish Times*, 14 Feb. 2003.

161. Coulter, "Old, Rich and Male? Must be a Lawyer."

162. Sexual Harassment at Work, Oasis; Irish National Pay Agreement, 2004, Finfacts Ireland.

163. Women in an Ireland of Equals, Building An Ireland of Equals.

164. Women's Health Council, "Women, Disadvantage and Health," October 2003, <http://www.whc.ie/publications/index.html> (July 2004).

165. Women in an Ireland of Equals, Building An Ireland of Equals, Sinn Féin.

166. Coulter, "Women's Earnings Remain 30 Percent below Men's."

167. Anne Lucey, "Women's Group Calls for Reform of Welfare System," *The Irish Times*, 30 Jan. 2004.

168. Ibid.

169. Coulter, "Women's Earnings Remain 30 Percent below Men's."

170. Human Development Reports, United Nations Development Programme.

171. Country Reports on Human Rights Practices, 2003, Ireland, U.S. Department of State.

172. UNESCO, "Progress of the World's Women 2002."

173. UNESCO, Education, <http://portal.unesco.org/education/> (Sep. 2003).

174. Coulter, "Old, Rich and Male? Must be a Lawyer."

175. How Does the Undergraduate Medical Education & Training System Impact on Your Organization? IMO Submission to HEA[1], <www.imo.ie/attachment.php?nAttId=479&doc_id=3823> (July 2004).

176. Hijacking Women's Groups, "Sarah Marriott listens to a gathering of women who want to wrest feminism from the academics," *The Irish Times*, 23 Sept. 1998.

177. Simon and Altstein, *Global Perspectives on Social Issues*; Julie Kay, "Ireland."

178. Simon and Altstein, *Global Perspectives on Social Issues*.

179. Ibid.

180. Ibid.; "Women of the World," *The Irish Times*, 7 March 2002.

181. Simon and Altstein, *Global Perspectives on Social Issues.*
182. Ibid.
183. "Abortion Policies, A Global Review, Ireland," United Nations, <http://www.un.org/esa/population/publications/abortion/profiles.htm> (Aug. 2003).
184. Bunreacht Na Héireann, Constitution of Ireland.
185. "Abortion Policies, A Global Review, Ireland," United Nations; Suzanne Breen, "Call for Liberalization of Abortion Law," *The Irish Times*, 6 Sept. 2003.
186. Julie Kay, "Ireland"; See *McGee v. The Attorney General*, 1974 IR 284.
187. Julie Kay, "Ireland."
188. Ibid.
189. CIA World Factbook, Ireland.
190. Julie Kay, "Ireland."
191. Women in an Ireland of Equals, Building An Ireland of Equals, Sinn Féin.
192. Julie Kay, "Ireland."
193. Women's Suffrage, A World Chronology of the Recognition of Women's Rights to Vote and to Stand for Election, Inter-Parliamentary Union, <http://www.ipu.org/wmn-e/suffrage.htm> (July 2004).
194. Equality before the Law, Oasis, Information on Public Services, An Irish Government Resource, <http://www.oasis.gov.ie/government_in_ireland/the_constitution/equality_before_the_law.html> (July 2004).
195. UNESCO, "Progress of the World's Women 2002;" Women in an Ireland of Equals, Building an Ireland of Equals, Sinn Féin, <http://sinnfein.ie/policies/document/187>.
196. The National Women's Council calls for Legislative Action to ensure equal representation of men and women in politics, 4 August 2004, National Women's Council of Ireland, <http://www.nwci.ie/documents/pr_040804.doc> (July 2004).
197. Office of the High Commissioner for Human Rights, Mary Robinson, United Nations High Commissioner for Human Rights (1997–2002), <http://www.unhchr.ch/html/hchr/unhc.htm> (July 2004).
198. Mary McAlesse, the current president, the official website of the President of Ireland, <http://www.irlgov.ie/aras/biographies.htm> (July 2004).
199. Country Profile: Ireland, 2004, *BBC News*, <http://news.bbc.co.uk/1/hi/world/europe/country_profiles/1038581.stm> (July 2004).
200. Ireland, Ireland in Brief, Embassy of Ireland, Washington D.C., <http://irelandemb.org/info.html> (July 2004).
201. Judicial Appointments Annual Report 2001–2002 Department for Constitutional Affairs (DCA), <http://www.dca.gov.uk/judicial/ja_arep2002/chapter1.html> (July 2004).
202. Yvonne Galligan, "Politicians' Words Prove Cheap over the Inclusion of Women in Politics," 3 Feb. 2004, *The Irish Times*.
203. The Irish Defense Forces, <http://www.military.ie/introduction/history.htm> (July 2004).
204. Parliament of Ireland, Parliamentary debates 2001, <http://www.gov.ie/debates-01/4dec/sect7.htm> (July 2004).
205. Ibid.; Jim Morahan, "Army Chief Vows to Stamp out Sexual Harassment," *Irish Examiner*, 21 August 2001.

206. John Breslin, "Army Bullying 'Rehash'," *Irish Examiner*, 14 Oct. 2004.

207. CIA World Factbook, Sweden, <http://www.cia.gov/cia/publications/factbook/geos/sw.html>.

208. The Sami in Finland, Virtual Finland, August 2000, <http://virtual.finland.fi/finfo/english/saameng.html> (July 2004).

209. General Board of Global Ministries, The United Methodist Church, Sweden, history, Country Profiles, <http://gbgm-umc.org/country_profiles/country_history.cfm?Id=157> (July 2004).

210. CIA World Factbook, Sweden.

211. General Board of Global Ministries, The United Methodist Church, Sweden, history.

212. The Constitution, The Swedish Parliament, <http://www.riksdagen.se/english/work/constitution.asp> (July 2004).

213. The Constitution, The Riksdagat at Work, Sveriges Riksdag, The Swedish Parliament, <http://www.riksdagen.se/english/work/constitution.asp> (July 2004).

214. The Constitution, The Swedish Parliament.

215. General Board of Global Ministries, The United Methodist Church, Sweden, history.

216. The Constitution, The Swedish Parliament.

217. Antoinette Hetzer, "The Swedish Model and the Role of Gender," Women in European Universities, <http://www.women-eu.de/download/HetzlerCP.pdf> (July 2004).

218. Shira J. Boss, "Equality May Mean Army Service in Sweden. A controversial proposal would make military service mandatory for women," *Christian Science*, 19 April 2000; "Sweden Wants Women to Beef up its Military," *The Manila Times*, 16 May 2004.

219. Country Reports on Human Rights Practices, 2003, Sweden, U.S. Department of State, released by the Bureau of Democracy, Human Rights, and Labor, Feb. 25, 2004, <http://www.state.gov/g/drl/rls/hrrpt/2003/27866.htm> (Aug. 2004).

220. Hetzer, "The Swedish Model and the Role of Gender;" CIA World Factbook, Sweden.

221. Equality between women and men, Sweden Institute, 18 March 2004, <http://www.sweden.se/templates/factsheet___4123.asp> (Aug. 2004).

222. Elisabet Ornerborg, "Sweden: Court Battles for Equal Pay—Women's Earnings in Sweden Remain Lower than Men's," *UNESCO Courier*, June 2000.

223. Hetzer, "The Swedish Model and the Role of Gender."

224. Ornerborg, "Sweden: Court Battles for Equal Pay."

225. Country Reports on Human Rights Practices, 2003, Sweden, U.S. Department of State.

226. Ornerborg, "Sweden: Court Battles for Equal Pay."

227. Hetzer, "The Swedish Model and the Role of Gender."

228. Equality between women and men, Sweden Institute, 18 March 2004.

229. Hetzer, "The Swedish Model and the Role of Gender."

230. Equality between women and men, Sweden Institute, 18 March 2004.

231. Number of employees at the government offices, government offices of Sweden, <http://sweden.gov.se/sb/d/4036/a/47754;jsessionid=abHsqhd3Y9p7> (Aug. 2004).

232. Equality between women and men, Sweden Institute, 18 March 2004.

233. Country Reports on Human Rights Practices, 2003, Sweden, U.S. Department of State.

234. Equality between women and men, Sweden Institute, 18 March 2004.

235. Ibid.

236. Ibid.

237. Hetzer, "The Swedish Model and the Role of Gender."

238. Equality between women and men, Sweden Institute, 18 March 2004.

239. Boss, "Equality May Mean Army Service in Sweden"; "Sweden Wants Women to Beef up its Military."

240. Hetzer, "The Swedish Model and the Role of Gender."

241. Equality between women and men, Sweden Institute, 18 March 2004.

242. Hetzer, "The Swedish Model and the Role of Gender."

243. Equality between women and men, Sweden Institute, 18 March 2004.

244. Hetzer, "The Swedish Model and the Role of Gender."

245. United Nations Educational, Scientific and Cultural Organization (UNESCO), "Progress of the World's Women 2002: Volume 2: Gender Equality and the Millennium Development Goals," United Nations Development Fund for Women (UNIFEM), 2002, <http://www.unifem.org/www/resources/progressv2/index.html> (July 2004).

246. UNESCO, Education, <http://portal.unesco.org/education/> (Sep. 2003).

247. General Board of Global Ministries, The United Methodist Church, Sweden, history.

248. Simon and Altstein, *Global Perspectives on Social Issues.*

249. Ibid.; Richard F. Thomasson, "Modern Sweden: The Declining Importance of Marriage," *Scandinavian Review* (August 1998): 83–89; Equality between women and men, Sweden Institute, 18 March 2004.

250. Simon and Altstein, *Global Perspectives on Social Issue.*

251. Equality between women and men, Sweden Institute, 18 March 2004.

252. Simon and Altstein, *Global Perspectives on Social Issues.*

253. David Popenoe, "Beyond the Nuclear Family: A Statistical Portrait of the Changing Family in Sweden," *Journal of Marriage and the Family* 49 (1987): 173–83.

254. Simon and Altstein, *Global Perspectives on Social Issues.*

255. "Abortion Policies, A Global Review, Sweden," United Nations, <http://www.un.org/esa/population/publications/abortion/profiles.htm> (Aug. 2003).

256. Ibid.; Simon, *Abortion: Statutes, Policies, and Public Attitudes the World Over* (Greenwood Publishing Group, 1998).

257. Equality between women and men, Sweden Institute, 18 March 2004.

258. Simon, *Abortion: Statutes, Policies, and Public Attitudes the World Over.*

259. Ibid.

260. General Board of Global Ministries, The United Methodist Church, Sweden, history; Paul Gallagher, "The Man who Told the Secret, It took a non-Swede to get the full story of a government sterilization program," *Columbia Journalism Review* (January/February 1998).

261. Equality between women and men, Sweden Institute, 18 March 2004.

262. "Abortion Policies, A Global Review, Sweden," United Nations.

263. Simon, *Abortion: Statutes, Policies, and Public Attitudes the World Over.*

264. Antoinette Hetzer, "The Swedish Model and the Role of Gender."

265. Ibid.

266. Ibid.

267. Equality between women and men, Sweden Institute, 18 March 2004.

268. Women in the Riksday, Sveriges Riksdag, The Swedish Parliament, <http://www.riksdagen.se/english/members/f08_kvin_en.asp> (Aug. 2004).

269. A summary of the History of Women in Sweden, Women's and Gender Studies in Sweden, San Diego State University, <http://www-rohan.sdsu.edu/~bzimmerm/sweden1/History_Page.html> (Sept. 2004).

270. Women in the Riksday, Sveriges Riksdag, The Swedish Parliament.

271. UNESCO, "Progress of the World's Women 2002."

272. Equality between women and men, Sweden Institute, 18 March 2004.

273. Ibid.; General Board of Global Ministries, The United Methodist Church, Sweden, history.

274. Boss, "Equality May Mean Army Service in Sweden;" "Sweden Wants Women to Beef up its Military."

275. Ibid.

276. Ibid.

277. CIA World Factbook, Germany, <http://www.cia.gov/cia/publications/factbook/geos/gm.html>.

278. Ibid.

279. Country Reports on Human Rights Practices, 2003, Germany, U.S. Department of State, released by the Bureau of Democracy, Human Rights, and Labor, Feb. 25, 2004, <http://www.state.gov/g/drl/rls/hrrpt/2003/27839.htm> (Aug. 2004).

280. Ibid.

281. Ibid.; CIA World Factbook, Germany.

282. Work and Life, Cross-national Differences, University of Wisconsin, <http://www.uwlax.edu/Sociology/miller/WEEK10.worklifeindifferentcountries.ppt> (June 2004), CIA World Factbook, Germany.

283. Anett Schenk, "Female Professors in Sweden and Germany," March 2003, <http://www.women-eu.de/download/TP%2003-03%20Schenk.pdf> (Oct. 2004).

284. Country Reports on Human Rights Practices, 2003, Germany, U.S. Department of State.

285. Study examines 'mobbing' at the workplace, European Foundation, 2002, <http://www.eiro.eurofound.eu.int/2002/08/feature/de0208203f.html> (Nov. 2004).

286. Country Reports on Human Rights Practices, 2003, Germany, U.S. Department of State.

287. Schenk, "Female Professors in Sweden and Germany."

288. Country Reports on Human Rights Practices, 2003, Germany, U.S. Department of State.

289. Battle for Equality Still Dominates, Deutsche Welle, 2003, <http://www.dw-world.de/dw/article/0,1564,801156,00.html> (May 2004).

290. The U.S. Library of Congress, Country Studies, Germany, 1988, <http://countrystudies.us/germany/> (Nov. 2003).

291. United Nations, "As Women's Anti-Discrimination Committee Considers Report Of Germany, Government, Emphasizes Right To Freedom From Violence As 'Political Priority,'" Committee on Elimination of Discrimination against Women 2004, <http://www.un.org/News/Press/docs/2004/wom1428.doc.htm> (June 2004).

292. Women in Germany, Spartacus Educational, <http://www.spartacus.schoolnet.co.uk/GERwomen.htm> (Feb. 2004).

293. The U.S. Library of Congress, Country Studies, Germany.

294. Ibid.

295. Ibid.

296. United Nations, "As Women's Anti-Discrimination Committee Considers Report Of Germany."

297. Work and Life, Cross-national Differences.

298. Valuing Parenthood, Australian Human Rights and Equal Opportunity Commission, 2002, <http://www.hreoc.gov.au/sex_discrimination/pml/report/sectionb.html>.

299. Work and Life, Cross-national Differences.

300. Country Reports on Human Rights Practices, 2003, Germany, U.S. Department of State.

301. United Nations, "As Women's Anti-Discrimination Committee Considers Report Of Germany."

302. Country Reports on Human Rights Practices, 2003, Germany, U.S. Department of State.

303. The U.S. Library of Congress, Country Studies, Germany.

304. United Nations Educational, Scientific and Cultural Organization (UNESCO), "Progress of the World's Women 2002: Volume 2: Gender Equality and the Millennium Development Goals," United Nations Development Fund for Women (UNIFEM), 2002,<http://www.unifem.org/www/resources/progressv2/index.html> (July 2004).

305. German Embassy, Washington D.C., Quickfacts: Education, 20 March 2002, <http://www.germany-info.org/relaunch/info/facts/education.html> (Feb. 2004).

306. Simon and Altstein, *Global Perspectives on Social Issues*.

307. The U.S. Library of Congress, Country Studies, Germany.

308. Simon and Altstein, *Global Perspectives on Social Issue*.

309. Ibid.; Federal Statistical Office, <http://statistic-bund.de/presse/englis\ch/pm/p623> (March 2004).

310. Simon and Altstein, *Global Perspectives on Social Issues*.

311. "Abortion Policies, A Global Review, Germany," United Nations, <http://www.un.org/esa/population/publications/abortion/profiles.htm> (Aug. 2003).

312. Simon, *Abortion: Statutes, Policies, and Public Attitudes the World Over*.

313. Ibid.

314. Ibid.

315. Ibid.

316. Ibid.

317. World Contraceptive Use, United Nations, 2003, <http://www.un.org/esa/population/publications/contraceptive2003/WallChart_CP2003.pdf> (Feb. 2004).

318. National Coalition on Health Care, Health Care in Germany, 2004, <http://www.nchc.org/facts/Germany.pdf> (Feb. 2004).

319. Ibid.

320. "Women and Smoking in Germany," International Network of Women Against Tobacco, <http://www.inwat.org/eurfactsheetgerman.htm> (Feb. 2004).

321. The U.S. Library of Congress, Country Studies, Germany.

322. Country Reports on Human Rights Practices, 2003, Germany, U.S. Department of State.

323. UNESCO, "Progress of the World's Women 2002."

324. "Women in National Parliaments," Inter-Parliamentary Union, 2004, <http://www.ipu.org/wmn-e/classif.htm>.

325. Country Reports on Human Rights Practices, 2003, Germany, U.S. Department of State.

326. The U.S. Library of Congress, Country Studies, Germany.

327. German Embassy, Washington D.C., Quickfacts: Education.

328. Country Reports on Human Rights Practices, 2003, Germany, U.S. Department of State.

329. Peter Finn, "German Women Gain Job Parity in Military," *Washington Post*, 3 Jan. 2001.

330. German Military Police Under Fire, Data Lounge, 1999, <http://archive.datalounge.com/datalounge/news/record.html?record=4435> (March 2004).

331. "Women join German Fighting Forces," *BBC News*, 2001, <http://news.bbc.co.uk/1/hi/world/europe/1097492.stm> (Feb. 2004).

332. "German army to lift ban on sex in barracks, Proposed changes would allow 'partnership relationships'," MSNBC, 21 April 2004, <http://www.msnbc.msn.com/id/4798107/> (April 2004).

333. Finn, "German Women Gain Job Parity in Military."

334. CIA World Factbook, Hungary, <http://www.cia.gov/cia/publications/factbook/geos/hu.html>.

335. UN Statistics Division, "Statistics and Indicators on Women and Men," 8 Mar. 2005, <http://unstats.un.org/unsd/demographic/products/indwm/indwm2.htm> (May 2005).

336. Péter Gaál, "Health Care Systems in Transition," Hungary, World Health Organization Regional Office for Europe, Vol. 6, no. 4, 2004, <http://www.euro.who.int/Document/E84926.pdf> (Feb. 2004).

337. CIA World Factbook, Hungary.

338. Péter Gaál, "Health Care Systems in Transition."

339. Hungary Constitution, Universität Bern, <http://www.oefre.unibe.ch/law/icl/hu00000_.html> (March 2004).

340. <http://www.nato.int/ims/2001/win/hungary.htm>; Hungary Constitution.

341. Hungary Constitution, Universität Bern.

342. Women 2000—An Investigation into the Status of Women's Rights in Central and South-Eastern Europe and the Newly Independent States, International Helsinki Federation for Human Rights, <http://www.ihfhr.org/documents/doc_summary.php?sec_id=3&d_id=1463> (Feb. 2004).

343. Country Reports on Human Rights Practices, 2003, Hungary, U.S. Department of State, released by the Bureau of Democracy, Human Rights, and Labor, Feb. 25, 2004, <http://www.state.gov/g/drl/rls/hrrpt/2003/27841.htm> (Aug. 2004).

344. Hungary, Reports to Treaty Bodies, Human Rights Committee, Vol. 5, <http://www.hri.ca/fortherecord2002/engtext/vol5eng/hungarytb.htm> (Feb. 2004).

345. Country Reports on Human Rights Practices, 2003, Hungary, U.S. Department of State.

346. Ibid.

347. Ibid.

348. CIA World Factbook, Hungary.

349. UN Statistics Division, "Statistics and Indicators on Women and Men," 8 Mar. 2005, <http://unstats.un.org/unsd/demographic/products/indwm/indwm2.htm> (May 2005).

350. CIA World Factbook, Hungary.

351. Hungary, Constitution, Universität Bern.

352. UN Statistics Division, "Statistics and Indicators on Women and Men."

353. Country Reports on Human Rights Practices, 2003, Hungary, U.S. Department of State.

354. UN Statistics Division, "Statistics and Indicators on Women and Men,"

355. Hungary, Reports to Treaty Bodies, Human Rights Committee.

356. UN Statistics Division, "Statistics and Indicators on Women and Men."

357. Country Reports on Human Rights Practices, 2003, Hungary, U.S. Department of State.

358. Women 2000—An Investigation into the Status of Women's Rights in Central and South-Eastern Europe and the Newly Independent States.

359. UN Statistics Division, "Statistics and Indicators on Women and Men."

360. Women 2000—An Investigation into the Status of Women's Rights in Central and South-Eastern Europe and the Newly Independent States; UN Statistics Division, "Statistics and Indicators on Women and Men."

361. Women 2000—An Investigation into the Status of Women's Rights in Central and South-Eastern Europe and the Newly Independent States.

362. Country Reports on Human Rights Practices, 2003, Hungary, U.S. Department of State.

363. Minnesota Advocates for Human Rights, "Hungary faced with first public sexual harassment at the workplace complaint," Stop Violence Against Women, 23 July 2004, <http://www.stopvaw.org/16Aug20044.html> (Dec. 2004).

364. Country Reports on Human Rights Practices, 2003, Hungary, U.S. Department of State.

365. Women 2000—An Investigation into the Status of Women's Rights in Central and South-Eastern Europe and the Newly Independent States.

366. United Nations Educational, Scientific and Cultural Organization (UNESCO), "Progress of the World's Women 2002: Volume 2: Gender Equality and the Millennium Development Goals," United Nations Development Fund for Women (UNIFEM), 2002, <http://www.unifem.org/www/resources/progressv2/index.html> (July 2004).

367. UNESCO, Education, <http://portal.unesco.org/education/> (Sep. 2003).

368. Simon and Altstein, *Global Perspectives on Social Issues*; Gulnar Nugman, World Divorce Rates, Heritage Foundation, 2002, <http://www.divorcereform.org/gul.html> (Sept. 2005).

369. Ibid.

370. Ibid.

371. Ibid.

372. Simon, *Abortion: Statutes, Policies, and Public Attitudes the World Over.*

373. "Hungary's Pending Law Restricting Abortion Will Be the Topic of an Open Forum Today," Center for Reproductive Rights, 28 April 2000, <http://www.crlp.org/pr_00_0328hung.html> (May 2004).

374. "Hungarian Government Fails to Ensure Women's Human Rights Advocates Criticize Hungary's Reproductive Rights Policies," Reproductive Rights, 22 March 2002, <http://www.crlp.org/pr_02_0322hungary.html> (May 2004).

375. Women 2000—An Investigation into the Status of Women's Rights in Central and South-Eastern Europe and the Newly Independent States.

376. The European Society of Contraception, Newsletter 1 no. 3, Sept. 2004, <http://www.contraception-esc.com/ESC_Newsletter3.htm> (Dec. 2004); Women 2000—An Investigation into the Status of Women's Rights in Central and South-Eastern Europe and the Newly Independent States.

377. Women 2000—An Investigation into the Status of Women's Rights in Central and South-Eastern Europe and the Newly Independent States.

378. The European Society of Contraception, 2004.

379. Susan A. Cohen, "Issues and Implications, A message to the President: Abortion Can be Safe, Legal and Still Rare," *The Guttmacher Report on Public Policy* Vol. 4, no. 1 (Feb. 2001).

380. "Hungarian Government Fails to Ensure Women's Human Rights," Center for Reproductive Rights.

381. The European Society of Contraception, 2004.

382. "Hungarian Government Fails to Ensure Women's Human Rights," Center for Reproductive Rights.

383. Cohen, "Issues and Implications."

384. "Abortion Policies, A Global Review, Hungary," United Nations, <http://www.un.org/esa/population/publications/abortion/profiles.htm> (Aug. 2003).

385. Hungary Constitution, Universität Bern.

386. Péter Gaál, "Health Care Systems in Transition."

387. Country Reports on Human Rights Practices, 2003, Hungary, U.S. Department of State.

388. Gaál, "Health Care Systems in Transition."

389. Ibid.

390. Ibid.

391. UN Statistics Division, "Statistics and Indicators on Women and Men."

392. European Forum, Hungary Update, 24 Aug. 2004, <http://www.europeanforum.net/country/hungary> (Feb. 2004).

393. Hungary Constitution, Universität Bern.

394. International Military Staff, Committee on Women in NATO Forces, Hungary.

395. Ibid.

396. Ibid.

397. Country Reports on Human Rights Practices, 2003, Hungary, U.S. Department of State.

398. CIA World Factbook, Poland, <http://www.cia.gov/cia/publications/factbook/geos/pl.html>.

399. UN Statistics Division, "Statistics and Indicators on Women and Men," 8 Mar. 2005, <http://unstats.un.org/unsd/demographic/products/indwm/indwm2.htm> (May 2005).

400. Country Reports on Human Rights Practices, 2003, Poland, U.S. Department of State, released by the Bureau of Democracy, Human Rights, and Labor, Feb. 25, 2004, <http://www.state.gov/g/drl/rls/hrrpt/2003/27858.htm> (Aug. 2004).

401. Joanna Wóycicka and Andrzej Dominczak, "Education of Women: Polish Women in the 90's," <http://free.ngo.pl/temida/edu.htm> (May 2004); CIA World Factbook, Poland.

402. Wóycicka and Dominczak, "Education of Women: Polish Women in the 90's."

403. Country Reports on Human Rights Practices, 2003, Poland, U.S. Department of State.

404. CIA World Factbook, Poland.

405. Jakub Wiśniewski, "The Impact of EU Accession on Status of Polish Women," AFAEMME, 29 Jan. 2004, <http://www.afaemme.org/docs/ponencias/grazynakaprovic.doc> (Feb. 2004).

406. UN Statistics Division, "Statistics and Indicators on Women and Men," 8 Mar. 2005, <http://unstats.un.org/unsd/demographic/products/indwm/indwm2.htm> (May 2005).

407. Ibid.

408. Country Reports on Human Rights Practices, 2003, Poland, U.S. Department of State.

409. Ibid.

410. Ibid.

411. Ibid.; Wiśniewski, "The Impact of EU Accession on Status of Polish Women."

412. Country Reports on Human Rights Practices, 2003, Poland, U.S. Department of State.

413. Ibid.

414. Ibid.; Wóycicka and Dominczak, "Education of Women: Polish Women in the 90's."

415. Ibid.

416. United Nations Educational, Scientific and Cultural Organization (UNESCO), "Progress of the World's Women 2002: Volume 2: Gender Equality and the Millennium Development Goals," United Nations Development Fund for Women (UNIFEM), 2002, <http://www.unifem.org/www/resources/progressv2/index.html> (July 2004).

417. UNESCO, Education, <http://portal.unesco.org/education/> (Sep. 2003).

418. Wiśniewski, "The Impact of EU Accession on Status of Polish Women."

419. Wóycicka and Dominczak, "Education of Women: Polish Women in the 90's."

420. Constitution of The Republic of Poland, chapter 1, The Senate Republic of Poland, April 2, 1997, <http://www.senat.gov.pl/k5eng/dok/konstytu/2.htm> (March 2004).

421. Angela Melchiorre, "At What Age are school children employed, married and taken to court," Poland, Right to Education Project, 2004, Second Edition, <http://www.right-to-education.org/content/age/poland.html> (Jan. 2005).

422. Urszula Nowakowska, "The Position of Women in the Family: Polish Women in the 90's," <http://free.ngo.pl/temida/family.htm>; Simon and Altstein, *Global Perspectives on Social Issues*.

423. Nowakowska, "The Position of Women in the Family: Polish Women in the 90's."

424. Simon and Altstein, *Global Perspectives on Social Issues*.

425. Ibid.; Nowakowska, "The Position of Women in the Family: Polish Women in the 90's."

426. Simon and Altstein, *Global Perspectives on Social Issues*.

427. Nowakowska, "The Position of Women in the Family: Polish Women in the 90's."

428. Simon and Altstein, *Global Perspectives on Social Issues*.

429. "Abortion Policies, A Global Review, Poland," United Nations, <http://www.un.org/esa/population/publications/abortion/profiles.htm> (Aug. 2003).

430. Simon and Altstein, *Global Perspectives on Social Issues*.

431. Gulnar Nugman, World Divorce Rates, Heritage Foundation, 2002, <http://www.divorcereform.org/gul.html> (Sept. 2005).

432. Ibid.; The Constitution of the Republic of Poland, Article 56 of the Family Code, <http://www.sejm.gov.pl/english/konstytucja/kon1.htm> (April 2004).

433. Simon and Altstein, *Global Perspectives on Social Issues*.

434. Ibid.; Country Reports on Human Rights Practices, 2003, Poland, U.S. Department of State.

435. Simon and Altstein, *Global Perspectives on Social Issues*.

436. Ibid.

437. "Abortion Policies, A Global Review, Poland," United Nations.

438. Ibid.; Simon, *Abortion: Statutes, Policies, and Public Attitudes the World Over*.

439. Legal abortion numbers rise in Poland, ClariNet; AFP, 21 Oct. 2003, <http://quickstart.clari.net/qs_se/webnews/wed/ds/Qpoland-abortion.REqo_DOL.html> (March 2004).

440. Simon, *Abortion: Statutes, Policies, and Public Attitudes the World Over*.

441. Ibid.; UN Statistics Division, "Statistics and Indicators on Women and Men."

442. Health Care in Poland, Travel Poland, <http://travel.poland.com/texts/en/t-pi-4-2.php> (Jan. 2004).

443. OECD Health Data 2004: A Comparative analysis of 30 countries, 2004 edition, Australian Institute of Health and Welfare, <http://www.aihw.gov.au/international/oecd/oecdhd04.html> (Feb. 2004).

444. Country Profile, Poland, *BBC News*, 2004, <http://news.bbc.co.uk/1/hi/world/europe/country_profiles/1054681.stm> (Sept. 2004).

445. Dorota Kawiorska, "SHA-Based Health Accounts in 13 OECD Countries: Country Studies, Poland, National Health Accounts 1999," 17 August 2004, <http://www.oecd.org/dataoecd/9/23/33664254.pdf> (Sept. 2004).

446. Simon Clarke, "Poverty in Poland," The University of Warwick, Russian Research Programme, <http://www.warwick.ac.uk/fac/soc/complabstuds/russia/Poverty_Poland.doc> (March 2004).

447. Wóycicka and Dominczak, "Education of Women: Polish Women in the 90's."

448. UNESCO, "Progress of the World's Women 2002."

449. Country Reports on Human Rights Practices, 2003, Poland, U.S. Department of State.

450. CIA World Factbook, Poland.

451. Poland—International Military Staff, Committee on Women in NATO Forces, Poland, 26 Aug. 2004, <http://www.nato.int/ims/2004/win/poland.pdf> (Sept. 2004).

452. Ibid.

453. Ibid.

454. Ibid.

455. CIA World Factbook, Romania, <http://www.cia.gov/cia/publications/factbook/geos/ro.html>; Country Profile, Romania, *BBC News*, 30 Nov. 2004, <http://news.bbc.co.uk/1/hi/world/europe/country-profile/1057466.stm> (Dec. 2004).

456. CIA World Factbook, Romania.

457. CIA World Factbook, Romania; The Gallup Organization, Public Opinion Barometer—May 2003, released 26 June 2003, <http://www.gallup.ro/english/poll/releases/pr030626/pr030626.htm#3> (July 2004).

458. Country Profile, Romania, *BBC News*, 30 Nov. 2004.

459. UN Statistics Division, "Statistics and Indicators on Women and Men," 8 Mar. 2005, <http://unstats.un.org/unsd/demographic/products/indwm/indwm2.htm> (May 2005).

460. Country Reports on Human Rights Practices, 2003, Romania, U.S. Department of State, released by the Bureau of Democracy, Human Rights, and Labor, Feb. 25, 2004, <http://www.state.gov/g/drl/rls/hrrpt/2003/27860.htm> (Aug. 2004).

461. CIA World Factbook, Romania.

462. Country Profile, Romania, *BBC News*, 30 Nov. 2004.

463. CIA World Factbook, Romania.

464. Country Reports on Human Rights Practices, 2003, Romania, U.S. Department of State; Minnesota Advocates for Human Rights Country Profile, Romania, Stop Violence Against Women, 2004, <http://www.stopvaw.org/Romania2.html>; Parliament of Romania, Romanian Constitution, Chamber of Deputies, <http://www.cdep.ro/pls/dic/site.page?den=act2_2&par1=1#t1c0s0a4> (Oct. 2004).

465. Country Reports on Human Rights Practices, 2003, Romania, U.S. Department of State.

466. Ibid.

467. CIA World Factbook, Romania.

468. UN Statistics Division, "Statistics and Indicators on Women and Men."

469. CIA World Factbook, Romania.

470. Minnesota Advocates for Human Rights Country Profile, Romania, 2004; Parliament of Romania, Romanian Constitution.

471. International Labour Organization (ILO), Law No. 202/2002 (19/4/2002) On Equal Opportunities between Women and Men—Romania, <http://www.ilo.org/public/english/employment/gems/eeo/law/romania/act6.htm> (May 2004).

472. International Labour Organization (ILO), Law No. 19/2000 Regarding the System of Public Pensions and Other Social Security Allowances—Romania, <http://www.ilo.org/public/english/employment/gems/eeo/law/romania/act4.htm> (March 2004).

473. UN Statistics Division, "Statistics and Indicators on Women and Men."

474. European Foundation, Legislation on maternity protection revised, Romania, <http://www.eiro.eurofound.eu.int/2004/04/feature/ro0404102f.html> (April 2004).

475. RADOR: News from Romania, 98–10–07, Hellenic Resources Institute, <http://www.hri.org/news/balkans/rador/1998/98-10-07.rador.html> (March 2004).

476. European Foundation, Legislation on maternity protection revised, Romania.

477. Ibid.; ILO 2002–2003 Collective Agreement, Romania, <http://www.ilo.org/public/english/employment/gems/eeo/law/romania/ca1.htm> (May 2004).

478. Country Reports on Human Rights Practices, 2003, Romania, U.S. Department of State.

479. Minnesota Advocates for Human Rights Country Profile, Romania, 2004.

480. ILO, Law No. 202/2002 (19/4/2002) On Equal Opportunities between Women and Men—Romania.

481. The Gallup Organization, Survey on Violence against Women in Bucharest, released May 27, 2003, <http://www.gallup.ro/english/poll/releases/pr030527/pr030527.htm#3> (June 2004).

482. Country Reports on Human Rights Practices, 2003, Romania, U.S. Department of State.

483. Minnesota Advocates for Human Rights Country Profile, Romania, 2004; Parliament of Romania, Romanian Constitution.

484. Country Reports on Human Rights Practices, 2003, Romania, U.S. Department of State.

485. Human Development Reports, United Nations Development Programme, 2003, <http://www.undp.org/hdr2003/indicator/cty_f_ROM.html> (Jan. 2005).

486. UN Statistics Division, "Statistics and Indicators on Women and Men."

487. Anita Cristea, "Position of Women on the Labour Market in Romania," Seeline Gender Project, <http://www.seeline-project.net/ECONOMIC/romania_research.htm> (May 2004).

488. ILO, More women enter the global labour force than ever before, but job equality, poverty reduction remain elusive, 5 March 2004, <http://www.ilo.org/public/english/region/ampro/cinterfor/temas/gender/news/art_oit.htm>.

489. Human Development Reports, United Nations Development Programme.

490. Marian Preda, Cristina Dobos, and Vlad Grigoras, "Romanian Pension System during the Transition: Major Problems and Solutions," European Institute of Romania, 2004, <http://www.ier.ro/PAIS/PAIS2/En/study9.pdf> (Oct. 2004).

491. Angela Melchiorre,"At What Age are school children employed, married and taken to court," Romania, Right to Education Project, 2004, Second Edition, <http://www.right-to-education.org/content/age/romania.html> (Jan. 2005).

492. Minnesota Advocates for Human Rights Country Profile, Romania, 2004; Parliament of Romania, Romanian Constitution.

493. Cristea, "Position of Women on the Labour Market in Romania."

494. Simon and Altstein, *Global Perspectives on Social Issues.*

495. Angela Melchiorre,"At What Age are school children employed, married and taken to court."

496. Simon and Altstein, *Global Perspectives on Social Issues.*

497. Ibid.

498. Ibid.

499. Ibid.

500. Ibid.

501. Percentage of Divorces in Selected Countries, InfoPlease, cited from the Human Development Report, 1999, United Nations, <http://www.infoplease.com/ipa/A0200806.html> (April 2004).

502. Simon and Altstein, *Global Perspectives on Social Issues.*

503. Ibid.

504. Ibid.

505. "Abortion Policies, A Global Review, Romania," United Nations, <http://www.un.org/esa/population/publications/abortion/profiles.htm> (Aug. 2003).

506. Simon, *Abortion: Statutes, Policies, and Public Attitudes the World Over* (Greenwood Publishing Group, 1998).

507. "Abortion Policies, A Global Review, Romania," United Nations.

508. Simon, *Abortion: Statutes, Policies, and Public Attitudes the World Over.*

509. "Abortion Policies, A Global Review, Romania," United Nations.

510. Simon, *Abortion: Statutes, Policies, and Public Attitudes the World Over.*

511. Abortions Outnumber Births in Romania, Planetwire.org, Media Analysis, 1–15 February 2004, <http://www.planetwire.org/details/4574> (March 2004).

512. Simon, *Abortion: Statutes, Policies, and Public Attitudes the World Over.*

513. "Abortion Policies, A Global Review, Romania," United Nations.

514. Abortions Outnumber Births in Romania.

515. UN Statistics Division, "Statistics and Indicators on Women and Men."

516. Contraceptive Use Among Married Men, 1990–2003, table 1, Information & Knowledge for Optimal Health (INFO) Project, Johns Hopkins School of Public Health, <http://www.infoforhealth.org/pr/m18/table1.html> (March 2004).

517. Contraceptive Use among Unmarried Men, 1993–2002, table 2, Information & Knowledge for Optimal Health (INFO) Project, Johns Hopkins School of Public Health, <http://www.infoforhealth.org/pr/m18/table2.html> (March 2004).

518. UN Statistics Division, "Statistics and Indicators on Women and Men," 8 Mar. 2005, <http://unstats.un.org/unsd/demographic/products/indwm/indwm2.htm> (May 2005).

519. Minnesota Advocates for Human Rights Country Profile, Romania, 2004; Parliament of Romania, Romanian Constitution.

520. European Observation on Health Care Systems, Health Care Systems in Transition, Romania, <http://www.euro.who.int/document/e71423.pdf> (June 2004).

521. Human Development Reports, United Nations Development Programme.

522. Minnesota Advocates for Human Rights Country Profile, Romania, 2004; Parliament of Romania, Romanian Constitution.

523. Human Development Report, Women's Political Participation, 2004.

524. UN Statistics Division, "Statistics and Indicators on Women and Men"; Human Development Report, Women's Political Participation, 2004.

525. Human Development Report, Women's Political Participation, 2004.

526. The Gallup Organization, Romanians support larger-scale participation of women in politics, 21 July 2003, <http://www.gallup.ro/english/poll/releases/pr030721/pr030721.htm> (Aug. 2003).

527. Human Development Report, Women's Political Participation, 2004.

528. Minnesota Advocates for Human Rights Country Profile, Romania, 2004; Parliament of Romania, Romanian Constitution.

529. CIA World Factbook, Romania.

530. International Military Staff, Committee on Women in NATO Forces, Romania, National Report, <http://www.nato.int/ims/2004/win/romania.pdf> (Dec. 2004).

531. Ibid.

532. CIA World Factbook, Russia, <http://www.cia.gov/cia/publications/factbook/geos/rs.html>.

533. UN Statistics Division, "Statistics and Indicators on Women and Men," 8 Mar. 2005, <http://unstats.un.org/unsd/demographic/products/indwm/indwm2.htm> (May 2005).

534. Country Reports on Human Rights Practices, 2003, Russia, U.S. Department of State, released by the Bureau of Democracy, Human Rights, and Labor, Feb. 25, 2004, <http://www.state.gov/g/drl/rls/hrrpt/2003/27861.htm> (Aug. 2004).

535. CIA World Factbook, Russia.

536. Ibid.

537. UN Statistics Division, "Statistics and Indicators on Women and Men," 8 Mar. 2005, <http://unstats.un.org/unsd/demographic/products/indwm/indwm2.htm> (May 2005).

538. Minnesota Advocates for Human Rights Country Profile, Russian Federation, <http://www.stopvaw.org/Russian_Federation.html>; The Constitution of the Russian Federation, Bucknell University, <http://www.departments.bucknell.edu/russian/const/ch2.html> (March 2004).

539. International Helsinki Federation For Human Rights, Women 2000—An Investigation into the Status of Women's Rights in Central and South-Eastern Europe and the Newly Independent States, <http://www.ihf-hr.org/documents/doc_summary.php?sec_id=3&d_id=1472> (Feb. 2004).

540. Country Reports on Human Rights Practices, 2003, Russia, U.S. Department of State.

541. UN Statistics Division, "Statistics and Indicators on Women and Men," 8 Mar. 2005, <http://unstats.un.org/unsd/demographic/products/indwm/indwm2.htm> (May 2005).

542. Country Reports on Human Rights Practices, 2003, Russia, U.S. Department of State.

543. International Helsinki Federation For Human Rights, Women 2000—An Investigation into the Status of Women's Rights in Central and South-Eastern Europe and the Newly Independent States.

544. Country Reports on Human Rights Practices, 2003, Russia, U.S. Department of State.

545. Human Development Reports, United Nations Development Programme, 2003, <http://www.undp.org/hdr2003/indicator/cty_f_RUS.html> (Jan. 2005).

546. Minnesota Advocates for Human Rights Country Profile, Russian Federation; The Constitution of the Russian Federation, Bucknell University.

547. Ibid.

548. International Helsinki Federation For Human Rights, Women 2000—An Investigation into the Status of Women's Rights in Central and South-Eastern Europe and the Newly Independent States.

549. Andrew Brooke, "Russian Women Lead the World," *The Moscow News,* <http://english.mn.ru/english/issue.php?2004-9-14>.

550. International Helsinki Federation For Human Rights, Women 2000—An Investigation into the Status of Women's Rights in Central and South-Eastern Europe and the Newly Independent States.

551. Minnesota Advocates for Human Rights Country Profile, Russian Federation; The Constitution of the Russian Federation, Bucknell University.

552. Angela Melchiorre,"At What Age are school children employed, married and taken to court," Russian Federation, Right to Education Project, 2004, Second Edition, <http://www.right-to-education.org/content/age/russian_federation.html> (Jan. 2005).

553. International Helsinki Federation for Human Rights, Women 2000—An Investigation into the Status of Women's Rights in Central and South-Eastern Europe and the Newly Independent States.

554. United Nations Educational, Scientific and Cultural Organization (UNESCO), "Progress of the World's Women 2002: Volume 2: Gender Equality and the Millennium Development Goals," United Nations Development Fund for Women (UNIFEM), 2002, <http://www.unifem.org/www/resources/progressv2/index.html> (July 2004).

555. UNESCO, Education, <http://portal.unesco.org/education/> (Sep. 2003).

556. Human Development Reports, United Nations Development Programme.

557. Ibid.

558. Minnesota Advocates for Human Rights Country Profile, Russian Federation; The Constitution of the Russian Federation, Bucknell University.

559. Simon and Altstein, *Global Perspectives on Social Issues.*

560. Ibid.

561. Gulnar Nugman, World Divorce Rates.

562. Simon and Altstein, *Global Perspectives on Social Issues.*

563. Ibid.

564. "Abortion Policies, A Global Review, Russia," United Nations, <http://www.un.org/esa/population/publications/abortion/profiles.htm> (Aug. 2003).

565. Rita J. Simon, *Abortion: Statutes, Policies, and Public Attitudes the World Over* (Greenwood Publishing Group, 1998).

566. "Abortion Policies, A Global Review, Russia," United Nations.

567. International Helsinki Federation for Human Rights, Women 2000—An Investigation into the Status of Women's Rights in Central and South-Eastern Europe and the Newly Independent States.

568. Simon, *Abortion: Statutes, Policies, and Public Attitudes the World Over.*

569. Ibid.

570. Ibid.; Anna Arutunyan, "Abortion in Russia: No Big Deal," *Moscow News,* 2004, <http://www.mosnews.com/feature/2004/11/25/abortion.shtml> (Dec. 2004).

571. "Abortion Policies, A Global Review, Russia," United Nations.

572. UN Statistics Division, "Statistics and Indicators on Women and Men."

573. International Helsinki Federation For Human Rights, Women 2000—An Investigation into the Status of Women's Rights in Central and South-Eastern Europe and the Newly Independent States.

574. Minnesota Advocates for Human Rights Country Profile, Russian Federation; The Constitution of the Russian Federation, Bucknell University.

575. Jeanne Whalen, "Russia's Health Care Is Crumbling: Dire Lack of Funds Creates Sick, Dwindling Populace And 'National Emergency,'" *Wall Street Journal*, 13 Feb. 2004.

576. Yelena Vansovich, "Life Is Better, Life Is Healthier, The Health Care Ministry sums up 2001," JRL, 21 March 2002, <http://www.cdi.org/russia/johnson/6148-6.cfm> (April 2004).

577. Whalen, "Russia's Health Care Is Crumbling."

578. International Helsinki Federation for Human Rights, Women 2000—An Investigation into the Status of Women's Rights in Central and South-Eastern Europe and the Newly Independent States.

579. Minnesota Advocates for Human Rights Country Profile, Russian Federation.

580. UNESCO, "Progress of the World's Women 2002."

581. "Women in National Parliaments," Inter-Parliamentary Union, 2004, <http://www.ipu.org/wmn-e/classif.htm>.

582. Women Warriors in the twentieth century, Gender Gap, <http://www.gendergap.com/military/Warriors-2.htm> (Sept. 2004).

583. CIA World Factbook, Russia.

584. Minnesota Advocates for Human Rights Country Profile, Russian Federation; The Constitution of the Russian Federation, Bucknell University.

585. Jennifer G. Mathers, "Women in the Russian Armed Forces: A Marriage of Convenience?" Minerva: Quarterly Report on Women and the Military, (Fall-Winter, 2000), <http://www.findarticles.com/p/articles/mi_m0EXI/is_2000_Fall-Winter/ai_73063469> (Nov. 2004).

586. Ibid.

587. Ibid.

Chapter Four

Middle East

EGYPT

Egypt is located in Northern Africa. It borders the Mediterranean Sea and is located between Libya and the Gaza Strip. Egypt has a population of 76,117,421 (July 2004 est.). Ninety-nine percent of Egyptians are of Eastern Hamitic stock (Egyptians, Bedouins, and Berbers). The remaining 1 percent is made up of Greek, Nubian, Armenian, and European (primarily Italian and French). Ninety-four percent of Egyptians are Muslim, the majority of whom are Sunni, while the remaining 6 percent is made up of Christians and other religions. Arabic is the official language, although many speak English and French.[1]

The female to male ratio is even. Life expectancy is seventy-one for women and sixty-seven for men.[2]

Constitution

Britain seized control of Egypt's government in 1882, but allegiance to the Ottoman Empire continued until 1914. Egypt became partially independent from the United Kingdom in 1922, but did not gain full sovereignty until shortly after World War II. The government of Egypt is a republic. The legal system is based on English common law, Islamic law, and the Napoleonic codes. The Constitution was ratified on September 11, 1971.[3]

In 1981, an Egyptian law was adopted that eliminated all forms of discrimination against women.[4] In addition, the Constitution states that persons (men and women) will be provided equal public duties and rights without discrimination based on gender, creed or religion. Yet, discrimination based on gender, homosexuality, and religion still happens. In fact, although homosexuality is

151

not legally criminalized, homosexuals are arrested via internet-based sting operations on the basis of debauchery.[5]

While rape is prohibited by law, marital rape is not. Those found guilty of rape face up to three years in prison with hard labor.[6]

Women, under the age of twenty-one, must obtain permission from their fathers to obtain passports and travel.[7]

Egyptian men who marry a foreigner can pass on their nationality to their children.[8] Egyptian women who marry non-nationals may not transfer their nationality to their children except in a few instances; when the child was born in Egypt and the nationality of the father is unknown, or when the child's relationship to the father cannot be legally established. It is estimated that one million children of women who marry foreigners cannot obtain citizenship.[9] This has a detrimental effect on children of an Egyptian mother and foreign father.

An amendment, whereby a mother may pass on her citizenship, is under consideration, except for children fathered by a Palestinian national.[10] See the sections Health Care, Work Force, and Education for further information.

Female Muslim heirs receive roughly one half the amount of a male heir. Christian widows of a Muslim man receive no inheritance rights. If a woman is the sole heir of her parents, she only receives one half of the inheritance. The remainder goes to designated male relatives. Contrarily, a sole male heir can receive the totality of his parent's inheritance.[11]

Both men and women have the right to vote at eighteen years of age. Voting is compulsory for men and women.[12]

Work Force and Economy

The purchasing power parity in Egypt is $295.2 billion (2004 est.). The labor force is made up of 20,190,000 million people (2004 est.). The unemployment rate is 9.9 percent (2004 est.). The population living below the poverty line is 16.7 percent.[13]

Women have been allowed to work outside their homes in Egypt for the past fifty-two years. In 1981, Egyptian law was ratified to grant women equal access to employment and training. However, the new Constitution encourages equality of men and women in the public sphere, if and only if, it does not interfere with Islamic principles.[14]

Unemployment, in 2002, was only 5.1 percent for men while it was 27.7 percent for women.[15] Women are encouraged to retire early. They are also encouraged to take part time positions for half the salary. In addition, recruitment in the private sector is geared toward men. Women are often left out of recruitment because of the possibility of maternity leave, which the company would have to pay.[16]

In 1981, women were granted the right to have paid maternity leave and unpaid childcare leave.[17] During maternity leave women are given full pay for a period of fifty days. A woman may take such leave only three times during her employment period. For companies that have fifty or more employees, women may take leave without pay for one year.[18] Companies that employ more than one hundred women must accommodate them by providing day care for their children.[19]

Women are prohibited from working in physically or morally dangerous jobs. Judicial positions are considered morally dangerous positions.[20] While nothing legally prohibits women from serving as a judge, there is only one female justice. Counselor Tahany al-Gabbani was appointed to the Supreme Court in 2003. She is the first woman to be appointed to the Supreme Court.[21] Other women have in the past, and continue to apply for judiciary positions. They have all been rejected.[22]

Sexual harassment is not prohibited by the law.[23] There are no statistics on how often sexual harassment occurs.

Children of Egyptian mothers and foreign-born fathers cannot gain employment without obtaining work permits and fulfilling resident requirements, even if they were born and raised in Egypt.[24]

The labor laws state that persons (male or female) must receive equal pay for equal work in the public sector.[25] The estimated annual income for women is $1,963 for women compared to $5,216 for men. Women earn 38 percent of what their male counterparts earn.[26]

Women make up 17 percent of private business owners and 25 percent of managerial positions in the four major national banks.[27] Women make up 9 percent of legislators, senior officials, and managers. Women make up 30 percent of professional and technical workers.[28]

Education

The Constitution states that religion must be taught in school.[29]

The government provides public education. Public education is compulsory for eight years of school. Since Egyptian mothers cannot pass on citizenship to their children, children born of foreign fathers are not considered citizens. Consequently, they are not granted a free education. In addition, such children are prohibited from entry into certain professional schools.[30]

In 2002, the female to male ratio for secondary level enrollment was 94 women for every 100 men.[31] Seventy-seven percent of age eligible females were enrolled in secondary school.[32] The ratio of female to male youth literacy (ages fifteen to twenty-four) in 2002 was 84 women to every 100 men.[33] Sixty-five percent of women ages fifteen to twenty-four were literate in 2002 compared to 57 percent in 1995.[34]

The adult literacy rate is 55.6 percent overall (43.6 for women and 67.2 percent for men).[35]

Public expenditure on education is roughly 3.7 percent of the GDP.[36]

Marriage

A non-Muslim woman does not have to convert to marry a Muslim man but a non-Muslim man must convert to marry a Muslim woman.[37]

The minimum legal age a person can marry is eighteen for men and sixteen for women. The average age is 26.4 for men and 21.6 for women. The percentage of men that are married is 46.1 percent compared to 43.3 percent of women. The divorce rate is 4.1 (per thousand of the total population).[38]

According to Islamic law, a husband may divorce his wife if she is infertile. In fact, men may obtain a divorce without any reason at all. This is called *talaq*. When involving *talaq* the husband is required to pay the remainder of the dowry to his wife and provide her with monetary support throughout the mandatory waiting period, and provide financial support for any children who are not yet legally adults. Couples may also divorce through mutual consent. It is more difficult for a wife to divorce her husband if he is unwilling.[39] The Egyptian Personal Status Laws, enacted in 1920, make women the legal subordinates to men.[40] In spite of this, in April 2000, a divorce law was passed that allows women to seek a divorce without proof of abuse or contractual violation through a system that is similar to *talaq*. Even under this law, it is still harder for women to divorce than men. Court-supervised mediation is required before a woman may be granted a divorce. She also must return any material property she gained through the marriage contract.[41] If a woman does divorce her husband without his consent her dowry will not be returned to her, nor may she receive alimony.[42] Men can seek a divorce without going through mediation and are not required to inform their wives of the dissolution of the marriage.[43] A man simply may go to the local marriage registrar to obtain a divorce.[44]

Judicial decree is the option most women choose in pursuing a divorce.[45] Women have the right to seek divorce in cases of a polygamous union in the first year of the second marriage. However, it is not her automatic right to be granted a divorce in these situations and she cannot seek a divorce after the first year of the polygamous marriage. In order to be granted a divorce the woman must prove that her husband's second marriage is detrimental to her mentally or physically. In reality, polygamous marriages are rare among the middle and upper classes.[46]

After a divorce, a mother has custody of her children.[47] Boys stay with their mothers until they are ten years old where upon they are returned to their fathers.[48] Girls are returned to their fathers when they are twelve years old. After the mother's period of custody has ended, the husband is entitled to regain the house, and the wife is required to leave.[49]

Women are entitled to only one year of alimony, an amount set by a judge who assesses the husband's financial status.[50] Alimony can be revoked if the wife does not obey the husband; that is, leaves the house without his consent.[51]

Egyptian women are only allowed passports with the permission of their spouse or male guardian. A husband may also forbid his wife to work outside the home if he can show that the work outside the home interferes with her duties at home.[52]

By law an Egyptian woman's material possessions are legally her own; she does not have to share them with her husband. Men, on the other hand, must legally provide for their wife and children as well as any other unmarried female in their extended family.[53]

Abortion and Contraceptives

The Penal Code of 1937 (sections 260 to 264) does not specifically allow abortions to save the life of the mother. However, the general principles of criminal law allow abortions to be performed because of necessity. Sometimes this is interpreted to include fetal impairment.[54] The abortion must be certified by three physicians. In addition, the husband's consent is required unless the doctor believes the operation is necessary.[55]

It is difficult for the prosecution to provide the necessary evidence to prove the crime of abortion.[56] The intent to perform an abortion is not enough evidence to convict a person of the offense of abortion. The prosecution has to prove that the woman was pregnant, and that there was an illegal interruption of the pregnancy. If a woman is found guilty of inducing an abortion they face imprisonment.[57] Physicians, surgeons, midwives, and pharmacists who perform an abortion are subject to hard labor.[58] There are roughly fifteen abortions for every one hundred pregnancies.[59]

Egypt has the longest history of contraceptive initiatives in the Middle East. The government gives direct support for contraceptive use.[60] Fifty-six percent of married women use contraceptives, this includes traditional and modern methods.[61] However, contraceptives are difficult for the poor to access. In addition, poor and rural women do not often use contraceptives due to the belief that contraceptives are harmful to a woman's health. Consequently, many women resort to self-induced abortions.[62] Between 1986 and 1992 the percentage of women between the ages of twenty and forty-five who had a child before the age of twenty was 30 percent in urban areas and 53 percent in rural areas.[63] The number of births for 1000 women between the ages fifteen and nineteen years old was 78 between 1990 and 1995.[64]

The fertility rate is 2.88 children per woman (2005 est.).[65]

Maternal mortality is 84 deaths for every 100,000 live births.[66]

Health Care

Under Article 16, citizens are guaranteed health services.[67] However, the public system does not cover every citizen. The health care system is made up of public and private providers. Individuals pay out of pocket expenses for medicine and private providers.[68] Consequently, the poor do not have adequate access to health care and pharmaceuticals.

Currently, children born from Egyptian mothers but foreign fathers are not entitled to state funded free medical care.[69]

The public health expenditure is 1.9 percent of the GDP.[70]

Women in Public Office

Women received the right to vote and stand for election in 1956. The first year a woman was elected or appointed to office was in 1957.[71]

In 2001, President Mubarak appointed eight women to the upper house of Parliament (The Shura Council).[72]

In 2004, women made up 2.9 percent of the members of the lower house and 6.8 of the members in the upper house.[73] This places Egypt in the bottom 5 percent in regard to women's share of seats in the national parliaments.[74] Women make up 6.1 percent of the employees at the ministerial level in government.[75]

Women in the Military

The Constitution mandates conscription but provides a variety of options for national service. Men are required to serve either in the police force, the prison-guard service, or in one of the military economic service units. Service usually begins when a man has completed high school. If he goes on to higher education, he may postpone service until he graduates. Typical service is three years. This number may be lowered or altered depending on one's education level. All males are required to register for the draft at age sixteen. Some men are eligible for exemption of military service. For example, exemption may be granted for men who have brothers who were killed in military service, or who are the bread-winners for their family. Women are not subject to conscription.[76]

The expenditure on the military is 2.7 percent of the GDP.[77]

IRAN

Iran is located in the Middle East between Iraq and Pakistan. It borders the Gulf of Oman, the Persian Gulf, and the Caspian Sea. The other bordering countries are: Afghanistan, Armenia, Azerbaijan, Turkey, and Turkmenistan.[78]

Iran has a population of 69,018,924 (July 2004 est.). The major ethnicities are Persian (51 percent), Azeri (24 percent), Gilaki and Mazandarani (8 percent), Kurd (7 percent), Arab (3 percent), Lur (2 percent), Baloch (2 percent), Turkmen (2 percent), while other groups make up the remaining 1 percent. Iran is the only country in the Middle East in which the official religion is Shiite Islam (89 percent). Of the remaining 11 percent, 9 percent are Sunni Muslim and 2 percent are Zoroastrian, Jewish, Christian, and Baha'i. The major languages are Farsi (also known as Parsi) and Farsi dialects (58 percent), Turkic and Turkic dialects (26 percent), Kurdish (9 percent), and Luri (2 percent). The last four percent are made up of Arabic (1 percent), Turkish (1 percent), and other languages.[79] Sixty percent of the Iranian population is under the age of twenty-five.[80]

There are 97 women to every 100 men. Life expectancy at birth is seventy-two for women and sixty-nine for men.[81]

Constitution

Iran was known as Persia until 1935. Iran became an Islamic republic in 1979 after the Shah was forced into exile. The government is a theocratic republic. The present Constitution was adopted in 1979 and revised in 1989.[82]

The Constitution states that men and women have the same rights and protections under the law. Women gained the right to vote under the rule of Reza Shah in 1963. Women have the right to vote, access to education, and employment and the right to be elected to public office. Yet, the Constitution also states that the Shari' a provisions, which restrict women rights and actions, is the supreme law.[83] For example Article 20 states, "All citizens of the country, both men and women, equally enjoy the protection of the law and enjoy all human, political, economic, social, and cultural rights, *in conformity with Islamic criteria.*"[84]

Article 21 states that the government must ensure the rights of women in all respects, in conformity with Islamic criteria, and accomplish the following goals:

1. create a favorable environment for the growth of woman's personality and the restoration of her rights, both the material and intellectual;
2. the protection of mothers, particularly during pregnancy and childbearing, and the protection of children without guardians;

3. establishing competent courts to protect and preserve the family;
4. the provision of special insurance for widows, and aged women and
   women without support; and
5. the awarding of guardianship of children to worthy mothers, in order to
   protect the interests of the children, in the absence of a legal guardian.
   Source: Islamic Republic of Iran Constitution.[85]

Men, not women, pass citizenship on to their children. In addition, husbands, not wives, may pass citizenship to their spouse.[86]

The legal age to vote for men and women is fifteen.[87]

In 2001, the government announced the formation of the "morality force." The morality force was designed to enforce the government's strict code of moral behavior. Press reports indicate that there were incidents where women were beaten, flogged, or imprisoned for listening to music, wearing makeup, or nail polish or clothing that was determined to be not modest enough; that is, clothing that did not cover their hair and all parts of their body except their face and hands.[88]

Women must wear a *hejab,* a headscarf that conceals the neck and hair. The *hejab* was banned during the rule of the Shah but reinstated during the rule of the Ayatollah Ruhollah Khomeini. The minimum covering acceptable is a headscarf and coat with long sleeves. In some areas, although it is not the law, women must wear a *chador,* a prayer outfit that conceals more of the body. At all times women must cover their body except the face, toes, and hands.[89] The law also prohibits the appearance in the media of any women, Iranian or not, who are uncovered.[90]

Women must be accompanied at all times by male guardians in accordance with personal status laws. At all times women must carry identification that proves her guardian is either a first- or second-degree relative. Members of the Islamic Revolutionary Committee may request these documents at any time.[91] Women must obtain the consent of their husbands, fathers or other male relatives in order to obtain a passport. Married women must gain written permission from their husbands in order to leave the country.[92]

Segregation of men and women is enforced in public spaces. Women are not allowed to socialize openly with men who are not relatives or who are unmarried.[93] Women must sit in specific reserved sections on buses.[94] Women must also enter public buildings, airports and universities through a separate entrance than men. In addition women must stay in "women only" areas when swimming, skiing, or at the beach. Women are prohibited from going to male sporting events, although this rule is not always enforced.[95] In 1998 the government passed a law that required the segregation of the sexes in regard to health care.

In 2004, Parliament passed a bill granting women superior inheritance laws. Women now inherit the majority of their husband's assets. Women may also divide the inheritance among themselves and their children.[101]

Work Force and Economy

Iran's purchasing power parity is $478.2 billion (2004 est.).[97] Forty percent of the population lives below the poverty line (2002 est.). Twenty-two million people make up the labor force. The unemployment rate was 15.7 percent in 2002.[98] 2004 statistics reveal a high unemployment rate of 34 percent (ages fifteen to twenty-four) with 22 percent unemployment for men and 41 percent for women.

The law grants women maternity leave, childcare, and pension benefits. The daily minimum wage, regardless of gender, is $2.50.[99]

After 1980, women were no longer able to be judges or study mining or agriculture. In 1992, the law changed in that women could be appointed as advisory judges.[100] In 1990, women made up 19 percent of the University professors.[101] Women are prohibited from seeking the presidency.[102] In 2001, 2 million women worked outside the home.[103]

Women earn roughly 28.5 percent of what their male counterparts earn. The estimated annual income for women is $2,835 compared to $9,946 for men.[104]

Education

Education for children and adolescents is compulsory, starting at age six.[105] Under the Constitution, Article 30, the government must provide all citizens (men and women) with free education from primary school. In addition, the government is required to provide free higher education.[106]

Gender is not a barrier in terms of education. In 1998, 52 percent of students entering universities were women, even though only one in ten applicants passes the university entrance exam.[107] In 2000, the ratio of female to male enrollment in secondary level education was 96 women to every 100 men. In 2002, 77 percent of girls eligible to enroll in secondary education were enrolled.[108] In 2000 the female to male ratio of student enrollment in tertiary school was 93 women to every 100 men.[109]

The ratio of female youth literacy (ages fifteen to twenty-four) compared to male youth literacy is 96 women to every 100 men. The female youth literacy rate in Iran is 92.7 percent compared to 87.5 percent in 1995.[110] In 1990, the literacy rate for women twenty-five and older was 43 percent compared to 64.7 for men.[111] In 2001, adult literacy was 70.4 percent for women and 83.5 percent for men.[112]

Public expenditure on education is 5 percent of the GDP.[113]

Marriage

The legal minimum age to marry is nine. The average age of marriage is 25.6 years for men and 22.4 for women. The percentage of men who are married is 79.3 compared to 97.1 of women. The divorce rate is 1.7 (per thousand of the total population). The marriage is only considered legal by the Islamic state when it occurs between two Muslims or those converted to Islam. Any children that result from intermarriage (marriage between a Muslim and non-Muslim) are illegitimate.[114]

Women must be granted permission to marry by their father or a male relative. In addition, the law allows for temporary marriages. In this practice a woman or girl may become the wife of a married or single Muslim male. This marriage can last any length of time, ranging from hours to years. According to Shi'a Islamic law a man may have as many of these temporary wives as he wishes. These wives are not given the same rights as those granted in a traditional marriage. A man may have up to four wives. According to Islamic law a Muslim woman may not marry a non-Muslim man.[115]

The Family Protection Act was passed in 1967.[116] The act granted women increased rights in the home and the workplace.[117] The act restricted polygamy, abolished men's unilateral right to obtain a divorce and granted women equal rights to child custody. However, in 1979, the act was declared to be not Islamic. In 1980, polygamy and men's unilateral right to obtain a divorce were reinstated. In addition, women's right to child custody and divorce were further limited. In 1992, the divorce law was amended in order to limit a man's right to divorce and to protect a woman's interest during divorce.[118] While women do have the right to divorce, a man does not have to cite a reason for divorce while women do.[119] Grounds for divorce for women are if her husband cannot provide for the family, if he is a drug addict, insane, or impotent. In December of 2002, a new law was enacted which made divorce for women less arbitrary and not as costly.[120] In 2002, Iran's Parliament approved a bill giving women equal right to divorce.[121]

Children are the born subjects of their father.[122] As of February 2002, divorced mothers have the right to keep their sons until they are seven years old. Prior to this date, women could only keep their sons until the age of two. When the son turns seven he is turned over to his father.[123] In addition, a woman who remarries must give custody of her children to her ex-husband. If a court finds that the ex-husband is an unfit parent, custody will be granted to the mother.[124] Nevertheless, a woman who requests a divorce is often ordered to return to her husband.[125]

Although Islamic divorce law does not recognize a woman's right to share the property that a couple acquired, a marriage contract that specifies this right, along with alimony, is honored.[126]

Abortion and Contraceptives

Abortion is not legal in Iran except to save the life of the woman.[127]

In 1961, abortion law was exactly the same as it is today. The only ground for an abortion was to save the life of the mother. In 1976, the Penal Code was amended to legalize abortion. A woman could have an abortion on social or economic grounds, if the abortion was performed during the first twelve weeks of pregnancy, if the couple gave their written consent, and if the abortion would have posed no danger to the health of the mother. If the woman was unmarried her own consent was sufficient. On the other hand, if she was in the process of a divorce she would have had to obtain the consent of her husband if the fetus was considered his legal obligation.[128]

After 1979, abortion was once again made illegal except to save the mother's life. Under the existing Penal Code, an abortion is considered a lesser crime involving bodily injury. The crime is punishable by financial payment to the victim's relatives. The compensation is dependant upon the stage of the pregnancy.[129]

Contraception and family planning became widely available in 1988.[130] In 1990, 65 percent of married women in the age of procreating used contraceptives.[131] In 1997, 73 percent of women use contraceptives (both traditional and modern forms of contraceptives).[132] The family planning program encourages spacing three or four years between pregnancies, limiting the number of children per family to three, and discourages pregnancies in women under eighteen or older than thirty-five years of age. There is strong encouragement for male sterilization. There is no charge for family planning services or for sterilization. Family benefits, paid maternity leave, housing subsidies, health care and insurance all end with the birth of the third child.[133] The fertility rate in 2004 was 1.93 births per woman.[134] The number of births for 1000 women between the ages of fifteen to nineteen between the years of 1990 to 1995 was 106.[135]

Health Care

Under the Constitution, Article 29, men and women have the right to health services, medical care and treatment. The state shall provide the services and financial support for such services for all citizens.[136]

In 1998, Parliament approved a new law requiring hospitals to segregate by sex all health care services. However, there are not enough trained women physicians and health care professionals to meet the needs of all the women and girls in Iran.[137]

Public expenditure on health care is 2.7 percent of the GDP.[138]

Women in Public Office

Women obtained the right to vote and stand for election in 1963. The first year a woman was elected or appointed to office was 1963.[139]

In 1999, women held 3 percent of the 290 seats in parliament.[140] In 2002, women held 4.1 percent of the seats in parliament, leaving Iran in the bottom 5 percent in regard to women's share of seats in the national parliaments. There has been virtually no change in regard to women's seats in parliament since 1987.[141] In the election of 1999, there were no female cabinet members. One woman served as a Presidential Advisor for Women's Affairs.[142]

In 2004, women held twelve (out of 290) of the Parliamentary seats.[143] Women made up 9.4 percent of the government at the ministerial level.[144]

Women in the Military

All male Iranians and those born to Iranian parents, twenty-one and older must complete a compulsory two-year military service.[145] This is compulsory for men only. Volunteers may enlist earlier.[146]

Since the beginning of 1986, women have been encouraged to receive military training. Women employed by the armed forces cannot receive military ranks; their employment status is that of office employees.[147]

Public expenditure on the military is four percent of the GDP.[148]

ISRAEL

Israel is located in the Middle East. It borders the Mediterranean Sea and is located between Egypt and Lebanon. The population in Israel is 6,199,008 (July 2004 est.). The primary ethnicity is Jewish (80.1 percent). The remainder is primarily Arab (1996 est.). The major religions are Judaism (80.1 percent), Islam (14.6 percent, mostly Sunni Muslim), Christianity (2.1 percent); the remaining 3.2 percent is made up of other religions (1996 est.). Hebrew is the official language. But, Arabic is used officially for the Arab minority and English is the most commonly used foreign language.[149] The number of women for 100 men is 102.[150] The life expectancy at birth is eighty-one for women and seventy-seven for men.[151]

Constitution

Israel has a multiparty parliamentary system.[152] Following World War II, the British withdrew from their occupation of Palestine. The UN then divided the area into Arab and Jewish states, an arrangement rejected by the Arabs. Israel declared its independence in May 1948. A series of wars have followed in which Israel has extended its boundaries. Israel does not have a formal constitution; some of the functions of a constitution are filled by the Declaration of Establishment (1948), the Basic Laws of the parliament (the "Knesset"), and the Israeli citizenship law. The legal system is based on a combination of English common law, British Mandate regulations, Turkish law, and, in personal matters, Jewish, Christian, and Muslim legal systems.[153]

The law prohibits discrimination based on sex, marital status, race, political beliefs, or age.[154] Israel's law provides equal rights for men and women in politics, the military, family, and work.[155] Women are also legally granted equal rights to men in regards to education, health, housing, and social welfare. Women are entitled to protection from sexual harassment, sexual exploitation, violence, and trafficking. Additionally, rape is illegal.[156]

Women were granted the right to vote in the late 1920's by the British government. In 1948, women were granted equality in Israel's Declaration of Independence. In 1950, the Women's Equal Rights Law granted women legal equality.[157] Israeli men and women have the right to vote at the age of eighteen.[158]

Discrimination based on gender and race still occur. Women continue to face discrimination in divorce and the work place. Israeli Arabs continue to face discrimination. It is difficult for Israeli Arabs to obtain housing. In addition, military service is a prerequisite for many social and economic benefits, including employment. However, service is not compulsory for Israeli Arabs and few enlist. Consequently, Israeli Arabs who do not perform military service are at a disadvantage.[159]

Work Force and Economy

The purchasing power parity of Israel is $120.9 billion (2004 est.). Eighteen percent of people live below the poverty line. The labor force is made up of 2.61 million people (2004 est.).[160] Women make up nearly half of the labor force.[161] Women continue to increase their participation.[162] The unemployment rate is 10.7 percent (2004 est.).[163] The unemployment rate for women is 10.6 percent and 10.1 percent for men.[164]

In 1998, Israel passed the Equal Employment Opportunity Law that prohibited sex discrimination in the work place.[165] The law prohibits discrimination against women in job training, conditions of employment, job advertising, promotion, dismissal and severance pay.[166] While the law prohibits sexual harassment,[167] there are no provisions for enforcement.[168] Sexual harassment remains a problem.[169]

Between 1979 and 1996 the number of women in the work force increased from 32 to 46 percent.[170]

Women make up 75 percent of the labor force in education, nursing, and social work.[171] They make up 32 percent of University professors and 20 percent of management positions.[172] Women make up less than 30 percent of the employment force in construction, agriculture, and industrial labor.[173] Women make up 2 percent of those in senior management positions in large companies.[174]

Under the law, there is equal pay for equal work including benefits and allowances.[175] However, overall women earn 79 to 80 percent of what men earn.[176] In addition, promotion, wages and benefits are not equal for women compared to men regardless of the 1996 Equal Employment Opportunity Law that prohibits the unequal allocation of fringe benefits.[177] Men continue to often gain more fringe benefits than women in similar jobs, such as overtime pay, cars, and travel allowance accounts.[178]

The difference between male and female wages negatively correlates with increased education.[179] For example women with four years of education earn 95 percent of what men earn with the same educational background.[180] But, women with sixteen years of education or more, earn 73 percent of what men earn with the same level of education.[181]

The estimated earned annual income is $14,201 (U.S.) for women compared to $26,636 (U.S.) for men.[182]

Women make up 26 percent of legislators, senior officials, and managers. Women make up 54 percent of professional and technical workers.[183]

In 2004, an amendment was added to the Employment Equal Opportunities Law adding pregnancy to the list of forbidden types of discrimination. Women cannot be denied employment, fired, or denied job advancement on account of their pregnancy.[184]

Women are given twelve weeks of maternity leave. Seventy-five percent of this is paid by social security.[185] They may take up to one year of leave without pay.[186] Working mothers also are given public subsidized preschool and day care services. Part-time workers receive the same full benefits, social security and tenure as full time employees.[187]

Prostitution is not illegal.[188] However, it is illegal to pimp prostitutes or run a brothel.[189]

The retirement age for women is sixty and sixty-five for men.[190] The age will slowly be raised to sixty-two for women.[191]

Israeli Arabs face discrimination in the workplace. In September 2003, the government approved an affirmative action plan to aid the hiring of Arabs to boards of government companies. Implementation has not yet occurred.[192]

Education

School is compulsory until age fifteen. Secondary school is free until age eighteen.[193]

In 2002, the ratio of female to male enrollment in secondary school was 102 women to every 100 men.[194] Female enrollment in secondary schools was 89 percent in 2000.[195] The ratio of female to male youth literacy (ages fifteen to twenty-four) was equal.[196]

Women make up 55.9 percent of students in higher education. Women make up 81 percent of students in teaching, 79.3 percent of students in nursing and medical assistance, 23.5 percent of students in engineering and architecture, and 31.4 percent of students studying math, statistics, and computer sciences.[197]

In 1990, literacy for women twenty-five and older was 90.7 percent compared to 93.3 percent in 1995.[198] In 2001, the adult literacy rate was 93.4 percent for women and 97.3 percent for men.[199] In 2000, the female to male ratio of student enrollment in tertiary school was 139 women to every 100 men.[200]

Marriage

Under the Marriage Law Act, the minimum age for men and women to marry is seventeen. Pregnancy alters the age of when a person can get married. Jewish, Muslim, and Christian religious laws all allow women to marry at a younger age than men.[201] The average age for men to marry is 27.5 years and 24.3 for women.

Marriages between parent and child, siblings, husband and sister in law (even if the original couple is divorced) are prohibited.[202] The divorce rate is 26 percent.[203] Single parents head six percent of the households in Israel.[204] Ninety-eight percent of Israeli women are or have been married.[205]

In 1953, the State of Israel granted the orthodox rabbinical courts complete jurisdiction over issues of marriage, divorce, and person status.[206] The grounds on which a court may grant a woman a divorce are if the husband has a physical defect that prohibits her from being able to cohabitate with him. A wife whose husband is unable to produce children, is also entitled to a divorce if she is childless and claims that she wishes to have a child. In addition, a woman may obtain a divorce if her husband unjustly refuses conjugal rights, or unjustly refuses to maintain her when he is in a position to do so or could be, or if he abuses her, is unfaithful to her, has intercourse with her against her will during her menstrual period, or causes her to transgress the dietary laws, knowing that she observes them.[207] While a court can decide in favor of a divorce, a woman still cannot get a divorce without the consent of her husband even if he abuses or abandons her. In 1998, there were 10,000 Israeli women whose husbands would not grant them a divorce.[208] A husband does not need his wife's consent in order to obtain a divorce. He may demand a divorce if his wife failed to bear children within a ten year span, and he has no children (even from another woman). Once divorced both parties are able to remarry. Upon divorce the wife is entitled to her dowry and her own property. If no pre-existing agreement between the couple exists, property is divided equally upon a divorce. In addition, a woman who is being divorced may be granted monetary compensation.[209]

Today there are thousands of "agunot's," women who may not have legitimate children or remarry because their husbands have disappeared or will not grant them a divorce. Rabbinical tribunals are allowed to sanction men who refuse to divorce their wives if there are ample grounds for divorce, such as abuse. However, sanctions are not always applied.[210]

Abortion and Contraceptives

The fertility rate is 2.47 births per woman (2004 est.).[211] This is higher than the fertility rate in most industrialized nations.[212] Having children is encouraged by the state and is rewarded.[213] Mothers are eligible for maternity grants.[214] David Ben-Gurion, the first Prime Minister of Israel, granted families with ten or more children a prize. The state pays for daycare and summer camps for families with four or more children. In addition there is a political lobbying group that represents the interests and rights of large families.[215] The number of births out of 1,000 women between the ages of fifteen to nineteen between the years of 1990 to 1995 was 23.[216]

Abortions are legal in Israel.[217] The grounds on which a woman can have an abortion is (1) to save her life; (2) to preserve her physical or mental health; (3) rape or incest; and (4) fetal impairment.[218] A woman cannot have an abortion for economic or social reasons. An abortion must be performed by a physician in a recognized medical institution with the written consent of the woman. Every legal abortion must be approved by a committee made up of two physicians and a social worker. The committee members must be appointed by the director of the hospital where the abortion will be performed, or by the Minister of Health.[219]

Prior to the creation of the State of Israel the abortion legislation in Palestine was based on the British Offences Against the Person Act of 1861. The new Israeli Government incorporated the Act into Israeli law. Consequently, Israel prohibited abortion until the Criminal Law Amendment of 1977. The Amendment permitted abortions in order to save the life of the mother or if the pregnancy would cause her physical or mental harm, if the woman was under the age of seventeen or over the age of forty, if the pregnancy resulted from a sexual offense, incest or extramarital intercourse, if the child was likely to have physical or mental deformation, or if the pregnancy would cause the mother or child difficult family or social circumstances. Illegal abortions can result in imprisonment for up to five years or a fine. In 1979, the law was amended to prohibit abortion on social and economic grounds.[220]

There is no time limit of gestation during which a woman can have an abortion. The costs for minors and for adults who have abortions on medical grounds are covered by the social insurance system.[221]

Contraceptive use among married women and those in consensual unions is 68 percent.[222] Women have access to emergency contraceptives without a prescription.[223]

Health Care

Public expenditure on health care is 5.1 percent of the GDP.[224] There is universal health care. In 1994, Parliament passed a health insurance bill that makes all Israeli citizens automatically insured regardless of one's age, religion, or financial status.[225] The bill was implemented in 1995.[226] Hospital stays are fully paid by the Health Maintenance Organization (HMO). Co-payments must be made by the patient for medications. This is economically difficult for those who are poor.[227]

Women in Public Office

Women were first able to stand for election and vote in 1948. The first woman was elected or appointed to Parliament in the same year.[228]

Israel's first and only female prime minister was Golda Meir.[229] She held office from 1969 to 1974. In 1999, the number of women in Parliament increased from nine to fifteen. In 1999, two women were appointed to cabinet posts. In 1993, 10.9 percent of those elected to local government bodies were women compared to 4.2 percent in 1950.[230] In 2002, women held 14.2 percent of the seats in the national parliament.[231] Nine women have served as mayors.[232]

Today, women hold 15 percent of the seats in Parliament.[233] Women make up 6.1 percent of employees at a ministerial level in government.[234]

Women in the Military

At age eighteen, upon the completion of secondary school, Israeli men serve three years in the military and women serve two years.[235] Service is not compulsory for Israeli Arabs.[236] Post the obligatory years of service, men must serve thirty days out of every year until they are fifty-four years of age.[237] Women's obligatory service is for a shorter period of time and they are assigned to participate in the reserves until age twenty-two.[238] Women are automatically exempt from service if they marry, are pregnant, or are religiously observant.[239] In addition, there is a ten-year minimum educational requirement. Nineteen percent of women do not enter military service because they do not meet the educational requirement. Eighteen percent are exempt from service because of their orthodox religious practices. All together roughly 55 percent of women enter military service compared to 95 percent of men.[240]

Women are usually excluded from all positions that involve combat. Female soldiers make up 30 percent of military positions, 65 percent of those women are assigned to secretarial, clerical, or administrative positions. In 1995, women made up 12.4 percent of high ranking retired or older officers assigned to the prestigious political or managerial posts.[241]

SYRIA

Syria is located in the Middle East between Lebanon and Turkey. It borders the Mediterranean Sea. The population of Syria is 18,016,874 (July 2004 est.). In addition, there are roughly 40,000 persons living in the Israeli-occupied area of Golan Heights, 20,000 of which are Arabs and 20,000 of which are Israeli settlers. The main ethnic group is Arab (90.3 percent); the remaining 9.7 percent are made up of Kurds, Armenians, and other ethnicities. Sunni Muslims make up 74 percent of the population, 16 percent of its people are Alawite, Druze, and other Muslim sects, and the remaining 10 percent are Jewish or Christians of various sects. Arabic is the official language. But, Kurdish, Armenian, Aramaic, Circassian are widely understood. French and English are spoken by some.[242]

There are 98 women for every 100 men. Life expectancy at birth is seventy-three years for women and seventy-one years for men.[243]

Constitution

France controlled Syria until its independence on April 17, 1947. Syria is a republic that has been under a military regime since March 1963. The Constitution was adopted on March 13, 1973. Syria's legal system is based on Islamic law and civil law. There are special religious courts.[244]

The age for both men and women to vote is eighteen years of age.[245] Voting is compulsory for men and women.[246]

The Constitution grants men and women equal rights and equal opportunities.[247] Under the Constitution (Article 25), all citizens are equal before the law in their duties and rights. The state ensures that citizens have equal opportunities. Under Article 26, all citizens have the right to participate in economic, social, political and cultural arenas. Under Article 3 of the Constitution, Islamic jurisprudence is a main source of legislation.[248]

Women still face discrimination in regard to personal status, inheritance, retirement, employment, and social security laws. Individuals who are Jewish or Kurd face social discrimination.[249] Many Kurds had their citizenship taken away in 1962.[250]

Rape is a felony. However, spousal rape is not illegal. In addition, the law provides for lesser sentence for crimes considered "honor crimes."[251]

Female heirs are usually given half the inheritance of male heirs. Male heirs must give financial support to female heirs in their family who inherit less. If the male heir fails to support the female heir she may sue him for support.[252]

Lastly, women are unable to pass on citizenship to their children, regardless of whether their child(ren) were born in Syria.[253]

Work Force and Economy

External factors like the war on terrorism and the Israeli-Palestinian conflict have adversely affected the economy. The purchasing power parity of Syria is $58.01 billion (2004 est.). Twenty percent of the population lives below the poverty line (2004 est.). The labor force is 4.97 million (2004 est.). The unemployment rate is 20 percent (2004 est.).[254] Unemployment is 24.1 percent for women and 8.3 percent for men.[255]

Women make up 20 percent of the labor force.[256] The estimated annual income for women is $1,549 (U.S.) compared to $5,496 for men.[257]

Sexual harassment is prohibited by law. In addition, the Constitution states that there shall be equal pay for equal work regardless of gender.[258]

Maternity leave is seventy-five days, 70 percent of which is paid by the woman's employer.[259] If an employer has 100 female employees in one place the employers must provide a nursery for the women's children who are between two months and three years old.[260]

Women make up 10 percent of lawyers, 7 percent of judges, 20 percent of university professors, and 57 percent of teachers (below the university level).[261] The female share of government employment is 26.9 percent.[262] Few women hold senior governmental positions. Women in the government primarily hold clerical and staff positions. The government does offer childcare for a small fee at the workplace and schools. Few women own a business.[263]

A wife loses her right to maintenance (similar to an allowance) if she works outside the home without her husband's permission.[264]

Education

Schools are government run.[265] Education is compulsory for boys and girls from age six to twelve.[266] The compulsory education age will be extended to age sixteen once there are sufficient financial resources.[267] The government provides free education for men and women from primary school through university.[268] Books are also free.[269]

Religious instruction in one's own denomination is mandatory. There is no religious study requirement at the university level.[270] In rural areas the drop out rate for women is high.[271] Under the Constitution, parents/guardians are obligated to enroll their school age child(ren) in school.[272]

The ratio of female to male primary school enrollment is 95 women to every 100 men. The ratio of female to male secondary school enrollment is 91 women to every 100 men.[273] The ratio of female youth literacy (ages fifteen to twenty-four) compared to male youth literacy in 2002 was 84 women to every 100 men.[274] The adult literacy rate is 74.2 percent for women and 91 percent for men.[275]

Marriage

Under the Constitution, Article 44, the family is considered the basic unit of society and is encouraged and protected by the state. The Constitution states that it will eliminate material and social obstacles hindering marriage.[276]

Religious courts deal with matters connected with personal status, such as marriage.[277]

The minimum age for marriage is eighteen for boys and seventeen for girls.[278] With parental consent men are eligible to marry at fifteen and women at thirteen.[279] The average age for women to marry is 25.1.[280] All marriages must be registered with authorities. Sanctions are imposed if the marriage is not registered.[281]

Although polygamous marriage is legal, only a small, male minority practice polygamy.[282] In addition, a court may not allow it.[283] Lineage in families traces to a common ancestor. Consequently, endogamy, marrying within one's lineage, is preferred. As a result it is common among Syrians of all socioeconomic classes to marry a first cousin, although this is less common among the middle class. Marriage between first cousins is frequent among Sunni, Kurd, and Turkoman Syrians but forbidden among Circassians and Christians. But, Circassians and Christians encourage marriage among more distant relatives.[284]

In both Muslim and Christian families the groom must pay a bride price called a *mahr*. A woman cannot marry without the consent of a male family member. In a middle class family it is not rare for a *mahr* to be comparable to several years' salary. The *mahr* or bride price, as often indicated in prenuptial agreements, serves as alimony in the event of a divorce or separation. The high price of the *mahr* is often used to deter a male from divorcing his wife. The bride price counteracts the ease by which a male can get a divorce.[285]

It is important that a woman is a virgin upon marriage in order to maintain the family honor. Prior to modern times men were bound to kill the offending woman. Presently, she would likely be banished to a town or city where she is not known.[286]

A male guardian can demand the annulment of a marriage if the woman failed to obtain his consent before marriage, or if the husband is not of the same social standing and the woman is not pregnant. A Muslim Syrian woman cannot marry a non-Muslim while a man can marry a non-Muslim. A husband can terminate paying support if his wife disobeys him. While a man can have four wives simultaneously, a woman can have one husband.[287]

If a woman obtains a job outside the home without prior permission from her husband, refuses sexual relations, or leaves the home without "justification," she surrenders all possible future financial support from her spouse.[288]

Under criminal law, a woman is punished twice as much for adultery compared to a man. Husbands may request a divorce on the basis of adultery. This claim is less successful for women.[289] In fact, a husband has the unilateral right to divorce his wife. Using *talaq*, by repeating "I divorce you" three times before the wife and a witness, a man can divorce his wife.[290] A man may divorce his wife for any reason.

For example, failure to produce a son may be used as grounds for divorcing a wife or taking a second wife.[291] In July 2003, the Syrian Court made a landmark ruling that confirmed that divorce by the Short Messaging System (SMS) was valid.[292] In that case a Syrian Judge ruled that an eighteen-month marriage was annulled when the husband sent his wife a text message that indicated that if she did not leave her parents home he would divorce her.[293] However, if a court rules that the *talaq* was arbitrary and impulsive, the husband may be ordered to support his wife for three years.[294] In addition, *talaq* does not count if it is said while drunk, or mentally or physically ill.[295] A woman who seeks a divorce must go to court and prove that her husband has abandoned his marital duties.[296] For instance, a woman can divorce her husband if he is mentally ill, if he does not give her financial support, or if he has been imprisoned for three years.[297] However, if a woman requests a divorce she runs the risk of not being permitted to obtain child support.[298]

Lastly, a husband may request that his wife be prohibited from going abroad, though this is rarely done.[299] Women are prohibited from traveling abroad with their children without their husband's permission.[300] Women must have proof that they have permission from their husband, regardless of whether the child is under full custody of the mother.[301]

In a divorce, the mother can have custody of her son(s) until the age of nine and daughter(s) until the age of eleven. Under some circumstances, a girl can remain in her mother's custody until she marries, and boys can remain with the mother if the child's father is deemed by the court to not be worthy of trust.[302]

Abortion and Contraceptives

Abortions are only allowed to save the life of the mother. Authorization for an abortion must be issued by two physicians. Under the Penal Code there are no stated exceptions to the general prohibition of abortion. Nevertheless, abortions may be performed to save the life of the woman under the general criminal law principles of necessity. A person who performs an abortion is subject to one to three years' imprisonment. A woman who induces her own abortion is subject to six months to three years' imprisonment. Penalties may be reduced if the abortion was induced to preserve the honor of a descendant or a relative to the second degree. A study in 1981 revealed that 9.6 percent of pregnancies result in abortion.[303]

The government gives direct support on contraceptive use. The Syrian Family Planning Association began providing family planning services in 1974.[304] The total fertility rate is 3.5 births per woman (2005 est.).[305] In 2003, contraceptive use, both traditional and modern, among married women was 36 percent.[306]

Health Care

Under Articles 46 and 47 of the Constitution, each citizen is entitled to health services, treatment, and medication.[307] Medical care is provided for boys and girls until age eighteen.[308]

There are both private and public health care systems. While wealthy individuals pay for private health care, those who live in rural areas have less access to health care.[309]

Services at government facilities are free for all citizens. Measles vaccinations are compulsory and free. Government employees and their dependents receive partially or fully covered private health care and pharmaceutical coverage.[310]

Women in Public Office

Women received the right to vote and to stand for election in 1949.[311] The first year a woman was appointed or elected to Parliament was 1973.[312]

Women held 10.4 percent of the seats in Parliament in 2002.[313] In 2004, women held 30 seats out of 250 (12 percent).[314] There were two female cabinet members.[315] Women hold 11.1 percent of the employment positions at the ministerial level.[316] There has been one female ambassador that has served the Syrian government.[317]

Women in the Military

Men have compulsory military service for thirty months (2004).[318] Although women are not obligated to serve in the military, some do.[319] Women were actively recruited for military service in the 1970s.[320] Presently, women are employed in more public relations type positions as opposed to military positions.[321]

NOTES

1. CIA World Factbook, Egypt, <http://www.cia.gov/cia/publications/factbook/geos/eg.html>.

2. UN Statistics Division, "Statistics and Indicators on Women and Men," 8 Mar. 2005, <http://unstats.un.org/unsd/demographic/products/indwm/indwm2.htm> (May 2005).

3. CIA World Factbook, Egypt.

4. Bahira Sherif, "Egypt: Multiple Perspectives on Women's Rights," *Women's Rights: A Global View*, ed. Lynn Walters (Westport, CT: Greenwood Press, 2001).

5. Country Reports on Human Rights Practices, 2003, Egypt, U.S. Department of State, released by the Bureau of Democracy, Human Rights, and Labor, Feb. 25, 2004, <http://www.state.gov/g/drl/rls/hrrpt/2003/27926.html> (Aug. 2004).

6. Ibid.

7. Ibid.

8. Sherif, "Egypt: Multiple Perspectives on Women's Rights."

9. Human Rights Watch, World Report 2002, Women's Human Rights, 2002, <http://www.hrw.org/wr2k2/women.html> (Sep. 2003).

10. Country Reports on Human Rights Practices, 2003, Egypt, U.S. Department of State.

11. Ibid.

12. CIA World Factbook, Egypt.

13. Ibid.

14. Sherif, "Egypt: Multiple Perspectives on Women's Rights."

15. UN Statistics Division, "Statistics and Indicators on Women and Men."

16. Sherif, "Egypt: Multiple Perspectives on Women's Rights."

17. Ibid.

18. "Law on Maternity Leave in the Private Sector, Egypt," International Labour Organization, 20 June 2002, <http://www.ilo.org/public/english/employment/gems/eeo/law/egypt/l_mlp.htm> (July 2004).

19. Sherif, "Egypt: Multiple Perspectives on Women's Rights."

20. Ibid.

21. Country Reports on Human Rights Practices, 2003, Egypt, U.S. Department of State.

22. Ashraf Khalil, "Egypt's First Female Judge May Remain 'The Only,'" *Women's E News*, 23 Sept. 2003, <http://www.womenenews.org/article.cfm/dyn/aid/1536/context/archive> (Oct. 2004).

23. Country Reports on Human Rights Practices, 2003, Egypt, U.S. Department of State.

24. Ibid.

25. Ibid.

26. Human Development Reports, United Nations Development Programme, 2003, <http://www.undp.org/hdr2003/indicator/cty_f_EGY.html> (Jan. 2005).

27. Country Reports on Human Rights Practices, 2003, Egypt, U.S. Department of State.

28. Human Development Reports, United Nations Development Programme.

29. Country Reports on Human Rights Practices, 2003, Egypt, U.S. Department of State.

30. Ibid.; United Nations Educational, Scientific and Cultural Organization (UNESCO), "Progress of the World's Women 2002: Volume 2: Gender Equality and the Millennium Development Goals," United Nations Development Fund for Women (UNIFEM), 2002, <http://www.unifem.org/www/resources/progressv2/index.html> (July 2004).

31. UNESCO, "Progress of the World's Women 2002."

32. Ibid.

33. Ibid.

34. Ibid.

35. Human Development Reports, United Nations Development Programme.

36. Ibid.

37. Country Reports on Human Rights Practices, 2003, Egypt, U.S. Department of State.

38. Rita J. Simon and Howard Altstein, *Global Perspectives on Social Issues: Marriage and Divorce* (Lanham, MD: Rowman & Littlefield Publishing Group, Inc., 2003).

39. Simon and Altstein, *Global Perspectives on Social Issues*.

40. Sherif, "Egypt: Multiple Perspectives on Women's Rights."

41. Simon and Altstein, *Global Perspectives on Social Issues*.

42. Country Reports on Human Rights Practices, 2003, Egypt, U.S. Department of State.

43. Simon and Altstein, *Global Perspectives on Social Issues*.

44. "Women in Egypt Want Broader Divorce Rights: Wide Coalition Pushed for Legal Equity," *The Washington Post*, April 14, 2000, pp. A16, A17.

45. Simon and Altstein, *Global Perspectives on Social Issues*.

46. Sherif, "Egypt: Multiple Perspectives on Women's Rights."

47. Ibid.

48. Simon and Altstein, *Global Perspectives on Social Issues*.

49. Sherif, "Egypt: Multiple Perspectives on Women's Rights."

50. Simon and Altstein, *Global Perspectives on Social Issues.*

51. Sherif, "Egypt: Multiple Perspectives on Women's Rights."

52. Ibid.

53. Ibid.

54. "Abortion Policies, A Global Review, Egypt," United Nations, <http://www.un.org/esa/population/publications/abortion/profiles.htm> (Aug. 2003).

55. Ibid.; Rita J. Simon, *Abortion: Statutes, Policies, and Public Attitudes the World Over* (Westport, CT: Greenwood Press, 1998).

56. "Abortion Policies, A Global Review, Egypt," United Nations.

57. Simon, *Abortion: Statutes, Policies, and Public Attitudes the World Over.*

58. "Abortion Policies, A Global Review, Egypt," United Nations.

59. Christopher Walker, "Abortions are Illegal and Common in Egypt," *Women's E News*, 12 April 2004, <http://www.womenenews.org/article.cfm/dyn/aid/1785/context/archive> (May 2004).

60. Simon, *Abortion: Statutes, Policies, and Public Attitudes the World Over.*

61. UN Statistics Division, "Statistics and Indicators on Women and Men."

62. Simon, *Abortion: Statutes, Policies, and Public Attitudes the World Over.*

63. Women in Development Network (WIDNET), Statistics—Asia & Pacific, Focus International, <http://www.focusintl.com/statangl.htm> (April 2004).

64. Ibid.

65. CIA World Factbook, Egypt.

66. Human Development Reports, United Nations Development Programme.

67. Constitution of the Arab Republic of Egypt, Universidad Autonoma de Madrid (UAM), Medina Project, <http://www.uam.es/otroscentros/medina/egypt/egypolcon.htm> (Dec. 2004).

68. Christian A Gericke, "Comparison of Health Care Financing Arangements in Egypt and Cuba: Lessons for Health Reform in Egypt," Berlin University of Technology, March 2004, <http://www.ww.tu-berlin.de/diskussionspapiere/2004/dp03-2004.pdf> (April 2004).

69. Paul Schemm, "Egypt May Soon Permit Women to Confer Citizenship," *Women's E News*, 3 Nov. 2003, <http://www.womenews.org/article.cfm/dyn/aid/1597/context/archive> (Dec. 2004).

70. Human Development Reports, United Nations Development Programme.

71. Ibid.

72. Country Reports on Human Rights Practices, 2003, Egypt, U.S. Department of State.

73. "Women in National Parliaments," Inter-Parliamentary Union, 2004, <http://www.ipu.org/wmn-e/classif.htm>.

74. UNESCO, "Progress of the World's Women 2002."

75. Human Development Reports, United Nations Development Programme.

76. The U.S. Library of Congress, Country Studies, Egypt, 1988, <http://countrystudies.us/egypt/> (Nov. 2003).

77. Human Development Reports, United Nations Development Programme.

78. CIA World Factbook, Egypt.

79. Ibid.

80. Ziba Mir-Hosseini, "Iran: Emerging Feminist Voices," *Women's Rights A Global View*, ed. Lynn Walter (Westport, CT: Greenwood Press, 2001).

81. UN Statistics Division, "Statistics and Indicators on Women and Men," 8 Mar. 2005, <http://unstats.un.org/unsd/demographic/products/indwm/indwm2.htm> (May 2005).

82. CIA World Factbook, Iran, <http://www.cia.gov/cia/publications/factbook/geos/ir.html>.

83. Mir-Hosseini, "Iran: Emerging Feminist Voices."

84. Ibid.; Islamic Republic of Iran Constitution, Iran Online, <http://www.iranonline.com/iran/iran-info/Government/constitution.html> (Nov. 2004).

85. Islamic Republic of Iran Constitution, Iran Online.

86. Mir-Hosseini, "Iran: Emerging Feminist Voices."

87. CIA World Factbook, Iran.

88. Country Reports on Human Rights Practices, 2002, Iran, U.S. Department of State, released by the Bureau of Democracy, Human Rights, and Labor, March 31, 2003, <http://www.state.gov/g/drl/rls/hrrpt/2002/18276.htm> (Aug. 2004).

89. Mir-Hosseini, "Iran: Emerging Feminist Voices."

90. Country Reports on Human Rights Practices, 2002, Iran, U.S. Department of State.

91. Mir-Hosseini, "Iran: Emerging Feminist Voices."

92. Country Reports on Human Rights Practices, 2002, Iran, U.S. Department of State.

93. Mir-Hosseini, "Iran: Emerging Feminist Voices."

94. Country Reports on Human Rights Practices, 2002, Iran, U.S. Department of State.

95. Mir-Hosseini, "Iran: Emerging Feminist Voices."

96. "Iranian Women Now Inherit All—Not Part—of Husbands' Assets," Peace Women, June 2004, <http://www.peacewomen.org/news/Iran/June04/assets.html> (July 2004).

97. CIA World Factbook, Iran.

98. Ibid.

99. Country Reports on Human Rights Practices, 2002, Iran, U.S. Department of State.

100. Mir-Hosseini, "Iran: Emerging Feminist Voices."

101. Women in Development Network (WIDNET), Statistics—Asia & Pacific.

102. Country Reports on Human Rights Practices, 2002, Iran, U.S. Department of State.

103. Ibid.

104. Human Development Reports, United Nations Development Programme, 2003, <http://www.undp.org/hdr2003/indicator/cty_f_IRN.html> (Jan. 2005).

105. Angela Melchiorre,"At What Age are school children employed, married and taken to court," Iran, Right to Education Project, 2004, Second Edition, <http://www.right-to-education.org/content/age/iran.html> (Jan. 2005).

106. Islamic Republic of Iran Constitution, Iran Online.

107. Mir-Hosseini, "Iran: Emerging Feminist Voices."

108. United Nations Educational, Scientific and Cultural Organization (UNESCO), "Progress of the World's Women 2002: Volume 2: Gender Equality and the Millennium Development Goals," United Nations Development Fund for Women (UNIFEM), 2002, <http://www.unifem.org/www/resources/progressv2/index.html> (July 2004).

109. UNESCO, Education, <http://portal.unesco.org/education/> (Sep. 2003).

110. UNESCO, "Progress of the World's Women 2002."

111. Women in Development Network (WIDNET), Statistics—Asia & Pacific.

112. Human Development Reports, United Nations Development Programme.

113. Ibid.

114. Simon and Altstein, *Global Perspectives on Social Issues*.

115. Country Reports on Human Rights Practices, 2002, Iran, U.S. Department of State.

116. Mir-Hosseini, "Iran: Emerging Feminist Voices."

117. Country Reports on Human Rights Practices, 2002, Iran, U.S. Department of State.

118. Mir-Hosseini, "Iran: Emerging Feminist Voices."

119. Country Reports on Human Rights Practices, 2002, Iran, U.S. Department of State.

120. Country Reports on Human Rights Practices, 2003, Iran, U.S. Department of State, released by the Bureau of Democracy, Human Rights, and Labor, Feb. 25, 2004, <http://www.state.gov/g/drl/rls/hrrpt/2003/27927.htm> (Aug. 2004).

121. International Events in 2002, *The Hindu*, <http://www.hinduonnet.com/revents/02/20020200.htm> (June 2004).

122. Simon and Altstein, *Global Perspectives on Social Issues*.

123. Country Reports on Human Rights Practices, 2003, Iran, U.S. Department of State.

124. Country Reports on Human Rights Practices, 2002, Iran, U.S. Department of State.

125. Simon and Altstein, *Global Perspectives on Social Issues*.

126. Country Reports on Human Rights Practices, 2002, Iran, U.S. Department of State.

127. Women in Development Network (WIDNET), Statistics—Asia & Pacific; "Abortion Policies, A Global Review, Iran," United Nations, <http://www.un.org/esa/population/publications/abortion/profiles.htm> (Aug. 2003).

128. Simon, *Abortion: Statutes, Policies, and Public Attitudes the World Over*.

129. Ibid.

130. Mir-Hosseini, "Iran: Emerging Feminist Voices."

131. Women in Development Network (WIDNET), Statistics—Asia & Pacific.

132. UN Statistics Division, "Statistics and Indicators on Women and Men."

133. Simon, *Abortion: Statutes, Policies, and Public Attitudes the World Over*.

134. CIA World Factbook, Iran.

135. Women in Development Network (WIDNET), Statistics—Asia & Pacific.

136. Islamic Republic of Iran Constitution, Iran Online.

137. Laila al-Marayati, "Discourse needed on Islam interpretation of rights," *Los Angeles Times*, 16 May 1998.

138. Human Development Reports, United Nations Development Programme.

139. Ibid.

140. Country Reports on Human Rights Practices, 2002, Iran, U.S. Department of State.

141. UNESCO, "Progress of the World's Women 2002."

142. Country Reports on Human Rights Practices, 2002, Iran, U.S. Department of State.

143. Human Development Reports, United Nations Development Programme; "Women in National Parliaments," Inter-Parliamentary Union, 2004, <http://www.ipu.org/wmn-e/classif.htm>.

144. Human Development Reports, United Nations Development Programme.

145. CIA World Factbook, Iran.

146. The U.S. Library of Congress, Country Studies, Iran, 1988, <http://countrystudies.us/iran/> (Nov. 2003); "Iran: Source and Quality of Manpower," 1987, <http://www.country-data.com/cgi-bin/query/r-6525.html>.

147. Ibid.

148. Human Development Reports, United Nations Development Programme.

149. CIA World Factbook, Israel, <http://www.cia.gov/cia/publications/factbook/geos/is.html>.

150. Women in Development Network (WIDNET), Statistics—Asia & Pacific.

151. UN Statistics Division, "Statistics and Indicators on Women and Men," 8 Mar. 2005, <http://unstats.un.org/unsd/demographic/products/indwm/indwm2.htm> (May 2005).

152. Chava Frankfort-Nachmias, "Israel: The Myth of Gender Equality," *Women's Rights: A Global View*, ed. Lynn Walters (Westport, CT: Greenwood Press, 2001).

153. CIA World Factbook, Israel.

154. Country Reports on Human Rights Practices, 2003, Israel and the occupied territories, U.S. Department of State, released by the Bureau of Democracy, Human Rights, and Labor, Feb. 25, 2004, <http://www.state.gov/g/drl/rls/hrrpt/2003/27929.htm> (Aug. 2004).

155. Frankfort-Nachmias, "Israel: The Myth of Gender Equality."

156. Country Reports on Human Rights Practices, 2003, Israel and the occupied territories, U.S. Department of State.

157. Frankfort-Nachmias, "Israel: The Myth of Gender Equality."

158. CIA World Factbook, Israel.

159. Country Reports on Human Rights Practices, 2003, Israel and the occupied territories, U.S. Department of State.

160. CIA World Factbook, Israel.

161. "Women in Israel," Jewish Virtual Library, A Division of The American–Israeli Cooperation Enterprise, 2004, <http://www.jewishvirtuallibrary.org/jsource/Society_&_Culture/women2004.html> cited from *Jerusalem Post*, 19 November 2004.

162. Israel Women's Network "Women in the Economy and the Labor Force in Israel," Women in Israel—Comendium of Data and Information 2002, <http://www.iwn .org.il/pdf%5Cch4sub1eng.pdf>, 83 (Oct. 2004).

163. CIA World Factbook, Israel.

164. UN Statistics Division, "Statistics and Indicators on Women and Men."

165. Frankfort-Nachmias, "Israel: The Myth of Gender Equality."

166. Ibid.

167. CIA World Factbook, Israel.

168. Frankfort-Nachmias, "Israel: The Myth of Gender Equality."

169. Country Reports on Human Rights Practices, 2003, Israel and the occupied territories, U.S. Department of State.

170. Frankfort-Nachmias, "Israel: The Myth of Gender Equality."

171. Ibid.

172. Women in Development Network (WIDNET), Statistics—Asia & Pacific.

173. Frankfort-Nachmias, "Israel: The Myth of Gender Equality."

174. Country Reports on Human Rights Practices, 2003, Israel and the occupied territories, U.S. Department of State.

175. Ibid.

176. Ibid.

177. Frankfort-Nachmias, "Israel: The Myth of Gender Equality."

178. Ibid.

179. Ibid.

180. Ibid.

181. Ibid.

182. Human Development Reports, United Nations Development Programme, 2003, <http://www.undp.org/hdr2003/indicator/cty_f_ISR.html> (Jan. 2005).

183. Ibid.

184. Israel Women's Network, Equal Opportunities at Work for Pregnant Women, The Knesset approved an amendment prohibiting an employer to discriminate against a female worker on the basis of pregnancy, <http://www.iwn.org.il/iwn.asp ?subject=dbmarquee.mdb&id=41&topic=IWN%20UPDATES> (Nov. 2005).

185. UN Statistics Division, "Statistics and Indicators on Women and Men."

186. Frankfort-Nachmias, "Israel: The Myth of Gender Equality."

187. Ibid.

188. Country Reports on Human Rights Practices, 2003, Israel and the occupied territories, U.S. Department of State.

189. Gideon Alon, "MKs okay bill to shut down brothel," *Daily Action*, 17 Oct. 2004, <http://www.bambili.com/bambili_news_en/katava_main.asp?news_id=2353 &sivug_id=3> (Nov. 2004).

190. Case Law in Israel—Supreme Court, International Labour Organization, 20 June 2002, <http://www.ilo.org/public/english/employment/gems/eeo/law/israel/cl _sc.htm> (July 2004).

191. Zvi Zrahiya, "Retirement age for women to rise gradually to 62," *Site News*, 1 March 2004, <http://www.bambili.com/bambili_news_en/katava_main.asp?news _id=1445> (April 2004).

192. Country Reports on Human Rights Practices, 2003, Israel and the occupied territories, U.S. Department of State.

193. Angela Melchiorre, "At What Age are school children employed, married and taken to court," Israel, Right to Education Project, 2004, Second Edition, <http://www .right-to-education.org/content/age/israel.html> (Jan. 2005).

194. Frankfort-Nachmias, "Israel: The Myth of Gender Equality;" United Nations Educational, Scientific and Cultural Organization (UNESCO), "Progress of the World's Women 2002: Volume 2: Gender Equality and the Millennium Development Goals," United Nations Development Fund for Women (UNIFEM), 2002, <http://www.unifem.org/www/resources/progressv2/index.html> (July 2004).

195. Ibid.

196. Ibid.

197. "Women in Israel," Jewish Virtual Library.

198. Women in Development Network (WIDNET), Statistics—Asia & Pacific.

199. Human Development Reports, United Nations Development Programme.

200. UNESCO Institute of Statistics, <http://portal.unesco.org/education/>.

201. Angela Melchiorre,"At What Age are school children employed, married and taken to court."

202. Simon and Altstein, *Global Perspectives on Social Issues*.

203. "World Divorce Statistics," *Divorce Magazine*, <http://www.divorcemag .com/statistics/statsWorld.shtml>; cited from Infoplease, Americans for Divorce Reform (May 2004).

204. Frankfort-Nachmias, "Israel: The Myth of Gender Equality."

205. Ibid.

206. Ibid.

207. Simon and Altstein, *Global Perspectives on Social Issues*.

208. Frankfort-Nachmias, "Israel: The Myth of Gender Equality."

209. Simon and Altstein, *Global Perspectives on Social Issues*.

210. Country Reports on Human Rights Practices, 2003, Israel and the occupied territories, U.S. Department of State.

211. CIA World Factbook, Israel.

212. Women in Development Network (WIDNET), Statistics—Asia & Pacific.

213. Frankfort-Nachmias, "Israel: The Myth of Gender Equality."

214. Maternity Benefits, National Insurance Institute of Israel, <http://www.btl .gov.il/English/newbenefits/maternity.htm> (Nov. 2005).

215. Frankfort-Nachmias, "Israel: The Myth of Gender Equality."

216. Women in Development Network (WIDNET), Statistics—Asia & Pacific.

217. Ibid.

218. "Abortion Policies, A Global Review, Israel," United Nations, <http://www .un.org/esa/population/publications/abortion/profiles.htm> (Aug. 2003).

219. Simon, *Abortion: Statutes, Policies, and Public Attitudes the World Over*.

220. Ibid.

221. Ibid.

222. "Israel—Contraceptive prevalence, any method," Israel—Globalis, 2004, <http://globalis.gvu.unu.edu/indicator_detail.cfm?IndicatorID=128&Country=IL>.

223. National Family Planning & Reproductive Health Association, Emergency Contraception is just that, Contraception, 30 June 2004, <http://www.nfprha.org/pac/factsheet/ecps.asp> (July 2004).

224. Israel—Globalis, 2003, <http://globalis.gvu.unu.edu/country.cfm?Country=IL>.

225. Mordechai Shani, "Israel has Rx for U.S. Healthcare," Physicians for a National Health Program, 10 September 2004, <http://www.pnhp.org/news/2004/september/israel_has_rx_for_us.php> (Oct. 2004).

226. "The Health Care System in Israel, A Historical Perspective," Israel Ministry of Foreign Affairs, The State of Israel, 26 June 2002, <http://www.mfa.gov.il/MFA/History/Modern%20History/Israel%20at%2050/The%20Health%20Care%20System %20in%20Israel-%20An%20Historical%20Pe> (July 2004).

227. Shani, "Israel has Rx for U.S. Healthcare."

228. Human Development Reports, United Nations Development Programme.

229. "Women's History Timeline, 1960–1969," Woman's Hour, BBC Radio 4, <http://www.bbc.co.uk/radio4/womanshour/timeline/1960.shtml> (May 2004).

230. Frankfort-Nachmias, "Israel: The Myth of Gender Equality."

231. UNESCO, "Progress of the World's Women 2002."

232. "Women in Israel," Jewish Virtual Library.

233. UN Statistics Division, "Statistics and Indicators on Women and Men."

234. Human Development Reports, United Nations Development Programme.

235. Frankfort-Nachmias, "Israel: The Myth of Gender Equality."

236. Country Reports on Human Rights Practices, 2003, Israel and the occupied territories, U.S. Department of State.

237. Frankfort-Nachmias, "Israel: The Myth of Gender Equality."

238. Ibid.; Cecile S. Landrum, "The Israeli Fighting Women: Myth and Fact," *Air & Space Power Chronicles*, 25 Oct. 2002, cited from *Air University Review*, Nov.–Dec. 1978, <http://www.airpower.maxwell.af.mil/airchronicles/aureview/1978/nov-dec/landrum.html> (Nov. 2004).

239. Frankfort-Nachmias, "Israel: The Myth of Gender Equality."

240. Landrum, "The Israeli Fighting Women: Myth and Fact."

241. Frankfort-Nachmias, "Israel: The Myth of Gender Equality."

242. CIA World Factbook, Syria, <http://www.cia.gov/cia/publications/factbook/geos/sy.html>.

243. UN Statistics Division, "Statistics and Indicators on Women and Men," 8 Mar. 2005, <http://unstats.un.org/unsd/demographic/products/indwm/indwm2.htm> (May 2005).

244. CIA World Factbook, Syria.

245. Ibid.

246. Country Reports on Human Rights Practices, 2003, Syria, U.S. Department of State, released by the Bureau of Democracy, Human Rights, and Labor, Feb. 25, 2004, <http://www.state.gov/g/drl/rls/hrrpt/2003/27938.htm> (Aug. 2004).

247. Country Reports on Human Rights Practices, 2003, Syria, U.S. Department of State.

248. Universität Bern, Constitution of Syria, International Constitutional Law, Jan. 2004, <http://www.oefre.unibe.ch/law/icl/sy00000_.html> (Feb. 2004).

249. Country Reports on Human Rights Practices, 2003, Syria, U.S. Department of State.

250. "Syria Clamps Down on Kurds," *BBC News*, 3 June 2004, <http://faculty-staff.ou.edu/L/Joshua.M.Landis-1/syriablog/2004/06/syria-clamps-down-on-kurds.htm> (July 2004); "Syria, the Silenced Kurds," *Human Rights Watch* 8, no. 4 (Oct. 1996), <http://hrw.org/reports/1996/syria.htm> (July 2004).

251. Country Reports on Human Rights Practices, 2003, Syria, U.S. Department of State.

252. Ibid.

253. "Syria, the Silenced Kurds."

254. CIA World Factbook, Syria.

255. UN Statistics Division, "Statistics and Indicators on Women and Men."

256. "Syrian Women Constitute 20 Percent of the Labor Force," Financial and Business, Syria Live, 23 Dec. 2001, <http://www.syrialive.net/financial/2001/122301 Syrian%20women%20constitute%2020%20percent%20of%20the%20labor%20force .htm> (Jan. 2005).

257. Human Development Reports, United Nations Development Programme, 2003, <http://www.undp.org/hdr2003/indicator/cty_f_SYR.html> (Jan. 2005).

258. Country Reports on Human Rights Practices, 2003, Syria, U.S. Department of State.

259. UN Statistics Division, "Statistics and Indicators on Women and Men."

260. "Decree no. 156 of 1976 on the implementation of article 139, pertaining to nurseries for children of women workers—Syria," International Labour Organization, 5 Dec. 2003, <http://www.ilo.org/public/english/employment/gems/eeo/law/syria/ act2.htm> (Jan. 2004).

261. Country Reports on Human Rights Practices, 2003, Syria, U.S. Department of State.

262. Economic Research Forum (ERF), Female Participation in Labor Force, Economic Trends in the MENA Region, 1998, <http://www.erf.org.eg/html/body-chap52.html> (July 2004).

263. "Gender: Syria," Programme on Governance in the Arab Region, United Nations Development Programme, <http://www.pogar.org/countries/gender.asp?cid=19> (March 2004).

264. Ibid.

265. "Syria—International Religious Freedom Report, 2004," released by the Bureau of Democracy, Human Rights, and Labor, Syria, <http://www.state.gov/g/drl/rls/ irf/2004/35508.htm>.

266. Country Reports on Human Rights Practices, 2003, Syria, U.S. Department of State.

267. Angela Melchiorre, "At What Age are school children employed, married and taken to court," Syria, Right to Education Project, 2004, Second Edition, <http://www.right-to-education.org/content/age/syria.html> (Jan. 2005).

268. Country Reports on Human Rights Practices, 2003, Syria, U.S. Department of State.

269. "Syria: Health & Education," Encyclopaedia of the Orient, LexicOrient, <http:// i-cias.com/e.o/syria_3.htm> (March 2004).

270. "Syria–International Religious Freedom Report, 2004."

271. Country Reports on Human Rights Practices, 2003, Syria, U.S. Department of State.

272. Angela Melchiorre, "At What Age are school children employed, married and taken to court."

273. Human Development Reports, United Nations Development Programme.

274. United Nations Educational, Scientific and Cultural Organization (UNESCO), "Progress of the World's Women 2002: Volume 2: Gender Equality and the Millennium Development Goals," United Nations Development Fund for Women (UNIFEM), 2002, <http://www.unifem.org/www/resources/progressv2/index.html> (July 2004).

275. Human Development Reports, United Nations Development Programme.

276. Universität Bern, Constitution of Syria.

277. Country Reports on Human Rights Practices, 2003, Syria, U.S. Department of State.

278. Human Rights Watch, World Report 2002, Women's Human Rights, 2002, <http://www.hrw.org/wr2k2/women.html> (Sep. 2003).

279. Emory University, "Syria," Islamic Family Law, <http://www.law.emory.edu/IFL/legal/syria.htm> (March 2004).

280. Angela Melchiorre, "At What Age are school children employed, married and taken to court."

281. Emory University, "Syria."

282. Country Reports on Human Rights Practices, 2003, Syria, U.S. Department of State.

283. Ibid.; The U.S. Library of Congress, Country Studies, Syria, 1988, <http://countrystudies.us/syria/> (Nov. 2003).

284. Ibid.

285. Ibid.

286. Ibid.

287. Human Rights Watch, World Report 2002, Women's Human Rights, 2002, <http://www.hrw.org/wr2k2/women.html> (Sep. 2003).

288. The U.S. Library of Congress, Country Studies, Syria; Emory University, "Syria."

289. Country Reports on Human Rights Practices, 2003, Syria, U.S. Department of State.

290. Human Rights Watch, World Report 2002, Women's Human Rights, 2002, <http://www.hrw.org/wr2k2/women.html> (Sep. 2003).

291. The U.S. Library of Congress, Country Studies, Syria.

292. Leela Jacinto, "I D4C U," *ABC News*, 1 Sept. 2004; AMAN News, <http://www.amanjordan.org/english/daily_news/wmview.php?ArtID=4813> (Oct. 2004).

293. Human Rights Watch, World Report 2002, Women's Human Rights, 2002, <http://www.hrw.org/wr2k2/women.html> (Sep. 2003); International Human Rights Commission, Women's Human Rights, World Reports 2002, <http://www.geocities.com/shahidkpk/women_2002.html> (March 2004); Jacinto, "I D4C U."

294. Ibid.

295. Ibid.

296. Human Rights Watch, World Report 2002, Women's Human Rights, 2002, <http://www.hrw.org/wr2k2/women.html> (Sep. 2003).

297. Emory University, "Syria."

298. Country Reports on Human Rights Practices, 2003, Syria, U.S. Department of State.

299. "Travel Considerations for Syria," Real Adventures, cited from U.S. State Department, <http://www.realadventures.com/listings/1024517.htm> (March 2004).

300. Country Reports on Human Rights Practices, 2003, Syria, U.S. Department of State.

301. Ibid.; "Travel Considerations for Syria," Real Adventures.

302. Emory University, "Syria," Real Adventures.

303. UN, "Abortion Policies: A Global Review."

304. Ibid.

305. CIA World Factbook, Syria.

306. "Syria—Contraceptive Prevalence: Any Method," Globalis—Syria, <http://globalis.gvu.unu.edu/indicator_detail.cfm?country=SY&indicatorid=128> (Jan. 2005); UN Statistics Division, "Statistics and Indicators on Women and Men."

307. Constitution of Syria.

308. Country Reports on Human Rights Practices, 2003, Syria, U.S. Department of State.

309. Citizenship and Immigration Canada, "Looking at Health Care, Syria," Cultural Profiles Project, <http://www.cp-pc.ca/english/syria/index.html> (Jan. 2005).

310. Ibid.

311. Human Development Reports, United Nations Development Programme; "Gender: Syria," Programme on Governance in the Arab Region.

312. Human Development Reports, United Nations Development Programme.

313. UNESCO, "Progress of the World's Women 2002."

314. Country Reports on Human Rights Practices, 2003, Syria, U.S. Department of State; UN Statistics Division, "Statistics and Indicators on Women and Men."

315. Country Reports on Human Rights Practices, 2003, Syria, U.S. Department of State.

316. Human Development Reports, United Nations Development Programme.

317. "Gender: Syria," Programme on Governance in the Arab Region.

318. CIA World Factbook, Syria.

319. Country Reports on Human Rights Practices, 2003, Syria, U.S. Department of State; "Syrian Arab Army," Global Security, <http://www.globalsecurity.org/military/world/syria/army.htm> (March 2004).

320. "Gender: Syria," Programme on Governance in the Arab Region.

321. "Syrian Arab Army," Global Security.

Chapter Five

Africa

GHANA

Ghana is located in Western Africa. It borders the Gulf of Guinea and is located between Togo and Cote d'Ivoire. The population of Ghana is 20,757,032 (2004 est.).[1]

The ethnic groups are: Black African 98.5 percent (the major tribes are: Akan 44 percent; Moshi-Dagomba 16 percent; Ewe 13 percent; Ga 8 percent; Gurma 3 percent; and Yoruba 1 percent), European and other 1.5 percent (1998). The major religions are Christianity (63 percent), indigenous sects (21 percent), and Islam (16 percent).[2]

English is the official language, although many speak African languages such as Akan, Moshi-Dagomba, Ewe, and Ga.[3] There are 101 women for every 100 men. Life expectancy at birth is age fifty-nine for women and fifty-six for men.[4]

Constitution

Ghana, which was created from the merger of the British colony of the Gold Coast and the Togoland trust territory, became the first country in colonial Africa to gain its independence. It did so in 1957. The Constitution was adopted in 1992. The government is a constitutional democracy. The legal system is based on English common law and customary law.[5]

Women and men have the right to vote at eighteen years of age.[6]

The Constitution addresses the status of women, sex discrimination, inheritance of spouses and children, marriage, and customary practices. Ghana's national population policy is intended to eliminate "laws that discriminate on the

185

basis of sex and harmful cultural practices . . . [and promote] women's education and employment."[7] Yet, women still face discrimination.

Statutory law reforms grant men and women equal rights to inheritance, however, judges have continued to apply customary law.[8]

Rural women can be forced out of their village by traditional village authorities (i.e., a shaman) if it is believed that they are a witch or they are pregnant out of wedlock. Although the Criminal Code protects women accused of witchcraft, women who are accused may be sent to penal villages or camps. Accused women are usually older widows who are blamed by other villagers for crop failure, illness, financial misfortune, or other difficulties.[9]

Chiefs oversee and enforce tribal laws that include marriage, divorce, property disputes, and child custody. The Criminal Code prohibits forced marriages.[10]

Work Force and Economy

Ghana has the purchasing power parity of $44.44 billion (2004 est.).[11]

The labor force is made up of 10 million people (2004 est.). The unemployment rate is 20 percent. Thirty-one percent of Ghanaians are living below the poverty line (1992 est.).[12]

Under Article 27 of the Constitution, men and women are granted equal rights in regard to training and promotion.[13]

Under the Constitution women are granted paid maternity leave.[14] The length of maternity leave is twelve weeks, 50 percent of which is paid by employers.[15] Under Article 27 of the Constitution, childcare is provided for children who are not old enough to attend school so that mothers, "who have the traditional care for children, realize their full potential."[16]

Financial return for experience is less for women than for men.[17] The estimated earned income for women is $1,802 (U.S.) compared to $2,419 for men.[18] Women earn 57 percent of what their male counterparts earn.[19] The female economic activity rate is 79.9 percent.[20]

Women hold more administrative positions and fewer managerial positions than men.[21] Women make up 67 percent of manufacturing employees and 85 percent of employees in wholesale and retail trading.[22]

Education

Public expenditure on education is 5 percent of the GDP.[23]

Under the Constitution, all people have the right to equal educational opportunities.[24]

Under the Education Act, basic education is supposed to be free and compulsory for all children between ages six and fifteen.[25] Education is compulsory for primary through junior secondary school (grades 1 to 9). However, education is not free. Government regulations state that schools can charge parents no more than $10 (U.S.) per term. Yet, parents are charged $50 per term. Additionally, parents are also required to purchase books and school uniforms. In response the government required that all fees above $10 be refunded to parents. Furthermore, bills for secondary schools now go through the District Directors of education before going to parents.[26]

There is a high female drop out rate. Presently, 77 percent of eligible female children are enrolled in primary school compared to 84 percent of boys. Forty-five percent of girls compared to 55 percent of boys are enrolled in junior secondary school (12 to 14 years).[27] Women make up less than half of the male student body at the University level (40 percent).[28] Enrollment of both boys and girls is significantly lower in rural areas. There are frequent reports of female students having been sexually harassed by male teachers and male classmates.[29]

In 2002, the ratio of female to male youth literacy (ages fifteen to twenty-four) is 95 women for every 100 men.[30] The female youth literacy rate in 2002 was 89.9 percent compared to 82.6 percent in 1995.[31] Literacy for women age fifteen and over is 67.1 percent and 82.7 percent for men.[32]

Marriage

Polygamy is commonly practiced. Marriages are often arranged or approved by senior kinsmen and the fathers of the potential husband and wife. Women in polygamous marriages do not inherit any of their husband's property except for gifts given to her by her husband. In Matrilineal marriages, where women continue to live at their maternal home, women and men inherit from their mother's family.[33]

The government respects both customary and common-law marriage and divorce practices. Many citizens are married under customary law as opposed to common law.[34] Between 1986 and 1992, 33 percent of married women were living in polygamous relationships.[35] The Customary Marriage and Divorce Registration Amendment Law of 1991 made the registration of customary law marriages or divorces optional rather than mandatory. Article 32 of the Constitution states, that, "no spouse may be deprived of a reasonable provision out of the estate of a spouse." This is chiefly designed to protect widows from being deprived of inheritance from their deceased husbands. In addition, the Criminal Code prohibits practices that "harass or penalize spouses whose husband or wife has recently died, and an individual who does so will be charged with a misdemeanor."[36]

The court may grant a divorce if it concludes that there has been an irreparable breakdown of the marriage (Matrimonial Cause Act, 1971).[37] The court determines child custody by taking into consideration the child(ren)'s best interest. The parent that is most capable of providing for the child's education and maintenance is usually granted custody.[38]

The government regulates the property rights of spouses in order to "ensure equal access to jointly acquired property and equal division of such property upon divorce" (Article 22 of the Constitution). The Intestate Succession Law of 1985 states that when a man dies intestate, "the surviving spouse receives three-sixteenths of the estate, the children receive nine-sixteenth, the parent receives one-eighth and the customary family receives one-eighth. If the decedent has no children one-half goes to the spouse, one-quarter to the surviving parent and one-quarter to the customary family." However, women do not normally obtain full control over the property to which they are entitled.[39]

Abortion and Contraceptives

Under the 1985 abortion law, abortions are legal in Ghana in order to save the life of the mother, to preserve the physical or mental health of the mother, if the pregnancy results from rape or incest, or if there is fetal impairment.[40] An abortion cannot be performed for economic or social reasons nor are abortions available upon request. Those who perform or aid in illegal abortions are subject to up to five years' imprisonment. An abortion must be performed by a registered physician. The doctor must have the consent of the mother. The abortion must be performed in a Government approved facility. Despite the legalization of abortions the lack of facilities and resources limit the access women have to obtain an abortion.[41]

Until 1985, abortions were governed by the Criminal Code of 1960. Abortions were illegal and could only be performed for medical or surgical treatment for the woman. The terms and restrictions were vague. Anyone who attempted to cause an abortion, including the woman herself, would be subject to ten years imprisonment.[42]

The Government gives direct support for contraceptive use.[43] In 1993, the percentage of married women in the procreating age group that used modern contraceptives was 20 percent.[44] In 2003, the contraceptive use for married women is 25.2 percent.[45] The fertility rate dropped from 6.4 (births per woman) in 1988 to 5.2 (births per woman) in 2000.[46] The number of births for 1,000 women between the ages fifteen and nineteen years in 1996 was 97. Although illegal, female genital mutilation is estimated at 15 to 30 percent.[47] Female genital mutilation [FGM] is a social practice that usually results in the removal of clitoris and some part of the labia [usually the labia minor].[48]

Health Care

The public health expenditure is 2.8 percent of the GDP. The private health expenditure is 1.9 percent of the GDP.[49]

Medical services are provided by the government, private clinics, missionaries, and traditional practices. People in rural areas have less access to medical services.[50]

Infectious diseases are a major problem.[51] The HIV/AIDS prevalence rate is 3.1 percent (2003 est.). There were 30,000 deaths that were HIV/AIDS related in 2003.[52]

Many people turn to both modern and traditional forms of medicine. Herbalists and Spiritualists are an important source of health care.[53]

Presently, the Government is creating national health insurance so that citizens will not have to pay for medical services or medicine. The system that has been in place is one in which patients had to pay for their medicine and likely other medical services.[54]

Women in Public Office

Women obtained the right to vote and stand for election in 1954. The first woman appointed to Parliament was in 1960.[55]

Eight percent of parliamentary seats were occupied by women in 1994.[56] In 2005, women made up nine percent of parliamentary seats. Women made up 8.6 percent of the employees at the ministerial level.[57]

Women in the Military

The expenditure on the military is 0.6 percent of the GDP.[58] Male Ghanaians must serve two years of national service. Women do not have to fulfill national service, but some women do serve in the military.[59] All employees must pass a physical examination and be at least eighteen years old.[60] Women are predominantly in administrative positions.[61] Military manpower is maintained by voluntary enlistment.[62]

Women were introduced to the army in 1957. Women make up roughly 2 percent of the military personnel. Women hold both officer and other ranks. However, the majority of women are in the nursing corps or the communication sector of the military. Women are also employed in the education, public relations, the military police and transportation sectors of the military.[63]

Advancement procedures are the same for men and women. However, people in the nursing corps have limited advancement potential.[64]

Recruits are required to have obtained at least a middle school or junior
secondary school education. This automatically reduces the number of
women compared to men since more men than women attend secondary
school.[65]
Women may not participate in combat.[66]

KENYA

Kenya is located in eastern Africa. It borders the Indian Ocean and is located
between Tanzania and Somalia. Kenya has a population of 32,021,856
(2004). The ethnic groups are Kikuyu (22 percent), Luhya (14 percent), Luo
(13 percent), Kalenjin (12 percent), Kamba (11 percent), Kisii (6 percent),
Meru (6 percent), other African ethnicities (12 percent); non-African (Asian,
European, and Arab) make up 1 percent. Forty-five percent of Kenyans are
Protestant, 33 percent are Roman Catholic, 10 percent follow indigenous beliefs, 10 percent are Muslim, and other religions together make up 2 percent.
English and Kiswahili are the official languages, although there are numerous
indigenous languages.[67]
Life expectancy for women at birth is 45.1 years compared to 44.79 for
men (2004 est.).[68] There are roughly 102 women for every 100 men.[69]

Constitution

Kenya gained independence from the United Kingdom in 1963.[70] Kenya is a
republic. Its legal system is based on Kenyan statutory law, Kenyan and English common law, tribal law, and Islamic law. Judicial review takes place in
the High Court.[71]
The Constitution, adopted in 1963, grants women and men equal protection. While the Constitution prohibits discrimination on the basis of sex,
women continue to face discrimination. Men, not women, can pass on their
citizenship to their child(ren). In addition, a married woman must gain her
husband's consent before she can obtain a national identity card and passport.
Unmarried women do not need male consent to obtain their identity card or
passport.[72]
Kenyan law states that women and men have equal inheritance rights. Yet,
women often receive less inheritance or are excluded from inheritance settlements all together. In most ethnic populations, under customary law, a woman
cannot inherit land. Presently, women possess 6 percent of land titles.[73]
The president, Mwai Kibaki, is head of government and chief of state.[74]
When he first became president he stated that a new Constitution would be in

place within the first one hundred days of his presidency. In January 2005, the one-hundred-day mark passed with no new constitution.[75]

Conflict between political parties is at the heart of the delay. The conflict is regarding the creation of a prime minister position and the altering of presidential powers that would result.[76]

In November 2005, the draft constitution was rejected by Kenyan voters. The draft constitution offered more rights to women. In fact, under the draft constitution, women are able to automatically pass their citizenship to their children. In addition, it granted women equal opportunities to men in regards to economic, cultural and political areas. In addition, customs, laws, culture, or tradition could not undermine the dignity, welfare, status or interests of women or men. Lastly, the draft constitution stated that it would protect women's rights and take into account a woman's unique status and natural maternal role in society.[77]

Work Force and Economy

The purchasing power parity is $33.03 billion (2004 est.). The labor force is 11.45 million (2004 est.). The unemployment rate is at 40 percent (2001 est.). Fifty percent of Kenyans live below the poverty line (2000 est.).[78] Female involvement in the labor force is 74.7 percent.[79]

While women have become active in urban small businesses they have difficulty moving into nontraditional fields. They are also promoted less often and are fired more often than men.[80] Women made up 83 percent of informal employment and 33 percent of self-employment in non-agricultural employment in 2000. Today, women make up 67 percent of the wages in non-agricultural informal employment.[81] Women earn 84 percent of what their male counterparts earn in non-agricultural employment.[82] The estimated earned income for women is $962 (U.S.) compared to $1,067 for men (90 percent). This makes Kenya one of the top nations, in terms of equality of wages between genders, in the world.[83]

Women are given two months of maternity leave, 100 percent of which is paid by the employer.[84]

Education

Public expenditure on education is 6.2 percent of the GDP.[85]

It is rare for women to have secondary education and as such they often are unable to get better paying jobs and positions of responsibility.[86] Only 28 percent of secondary school age girls are enrolled in school.[87] Female illiteracy for women twenty-five and older in 1990 was 54.2 percent compared to 26 percent for men.[88] If they are found to have become pregnant, many women are kicked out of school.[89]

Today, 78.5 percent of adult women are literate compared to 90 percent of men.[90]

Marriage

Kenya is made up of a diversity of religions and cultures. Consequently, a number of different family law systems exist.[91]

Under statutory law, the minimum age to marry is eighteen. Under Islamic law, a woman may marry at the age of puberty. That means that a girl can marry at as young as nine or eleven years of age.[92]

Most people are governed by some combination of customary and religious law. Under customary law, a marriage is an alliance between two families, that of the husband and wife. A dowry is common in a customary law marriage.[93]

Polygamous marriages are recognized under customary law. Unmarried cohabiting couples and polyandrous relationships are not acknowledged under customary law.[94]

In some areas wife inheritance is practiced. This is a practice whereby a widow becomes the responsibility of a male member of her husband's family. If a brother-in-law is unable to take the widow, she then becomes the responsibility of a cousin-in-law, or a family friend of her husband's family. Under this tradition, it was formerly taboo for the man to have conjugal relations with an inherited widow. However, it is no longer taboo. Some widows are widowed because their husband died of AIDS. Consequently, this tradition has contributed to the spread of AIDS.[95]

Parental Responsibilities

Custody of young children is ordinarily granted to the mother, except among Muslims. Under Islamic law, the mother is awarded custody of sons under the age of seven and girls under the age of nine.[96]

A child born out of wedlock is the sole responsibility of the mother. The child's mother must provide all of the child's necessities, including education. However, the father of a woman who bears a child out of wedlock may apply for pregnancy compensation from the father of the child under customary law. The amount, however, only covers a small portion of the medical expenses related to the birth of a child.[97] Presently, under the Affiliation Act, women can sue for child support.[98]

Separation and Divorce

Under statutory law, a person can apply for divorce after three years of marriage. A person can also apply for a divorce earlier on the grounds of: "exceptional depravity or hardship."[99]

A woman can sue her husband on grounds of cruelty, adultery, mental illness or desertion. A wife may also sue for divorce on grounds of rape, sodomy, or bestiality.[100]

A husband may sue for damages from a man having an adulterous relationship with his wife. Contrarily, a wife has no right to sue a woman for having an adulterous relationship with her husband.[101]

Under Islamic law, a husband can instantly divorce his wife by stating three *talaqs* ("I divorce thee"). After the *talaqs* are stated, a woman loses all maintenance. In addition, a Muslim woman is unable to divorce her husband without his consent.[102]

Also a woman's right to separation and divorce depends on whether she was in a monogamous or polygamous marriage. The rights of women in a monogamous marriage are much greater than those of women in a polygamous marriage.[103]

In addition to granting a divorce, courts are empowered to order the husband to pay alimony to the wife. Under Islamic law, mothers normally do not get alimony beyond 3 months after divorce.[104]

Abortion and Contraceptives

Kenya permits abortion if the mother's life is in danger or to preserve the physical or mental health of the mother. In addition, an abortion may be performed if there is fetal impairment, or if the pregnancy is the result of rape or incest. An abortion cannot be performed for economic or social reasons. It must be performed by a certified physician with the consent of the woman and her husband.[105] It must be performed in a hospital after two medical opinions have been obtained, one of which must be from the physician who is treating her and the other from a psychiatrist.[106]

Abortions account for over 20 percent of maternal deaths.[107]

The fertility rate in Kenya has dropped from 8.1 (births per woman) between the years 1970 to 1975 to 4 (births per woman) between the years 2000 to 2005.[108]

Kenya has a low contraceptive use rate. Contraceptives are not widely accessible. Contraceptive use is roughly 39.3 percent.[109] A woman must obtain the consent of her husband before having voluntary sterilization.[110]

Female genital mutilation is estimated at 38 percent or higher.[111]

Health Care

The public health expenditure is 1.7 percent of the GDP while the private health expenditure is 6.2 percent of the GDP.[112] The government, churches, spiritual and holistic healers, volunteers, and private groups provide health services. Health care is expensive. Consequently, many do not seek medical attention until they are seriously ill.[113] The adult HIV prevalence rate is 6.7 percent (2003 est.).[114] There are twice as many women than men who are HIV positive.[115] Many doctors and health care providers are underpaid. In addition, in many areas there is a lack of medicine.[116]

Women in Public Office

In 1963, women obtained the right to vote, without restriction. The first year a woman was appointed and elected to Parliament was 1969.[117]

Kenyan women held 3.6 percent of the seats in the national parliament in November 2002 compared to three percent in 1999.[118] This placed Kenya in the lowest 5 percent of the world in regard to women's share of seats in national parliaments.[119] As of December 2002, there were fifteen women (nine elected and six nominated) in the national assembly that is composed of 222 seats (7.1 percent).[120] There are three female ministers and three female assistant ministers.[121] Women make up 1.4 percent of employees at the ministerial level.[122]

Women in the Military

Some women do participate in the military. February 2002 was the first time in Kenyan's naval history that a female officer, Lt. Regina Ndinda Musau, was on board a Kenyan ship that was taking part in military simulation maneuvers. In addition, there were six women who were soldiers in the infantry during the maneuvers. Women have yet to participate in actual combat.[123]

NIGERIA

Nigeria is located in western Africa. It borders the Gulf of Guinea and is between Cameroon, Niger, Chad, and Benin. Nigeria has a population of 137,253,133 with more than 250 ethnic groups (2004 est.). The majority groups are Hausa and Fulani that make up 29 percent, Yoruba (21 percent), Igbo (Ibo) (18 percent), Ijaw (10 percent), Kanuri (4 percent), Ibibio (3.5 percent), Tiv (2.5 percent), and other (12 percent). The major religions in Nigeria are Muslim (50 percent), Christianity (40 percent), and indigenous religions (10 percent).[124] The majority of Christians live in the south, while the majority of Muslims live in the northern part of the country.[125] English is the official language, although Hausa, Yoruba, Igbo (Ibo), and Fulani are also spoken.[126]

There are 99 women for every 100 men.[127] The life expectancy at birth for women is 52 years and 51.2 for men.[128]

Constitution

Nigeria gained independence from the United Kingdom on October 1, 1960. The present Constitution was adopted in 1999, after the end of sixteen years of military rule. The government is a republic transitioning from military to civilian rule. The legal system is based on English common law, Islamic Shari' a law (in some northern states), and traditional law.[129] The president is Olusegun Obasanjo.[130]

The Constitution prohibits discrimination based on gender, political opinion, ethnic groups, religion, community, or place of origin. However, discrimination against women continues to exist.[131] A woman's testimony, before a court, is given less credence than a man's testimony.[132] In Shari'a courts the testimony of women or non-Muslims is given less weight.[133]

While, legally, women must obtain permission from a male family member before being able to obtain a passport the law is not frequently enforced.[134]

Women do not have the same rights as men in regard to inheritance and property rights. In addition, it is difficult for women to obtain credit.[135] In 1997, the Supreme Court granted women equal inheritance rights to those of men. Regardless of the Supreme Court ruling, judges have continued to apply customary law to inheritance cases involving women.[136]

Nigerian men, not women, can pass on their citizenship to their spouse.[137]

Under statutory law, women may own land. However, under customary law, they cannot own land. On occasion, women can obtain land through marriage or family.[138]

Men and women are often segregated in healthcare and transportation.[139]

Both women and men are eligible to vote at eighteen years of age.[140]

Work Force and Economy

Nigeria has a purchasing power parity of $114.8 billion (2004 est.). It has a labor force of. 54.36 million (2004 est.).[141] The unemployment rate is 2.7 percent (2004 est.).[142] Sixty percent of the population lives below the poverty line (2000 est.).[143]

Under the Constitution, Article 17, women and men are granted equal pay for equal work. While discrimination on the basis of gender is prohibited,[144] women do not receive equal pay for equal work.[145] The estimated income for women is $562 (U.S.) compared to $1,322 for men (43 percent). The female economic activity rate is 47.8.[146]

The number of women in the business sector is continually increasing.[147] In addition, the number of women in the areas of politics, armed forces, medicine, law, and education also continues to increase.[148] However, some businesses or employers fire a woman when they learn she is pregnant.[149]

Maternity leave is twelve weeks, 50 percent of which is paid by employers.[150] Women in the south have more access to political, professional, and influential positions compared to the north.[151]

Education

Public expenditure on education is 0.9 percent of the GDP (1990 est.).[152]

"When practical," the Constitution, under Article 18, states that the government "must provide free, compulsory, and universal primary, secondary, university education, and an adult literacy program." However, free and universal education is rarely provided.[153] Girls in rural areas have less access to education while girls in the south have more access to education.[154]

The female to male youth literacy rate (ages fifteen to twenty-four) in 2002 was 95 women to every 100 men. The female youth literacy rate was 86.1 percent in 2002 compared to 76 percent in 1995.[155] In 2000, the illiteracy rate of women was 15.7 percent compared to 10.4 percent of men compared to 1970 where the illiteracy rate was 78.6 percent and 49.9 percent respectively.[156] In 2002, the adult literacy rate was 59.4 percent for women and 74.4 percent for men.[157]

Some areas enforce a dress code for students. Under Shari'a law, which exists in the State of Zamfara in Northern Nigeria, female high school students may not wear skirts or Western forms of dress.[158] Female high school students must also wear hijabs. Students who fail to follow the dress code may be subject to public flogging.[159]

Marriage

The median age of marriage (first marriage) for women is eighteen.[160]

There are three types of marriages in Nigeria: religious, customary, and civil. All three regulate matters dealing with marriage, divorce, and child custody. Nine traditionally Muslims northern states have adopted Islamic law.

Polygamy and early marriage (early teens) are recognized by both religious and customary marriages. In 1999, 36 percent of all married women were in polygamous marriages.[161]

Under the Penal Code, husbands may use physical force to discipline their wives. The force may not cause facial disfigurement, loss of sight, hearing, speech, or life threatening injuries.[162]

Women are often unable to inherit their husband's property.[163]

Some widows, predominantly in eastern Nigeria, have to endure confinement that can last from weeks to a year. Under confinement, a widow is required to shave her head, dress in black, and live with other restrictions.[164]

Some widows face wife inheritance.[165] Under this practice, a widow becomes the responsibility of a male member of her husband's family. If a brother in law is unable to take the widow, she then becomes the responsibility of a cousin in law, or a family friend of her husband's family. Under this tradition, it was formerly taboo for the man to have conjugal relations with an inherited widow. However, it is no longer taboo.[166]

A woman may sue for divorce as an adult if she was married as a minor.[167] The court is at liberty to decide whether maintenance will be granted.

A man may divorce if his wife has committed adultery. However, adultery committed by a husband is not grounds for divorce. A divorced woman accused of adultery cannot receive maintenance.

Women believed to have committed adultery were sometimes sentenced to harsh punishments by courts.[168]

Abortion and Contraceptives

Although abortions are illegal, Nigeria recorded 600,000 unsafe abortions in 1998. This gives Nigeria one of the highest unsafe abortion rates in the world. Northern and southern Nigeria have different abortion laws. Both allow abortions to save the life of the mother. However, southern Nigeria allows an abortion in order to preserve the physical or mental health of the mother. In both regions a woman must get certification from two physicians that the birth poses a threat to her life. Under the Penal Code, a person who performs an illegal abortion is subject to up to fourteen years in prison and/or the payment of a fine. This applies to a woman who tries to abort her own fetus. Although the law states the existence of legal grounds for a woman to have an abortion, there are often severe consequences for the patient and the physician performing the abortion. Illegal abortions are increasing and are considered to be a major cause of the high Nigerian maternal mortality rate that is over 1,000 per 100,000 live births. In 1984, there were 500,000 illegal abortions performed during that year. Reports indicate that women fifteen to nineteen are at the greatest risk group for seeking an illegal abortion. In addition, there is a large social stigma for women who raise a child out of wedlock.[169]

Since 1988, the government has actively supported and promoted the availability and distribution of family planning services. Nevertheless, the availability of family planning services is still believed to be limited. In addition, the use of contraceptives is low.[170] The prevalence rate of modern contraceptive use is 15 percent (2003 est.).[171] The fertility rate is 5.32 births per woman (2004 est.).[172]

Female circumcision and genital mutilation are practiced. Nearly half of all women between the ages of 45 and 49 have been circumcised. The rate of circumcisions for women, under the age of thirty, has dropped to 25 percent.[173]

Health Care

Nigeria has one of the lowest health budgets in Africa. The public health expenditure is 0.8 percent of the GDP. The private health expenditure is 2.6 percent of the GDP.[174]

While the Constitution ensures that all persons are entitled to adequate health and medical facilities, there is limited access. In addition, the quality of facilities and health services is low.[175]

The HIV/AIDS adult prevalence rate is 5.4 percent (2003 est.).[176] It is estimated that twice as many women are infected as men.[177]

Women in Public Office

Women obtained the right to vote and stand for election in 1958.[178] Women occupied 3.2 percent of the seats in the national parliament in 2002, placing Nigeria in the bottom 5 percent for women's share of seats in national parliaments.[179] Women occupy 6.4 percent of the seats in the House and 3.7 percent of the seats in the Senate.[180] Women make up 22.6 percent of the employees at the ministerial level.[181]

Some political parties waive filing fees for women seeking political office in order to encourage women to participate.[182]

Women in the Military

One point one percent of the GDP is spent on the military.[183]

While women make up roughly 30 percent of the military personnel, few women are in high-ranking positions.[184] The highest ranking women in 1984 were one Army colonel, one Air Force wing commander, and one Navy com-

mander, all in the medical corps. In 1989, the navy announced that it was sus-
pending recruitment of women, except nurses, until adequate and appropriate
conditions of service had been devised, such as accommodations, training,
promotions, and authorization for marriages and pregnancies.[185]

SOUTH AFRICA

South Africa is located at the southernmost tip of Africa. The bordering countries are Botswana, Lesotho, Mozambique, Namibia, Swaziland, and Zim-
babwe. The population is 42,718,530. The major ethnicities are Black (75.2
percent), White (13.6 percent), mixed Black and White (8.6 percent), and Indian (2.6 percent). The major religions are Christian (68 percent), Indigenous
and Animist (28.5 percent), Muslim (2 percent), and Hindu (1.5 percent).
There are eleven official languages in South Africa, including Afrikaans, English, Ndebele, Pedi, Sotho, Swazi, Tsonga, Tswana, Venda, Xhosa, and Zulu.[186]
    Life expectancy at birth for women is 51.9 years compared to 46 for
men.[187] There are 105 women for every 100 men.[188]

Constitution

South Africa gained independence from the United Kingdom on May 31, 1910.
Between 1910 and 1996 the Union of South Africa operated under a social policy of Apartheid that resulted in the official, and overt, separation of the races
in all areas including political, legal, and economic rights. In 1996, apartheid
was brought to an end. The result was a Black majority rule in the government.
The present constitution was signed by former President Nelson Mandela on
December 10, 1996. The Constitution became effective on February 3, 1997.[189]
    The Chief of State, President Thabo Mbeki, is in his second five-year term.[190]
    Under the Constitution, all persons are equal before the law and have the
right to equal protection.[191] The Constitution prohibits discrimination on the
basis of sex, race, ethnic or social origin, disability, age, color, culture, pregnancy, language, or marital status. Yet, discrimination in the areas of employment, family law, and property law continue to occur against women and
Blacks.[192]
    It is more difficult for women than men to obtain land or credit.[193]
    In 2003, the Black Administration Act was found to be unconstitutional and
discriminatory. The Act prevented Black women and Black children or illegitimate children from inheriting their parent's estate if there was no will in place.[194]
    The voting age for men and women is eighteen.[195]

Work Force and Economy

South Africa has the purchasing power parity of $456.7 billion (2003 est.). The percentage of South Africans that live below the poverty line is 50 percent (2000 est.). The labor force is made up of 16.35 million people (2003). The unemployment rate is 31 percent (2003 est.).[196] The majority of unemployed persons are Black.[197]

The wealthiest 20 percent of the population on average earn forty-five times more than the poorest 20 percent of the population. The wealthy are predominantly White while the poor are majority Black, a remnant of Apartheid. The majority of poor people are women, many of whom are Black.[198]

Fifty-eight percent of employed women work in informal employment in the non-agricultural sector and 27 percent of those women are self-employed. Seventy-three percent of the wages women earn is in informal employment compared to 77 percent of men.[199]

While discrimination against women in the work place is prohibited, it still occurs.[200]

New laws give full labor rights to male and female farm workers. But female farm workers are more likely to be temporary or seasonal workers than men. In addition, women do more menial labor. Employers view women's labor as a supplement to men's labor even when women work the same position and the same hours as men. Employers often deny female farm workers statutory maternity benefits.[201]

Women obtain twelve weeks of maternity leave, 45 percent of which is paid by unemployment insurance.[202]

Under labor laws, employers are required to take appropriate measures when they learn of an instance of sexual harassment. Aggressors can face disciplinary sanctions and/or criminal and civil charges.[203] Regardless, sexual harassment continues to be a problem.[204]

The female labor activity rate is 47.3 percent.[205] Women do not earn equal wages for equal work regardless of the fact that women tend to be educated more than men by one to two years.[206] The estimated female income is $6,371 (U.S.) and $14,202 for men (women earn 44.85 percent of men).[207]

In companies with 150 or more employees women make up 18 percent of those in senior management positions. Women make up the majority of employees in the welfare and health fields.[208]

Education

Public expenditure on education is 5.7 percent of the GDP.[209] Education is compulsory for children age seven to fifteen. There is a higher drop out rate for girls than boys. In addition, fewer women pass lower secondary school than men.[210]

The ratio of female to male enrollment in secondary schools is 110 women to every 100 men. Female enrollment in secondary education is 95 percent.[211] The female to male ratio of student enrollment in tertiary school is 123 women for every 100 men.[212]

The ratio of male to female youth (ages fifteen to twenty-four) literacy is 100 percent. The female youth literacy rate was 91.7 percent compared to 89.9 percent in 1995.[213] The adult literacy rate for women is 85.3 percent and 86.7 percent for men.[214]

Marriage

The government has sole authority for passing laws regulating marriage and matrimonial causes.[215] Individuals under the age of twenty-one require permission from their parents.[216] In addition, boys from fourteen to eighteen and girls twelve to fifteen require permission from the High Court or Minister of Home Affairs. Boys under fourteen and girls under twelve cannot marry.[217] The average age for men to marry is 28.9 compared to 26.8 for women.[218]

Under the Customary Marriage Act, existing customary marriages, both polygamous and monogamous, are recognized as valid and should be registered with the government. Under the Act, traditional marriages are fully acknowledged and constitutional protections are extended to protect women and children who are involved in customary unions. Previous to the Act, wives and children of untraditional marriages were considered illegitimate and denied legal inheritance rights.[219]

Under the existing law, all assets are shared equally by a couple unless this right is waived by either party in a prenuptial agreement. A decree by the court is needed to dissolve a customary marriage. A woman who does not want to be in a polygamous marriage may dissolve her marriage when her husband takes an additional wife. The Act also prohibits the tradition of forcing a widow to marry the brother of her deceased husband. The Act does not extend to marriages contracted under other religious customs, such as those of Hinduism or Islam.[220]

The Matrimonial Act of 1984 guarantees that the poorer spouse may claim an amount equal to half of the difference between the values of the two estates. This is to insure that the poorer spouse, most likely female, would acquire or inherit an amount from her deceased or estranged husband proportionate with the length of the marriage.[221]

Under Section 3 of the Divorce Act of 1979, a marriage may be dissolved if there is an irretrievable breakdown of the marriage or if one party to the marriage is affected by mental illness or is in a coma. The court will not grant a divorce until it is satisfied that the provisions made for the welfare of the children are satisfactory, and an advocate has been appointed who has submitted his/her report and recommendation. The court always awards custody according to the best interest of the children. Custody is usually given to the mother. If the children are able to offer an opinion as to which parent should be awarded custody, the court will consider their wishes. In common law, the parent that has not been awarded custody has the right of reasonable access to the children. In addition, this parent must pay child support until the child can support himself/herself. The court may also award spousal support. The court will consider the spouses' earning capacities, financial needs, and obligations. In addition, the court will consider their ages, the duration of the marriage, their standard of living prior to divorce, their conduct relative to their marriage's breakdown, and the type of asset division they are entitled to.[222]

Abortion and Contraceptives

Abortions are legal in South Africa. An abortion may be performed to save the life of the woman, to preserve her physical or mental health, if the pregnancy resulted from rape or incest, if there is fetal impairment or because of economic or social reasons. Abortions are available on request. The abortion must be performed by a physician in a government hospital or other approved medical institution. An abortion requires the approval of two independent physicians other than the physician performing the abortion. One of the independent physicians must be a psychiatrist if the abortion is being performed on mental health grounds. One of the physicians must be a district surgeon if the pregnancy resulted from rape or incest. The independent physicians may not assist in the abortion. Abortions for rape, incest or intercourse with a mentally challenged woman cannot be granted without a certificate from the local magistrate.[223]

The total fertility rate is 2.18 births per woman.[224] Forty-eight percent of married women use modern contraceptives. The government supports family planning services. Contraceptives are provided free of charge at all government medical institutions.[225] Contraceptive prevalence is 56 percent.[226]

Health Care

Until 1990, Blacks received lesser quality health care than Whites purely on the basis of race. Today, the social policy has altered. Presently, persons of all races legally have the right to equal health care. But there is still a divide between the quality of health care that Blacks receive compared to Whites. This is because the wealthy, who are primarily White, have access to superior private health care while the poor, predominantly Black, do not.[227]

The public health expenditure is 3.6 of the GDP. The private health expenditure is 5.1 percent of the GDP.[228] Under the Constitution, everyone has the right to have access to health care services when there are adequate resources.[229]

The HIV prevalence rate is 21.5 percent.[230] For pregnant women, the HIV prevalence rate is 26.5 percent.[231] There are 5.3 million people living with HIV/AIDS (2003 est.).[232]

Pregnant women and children under six years of age receive free health care. Children in primary school in poorer areas receive free food. In addition, poor urban areas have access to community health centers. Those living in rural areas have less access to health care. Many people turn to folk medicine to cure ailments.[233]

Women in Public Office

Women obtained the right to vote and the right to stand for election in 1994.[234]

Women occupied 30 percent of the seats in the national parliament in 2002.[235] Today, women make up 32.75 percent of the seats in Parliament.[236] Women make up 32.3 percent of the seats in provincial legislatures.[237] Women make up 38.1 percent of the employees at the ministerial level.[238] Women make up 50 percent of the persons in deputy ministerial positions.[239]

Women in the Military

Two percent of the GDP is spent on the military.[240] South African women have long participated in the military. Women served in supporting roles in the South African Defense Force ('SADF') in World War I and World War II. Presently, women are primarily assigned to administrative positions. Women may not serve in combat positions and hold few leadership positions.[241]

NOTES

1. CIA World Factbook, Ghana, <http://www.cia.gov/cia/publications/factbook/geos/gh.html>.

2. Ibid.

3. Ibid.

4. UN Statistics Division, "Statistics and Indicators on Women and Men," 8 Mar. 2005, <http://unstats.un.org/unsd/demographic/products/indwm/indwm2.htm> (May 2005).

5. CIA World Factbook, Ghana.

6. Ibid.

7. Rita J. Simon and Howard Altstein, *Global Perspectives on Social Issues: Marriage and Divorce* (Lanham: Rowman & Littlefield Publishing Group, Inc., 2003).

8. Human Rights Watch, World Report 2002, Women's Human Rights, 2002, <http://www.hrw.org/wr2k2/women.html> (Sep. 2003).

9. Country Reports on Human Rights Practices, 2002, Ghana, U.S. Department of State, released by the Bureau of Democracy, Human Rights, and Labor, February 25, 2004, <http://www.state.gov/g/drl/rls/hrrpt/2003/27730.htm> (Dec. 2004).

10. Country Reports on Human Rights Practices, 2002, Ghana, U.S. Department of State.

11. CIA World Factbook, Ghana.

12. Ibid.

13. Ghana Review International (GRi), Constitution of Ghana, chapter 5, Fundamental Human Rights and Freedoms, 1992, <http://www.ghanareview.com/parlia/Gconst5.html> (Dec. 2004).

14. Ibid.

15. UN Statistics Division, "Statistics and Indicators on Women and Men."

16. Ghana Review International (GRi), Constitution of Ghana.

17. Dorte Verner, "Wage and Productivity Gaps: Evidence from Ghana," Centre for the Study of African Economies, 20 Jan. 2000, <http://www.csae.ox.ac.uk/conferences/2000-OiA/pdfpapers/verner2.pdf>.

18. Human Development Reports, United Nations Development Programme, 2003, <http://hdr.undp.org/reports/global/2004/pdf/hdr04_HDl.pdf> (Dec. 2005).

19. Verner, "Wage and Productivity Gaps."

20. Human Development Reports, United Nations Development Programme.

21. Verner, "Wage and Productivity Gaps."

22. The World Bank Group, "Ghana: Women's role in improved economic performance," Africa Region Findings, no. 145 (Oct. 1999), <http://www.worldbank.org/afr/findings/english/find145.htm> (Dec. 2004).

23. Country Reports on Human Rights Practices, 2002, Ghana, U.S. Department of State.

24. Ibid.; Angela Melchiorre, "At What Age are school children employed, married and taken to court," Ghana, Right to Education Project, 2004, Second Edition, <http://www.right-to-education.org/content/age/ghana.html> (Jan. 2005).

25. Ibid.

26. Country Reports on Human Rights Practices, 2002, Ghana, U.S. Department of State.

27. Ibid.

28. Ibid.; United Nations Educational, Scientific and Cultural Organization (UNESCO), Education, <http://portal.unesco.org/education/> (Dec. 2004).

29. Country Reports on Human Rights Practices, 2003, Ghana.

30. UNESCO, Education.

31. United Nations Educational, Scientific and Cultural Organization (UNESCO), "Progress of the World's Women 2002: Volume 2: Gender Equality and the Millennium Development Goals," United Nations Development Fund for Women (UNIFEM), 2002, <http://www.unifem.org/www/resources/progressv2/index.html> (Dec. 2004).

32. CIA World Factbook, Ghana.

33. The U.S. Library of Congress, Country Studies, Ghana, 1988, <http://countrystudies.us/ghana/> (Dec. 2004).

34. Simon and Altstein, *Global Perspectives on Social Issues*.

35. Women in Development Network (WIDNET), Statistics—Africa, Focus International, <http://www.focusintl.com/statangl.htm> (April 2004).

36. Simon and Altstein, *Global Perspectives on Social Issues*.

37. Between 1986 and 1992, 33 percent of married women were living in polygamous relationships. Simon and Altstein, *Global Perspectives on Social Issues*.

38. Ibid.

39. Ibid.

40. "Abortion Policies, A Global Review, Ghana," United Nations, <http://www.un.org/esa/population/publications/abortion/profiles.htm> (Dec. 2004).

41. Ibid.

42. Ibid.

43. Ibid.

44. Arjun Adlakha, "Population Trends: Ghana," International Brief, U.S. Department of Commerce, July 1996, <http://www.census.gov/ipc/prod/ib96_01.pdf> (Nov. 2005).

45. Globalis, "Ghana—Contraceptive prevalence, any method, 2003, <http://globalis.gvu.unu.edu/indicator_detail.cfm?country=GH&indicatorid=128> (Dec. 2004).

46. "Abortion Policies, A Global Review, Ghana," United Nations.

47. Arjun Adlakha, "Population Trends: Ghana;" Country Reports on Human Rights Practices, 2002, Ghana, U.S. Department of State.

48. Definition of infibulation available at <http://www.nationmaster.com/encyclopedia/Infibulation>.

49. Human Development Reports, United Nations Development Programme.

50. Citizenship and Immigration Canada, "Looking at Health Care, Ghana," Cultural Profiles Project, <http://www.settlement.org/cp/english/ghana/health.html> (Dec. 2004).

51. Felicity Smith, "Reflections on Health Care in Ghana," *The Pharmaceutical Journal* 268, (1 June 2002): 768.

52. CIA World Factbook, Ghana.

53. Smith, "Reflections on Health Care in Ghana."

54. Ibid.

55. Human Development Reports, United Nations Development Programme.

56. Women in Development Network (WIDNET), Statistics—Africa; UNESCO, "Progress of the World's Women 2002."

57. Human Development Reports, United Nations Development Programme.

58. Ibid.

59. CIA World Factbook, Ghana.

60. Photius Coutsoukis, "Ghana Manpower," cited from The U.S. Library of Congress; CIA World Factbook, <http://www.photius.com/countries/ghana/economy/ghana_economy_manpower.html> (Dec. 2004).

61. The U.S. Library of Congress, Country Studies, Ghana.

62. Ibid.

63. Mercy Adoley Yebuah, "Women and the Military: The Ghanaian Case," Universitetet i Bergen, <http://ugle.svf.uib.no/admorg/default.asp?strId=1897&kategori=425> (Dec. 2004).

64. Ibid.

65. Coutsoukis, "Ghana Manpower."

66. Yebuah, "Women and the Military: The Ghanaian Case."

67. CIA World Factbook, Kenya, <http://www.cia.gov/cia/publications/factbook/geos/ke.html>.

68. Ibid.

69. UN Statistics Division, "Statistics and Indicators on Women and Men," 8 Mar. 2005, <http://unstats.un.org/unsd/demographic/products/indwm/indwm2.htm> (Dec. 2004).

70. Newsletter, Growth Through Learning 7, (Fall 2001), <www.growththroughlearning.org/Newsletters/f01.html> (Dec. 2004).

71. CIA World Factbook, Kenya.

72. Country Reports on Human Rights Practices, 2003, Kenya, U.S. Department of State, released by the Bureau of Democracy, Human Rights, and Labor, February 25, 2004, <http://www.state.gov/g/drl/rls/hrrpt/2003/27733.htm> (Nov. 2004).

73. Ibid.

74. CIA World Factbook, Kenya.

75. Joyce Mulama, "Challenges 2004–2005: The Kenyan Constitution that Wasn't," Terraviva Africa, 3 Jan. 2005, <http://www.ipsterraviva.net/Africa/viewstory.asp?idnews=12> (Jan. 2005).

76. Ibid.

77. "Kenyans reject new constitution," *BBC News*, 22 Nov. 2005, <http://news.bbc.co.uk/1/hi/world/africa/4455538.stm> (Nov. 2005); Kenya Constitution, "The Draft Constitution of Kenya 2004: Chapter 6," 2004, <http://www.kenyaconstitution.org/docs/chapter6.htm> (Dec. 2004).

78. CIA World Factbook, Kenya.

79. Human Development Reports, United Nations Development Programme, 2003, <http://www.undp.org/reports/global/2004/pdf/hdr04_HDI> (Nov. 2005).

80. Country Reports on Human Rights Practices, 2003, Kenya, U.S. Department of State.

81. United Nations Educational, Scientific and Cultural Organization (UNESCO), "Progress of the World's Women 2002: Volume 2: Gender Equality and the Millennium Development Goals," United Nations Development Fund for Women (UNIFEM), 2002, <http://www.unifem.org/www/resources/progressv2/index.html> (Nov. 2004).

82. United Nations Population Fund, "The State of the World Population," chapter 5, "Counting the Cost of Gender Inequality," 2000, <http://www.unfpa.org/swp/2000/pdf/english/chapter5.pdf> (Nov. 2004).

83. Human Development Reports, United Nations Development Programme.

84. UN Statistics Division, "Statistics and Indicators on Women and Men."

85. Human Development Reports, United Nations Development Programme.

86. UNESCO, "Progress of the World's Women 2002."

87. Ibid.

88. Women in Development Network (WIDNET), Statistics—Africa (April 2004).

89. Vicky W. Mucai-Kattambo, et al, "Law and the Status of Women in Kenya," International Environmental Law Research Centre, <http://www.ielrc.org/content/a9501.pdf> (Nov. 2004).

90. Human Development Reports, United Nations Development Programme.

91. Simon and Altstein, *Global Perspectives on Social Issues.*

92. Mucai-Kattambo, et al, "Law and the Status of Women in Kenya."

93. Simon and Altstein, *Global Perspectives on Social Issues.*

94. Ibid.

95. Stephen Buckley, "Wife Inheritance Spurs AIDS Rise in Kenya," *Washington Post*, 8 Nov. 1997, <http://www.washingtonpost.com/wp-srv/inatl/longterm/africanlives/kenya/kenya_aids.htm> (Nov. 2004).

96. Simon and Altstein, *Global Perspectives on Social Issues.*

97. Ibid.

98. Lynn M. Thomas, "Politics of the Womb: Reproduction and the State in Kenya," (Berkeley: University of California Press, 2003) 156.

99. Simon and Altstein, *Global Perspectives on Social Issues.*

100. Ibid.

101. Ibid.

102. Mucai-Kattambo, et al, "Law and the Status of Women in Kenya."

103. Ibid.

104. Simon and Altstein, *Global Perspectives on Social Issues.*

105. "Abortion Policies, A Global Review, Kenya," United Nations, <http://www.un.org/esa/population/publications/abortion/profiles.htm> (Dec. 2004).

106. Simon and Altstein, *Global Perspectives on Social Issues.*

107. Rita J. Simon, *Abortion: Statutes, Policies, and Public Attitudes the World Over* (Westport, CT: Greenwood Publishing Group, 1998).

108. Human Development Reports, United Nations Development Programme.

109. Globalis, "Kenya—Contraceptive prevalence, any method, 2003, <http://globalis.gvu.unu.edu/indicator_detail.cfm?country=KE&indicatorid=128> (Jan. 2005).

110. Mucai-Kattambo, et al, "Law and the Status of Women in Kenya."

111. Country Reports on Human Rights Practices, 2003, Kenya, U.S. Department of State.

112. Human Development Reports, United Nations Development Programme.

113. Citizenship and Immigration Canada, "Looking at Health Care, Kenya," Cultural Profiles Project, <http://www.settlement.org/cp/english/kenya/health.html> (Nov. 2004).

114. CIA World Factbook, Kenya.

115. "A Dose of Reality: Women's Rights in the Fight Against HIV/AIDS," Human Rights Watch, <http://hrw.org/english/docs/2005/03/21/africa10357.htm> (Nov. 2005).

116. Citizenship and Immigration Canada, "Looking at Health Care, Kenya."

117. Human Development Reports, United Nations Development Programme.

118. "Women in National Parliaments," Inter-Parliamentary Union, 2004, <http://www.ipu.org/wmn-e/classif.htm>; Women in Development Network (WIDNET), Statistics—Africa (April 2004).

119. UNESCO, "Progress of the World's Women 2002."

120. Country Reports on Human Rights Practices, 2003, Kenya, U.S. Department of State; Human Development Reports, United Nations Development Programme.

121. Country Reports on Human Rights Practices, 2003, Kenya.

122. Human Development Reports, United Nations Development Programme.

123. "Joint Military Exercises Kick Off in Tanzania," *The East African*, 11 Feb. 2002, <http://www.nationaudio.com/News/EastAfrican/18022002/Regional/Regional5 .html> (Dec. 2004).

124. CIA World Factbook, Nigeria, <http://www.cia.gov/cia/publications/factbook/ geos/ni.html> (Dec. 2004).

125. "Nigerian Index," Universität Bern, International Constitutional Law, 1999, <http://www.oefre.unibe.ch/law/icl/ni__indx.html> (August 2003).

126. CIA World Factbook, Nigeria.

127. UN Statistics Division, "Statistics and Indicators on Women and Men," 8 Mar. 2005, <http://unstats.un.org/unsd/demographic/products/indwm/indwm2.htm> (Oct. 2004).

128. Human Development Reports, United Nations Development Programme, 2003, <http://hdr.undp.org/reports/global/2004/pdf/hdr04_HDI.pdf> (Oct. 2004).

129. CIA World Factbook, Nigeria.

130. Country Reports on Human Rights Practices, 2003, Nigeria, U.S. Department of State, released by the Bureau of Democracy, Human Rights, and Labor, February 25, 2004, <http://www.state.gov/g/drl/rls/hrrpt/2003/27743.htm> (Oct. 2004).

131. Ibid.

132. Nigeria Country Report, Country Information and Policy Unit, Immigration and Nationality Directorate, April 2004, <http://www.ecoi.net/pub/panja1_02782nig .pdf> (Oct. 2004).

133. Country Reports on Human Rights Practices, 2003, Nigeria, U.S. Department of State.

134. Ibid.

135. Ibid.

136. Human Rights Watch, World Report 2002, Women's Human Rights, 2002, <http://www.hrw.org/wr2k2/women.html> (Sep. 2003).

137. Ada Okoye, "Sharing the Citizenship of Women: A Comparative Gendered Analysis of the Concept of 'Legal Personhood' in Africa," Africa Gender Institute, Gender and Women's Studies for Africa's Transformation (GWS), <http://www .gwsafrica.org/knowledge/ap3.html> (Oct. 2004).

138. Country Reports on Human Rights Practices, 2003, Nigeria, U.S. Department of State.

139. Ibid.

140. CIA World Factbook, Nigeria.

141. Ibid.

142. Applied Language Solutions, "Economy of Nigeria," Country Guides, <http:// www.appliedlanguage.com/country_guides/nigeria_country_economy.shtml> (Nov. 2004).

143. CIA World Factbook, Nigeria.

144. Nigeria Law, Constitution of the Federal Republic of Nigeria, 1999, <http:// www.nigeria-law.org/ConstitutionOfTheFederalRepublicOfNigeria.htm> (Oct. 2004).

145. Country Reports on Human Rights Practices, 2003, Nigeria, U.S. Department of State.

146. Human Development Reports, United Nations Development Programme.

147. Country Reports on Human Rights Practices, 2003, Nigeria, U.S. Department of State.

148. Andrew F. Uduigwomen, "A Philosophy of Education for Nigerian Women: Problems and Prospects," *The African Symposium* 4, no. 1 (March 2004), <http://www2.ncsu.edu/ncsu/aern/udomen.html> (Nov. 2004).

149. Country Reports on Human Rights Practices, 2003, Nigeria, U.S. Department of State.

150. UN Statistics Division, "Statistics and Indicators on Women and Men."

151. The U.S. Library of Congress, Country Studies, Nigeria, 1988, <http://countrystudies.us/nigeria/> (Nov. 2003).

152. Human Development Reports, United Nations Development Programme.

153. Country Reports on Human Rights Practices, 2003, Nigeria, U.S. Department of State.

154. Ibid.; The U.S. Library of Congress, Country Studies, Nigeria.

155. United Nations Educational, Scientific and Cultural Organization (UNESCO), "Progress of the World's Women 2002: Volume 2: Gender Equality and the Millennium Development Goals," United Nations Development Fund for Women (UNIFEM), 2002, <http://www.unifem.org/www/resources/progressv2/index.html> (Oct. 2004).

156. Ibid.

157. Human Development Reports, United Nations Development Programme.

158. Nigeria Country Report, Country Information and Policy Unit.

159. Paul Marshall, "Outside Encouragement, Sharia Rules Nigeria—With the Help of Foreign Islamists," *National Review*, May 5, 2004, <http://www.nationalreview.com/comment/marshall200405050847.asp> (Oct. 2004).

160. Simon and Altstein, *Global Perspectives on Social Issues*.

161. Ibid.

162. Country Reports on Human Rights Practices, 2003, Nigeria, U.S. Department of State.

163. Ibid.

164. Ibid.

165. Ibid.

166. Buckley, "Wife Inheritance Spurs AIDS Rise in Kenya."

167. Simon and Altstein, *Global Perspectives on Social Issues*.

168. Country Reports on Human Rights Practices, 2003, Nigeria, U.S. Department of State.

169. Simon and Altstein, *Global Perspectives on Social Issues*.

170. Ibid.

171. Globalis, "Nigeria—Contraceptive prevalence, any method," 2002, <http://globalis.gvu.unu.edu/indicator_detail.cfm?country=NG&indicatorid=128> (Oct. 2004).

172. CIA World Factbook, Nigeria.

173. Simon and Altstein, *Global Perspectives on Social Issues*.

174. Human Development Reports, United Nations Development Programme.

175. Nigeria Law, Constitution of the Federal Republic of Nigeria, 1999.

176. CIA World Factbook, Nigeria.

177. United States Agency for International Development (USAID), "Nigeria," Country Health Statistical Report, March 2004, <http://www.dec.org/pdf_docs/PNACX851.pdf> (Oct. 2004).

178. Human Development Reports, United Nations Development Programme.

179. UNESCO, "Progress of the World's Women 2002"; "Women in National Parliaments," Inter-Parliamentary Union, 2004, <http://www.ipu.org/wmn-e/classif.htm>.

180. "Women in National Parliaments," Inter-Parliamentary Union, 2004,<http://www.ipu.org/wmn-e/classif.htm> (Oct. 2004).

181. Human Development Reports, United Nations Development Programme.

182. Country Reports on Human Rights Practices, 2003, Nigeria, U.S. Department of State.

183. Human Development Reports, United Nations Development Programme.

184. The U.S. Library of Congress, Country Studies, Nigeria.

185. Ibid.

186. CIA World Factbook, South Africa, <http://www.cia.gov/cia/publications/factbook/geos/sf.html>.

187. Human Development Reports, United Nations Development Programme, 2003, <http://hdr.undp.org/reports/global/2004/pdf/hdr04_HDI.pdf> (Sep. 2004).

188. UN Statistics Division, "Statistics and Indicators on Women and Men," 8 Mar. 2005, <http://unstats.un.org/unsd/demographic/products/indwm/indwm2.htm> (Sep. 2004).

189. CIA World Factbook, South Africa.

190. Ibid.; "Learning English—Words in the News," *BBC*, 28 April 2004, <http://www.bbc.co.uk/worldservice/learningenglish/newsenglish/witn/2004/04/040428_south_africa_celebrates.shtml> (Sep. 2004).

191. South African Government Information, Constitution of the Republic of South Africa, 1996, Chapter 2 - Bill of Rights, <http://www.info.gov.za/documents/constitution/1996/96cons2.htm>.

192. Country Reports on Human Rights Practices, 2003, South Africa, U.S. Department of State, released by the Bureau of Democracy, Human Rights, and Labor, February 25, 2004, <http://www.state.gov/g/drl/rls/hrrpt/2003/27752.htm> (Sep. 2004).

193. Ibid.

194. Ibid.

195. CIA World Factbook, South Africa.

196. Ibid.

197. USAID Budget, "South Africa, The Development Challenge," <http://www.usaid.gov/policy/budget/cbj2005/afr/za.html> (Sep. 2004).

198. Zarina Maharaj, "Gender Inequality and the Economy: Empowering Women in the new South Africa," Africa Action, 9 Aug. 1999, <http://www.africaaction.org/docs99/gen9908.htm> (Sep. 2005).

199. United Nations Educational, Scientific and Cultural Organization (UNESCO), "Progress of the World's Women 2002: Volume 2: Gender Equality and the Millennium Development Goals," United Nations Development Fund for Women

(UNIFEM), 2002,<http://www.unifem.org/www/resources/progressv2/index.html> (Sep. 2004).

200. Country Reports on Human Rights Practices, 2003, South Africa, U.S. Department of State.

201. Human Rights Watch, World Report 2002, Women's Human Rights, 2002, <http://www.hrw.org/wr2k2/women.html> (Sep. 2003).

202. UN Statistics Division, "Statistics and Indicators on Women and Men."

203. "Code of Good Practice—Sexual Harassment," Labour Protect, <http://www.labourprotect.co.za/sexual_harassment.htm> (Sep. 2004).

204. Country Reports on Human Rights Practices, 2003, South Africa, U.S. Department of State.

205. Human Development Reports, United Nations Development Programme.

206. Country Reports on Human Rights Practices, 2003, South Africa, U.S. Department of State; Zarina Maharaj, "Gender Inequality and the Economy: Empowering Women in the new South Africa."

207. Human Development Reports, United Nations Development Programme.

208. Country Reports on Human Rights Practices, 2003, South Africa, U.S. Department of State.

209. Human Development Reports, United Nations Development Programme.

210. Country Reports on Human Rights Practices, 2003, South Africa, U.S. Department of State.

211. UNESCO, "Progress of the World's Women 2002."

212. UNESCO, Education, <http://portal.unesco.org/education/> (Sep. 2004).

213. UNESCO, "Progress of the World's Women 2002."

214. Human Development Reports, United Nations Development Programme.

215. Simon and Altstein, *Global Perspectives on Social Issues*.

216. Country Reports on Human Rights Practices, 2003, South Africa, U.S. Department of State.

217. Angela Melchiorre,"At What Age? . . . Are school children employed, married and taken to court," Australia, Right to Education Project, 2004, 2221. ed., <http://www.right-to-education.org/content/age/south_africa.html> (Sep. 2004).

218. Simon and Altstein, *Global Perspectives on Social Issues*.

219. Ibid.

220. Ibid.

221. Ibid.

222. Ibid.

223. "Abortion Policies, A Global Review, Australia," United Nations, <http://www.un.org/esa/population/publications/abortion/profiles.htm> (Sep. 2004).

224. CIA World Factbook, South Africa.

225. "Abortion Policies, A Global Review, Australia," United Nations.

226. Human Development Reports, United Nations Development Programme.

227. Citizenship and Immigration Canada, "Looking at Health Care, South Africa," Cultural Profiles Project, <http://www.cp-pc.ca/english/southafrica/index.html> (Jan. 2004).

228. Human Development Reports, United Nations Development Programme.

229. South African Government Information, Constitution of the Republic of South Africa, 1996.

230. Human Development Reports, United Nations Development Programme.

231. USAID Budget, "South Africa, The Development Challenge."

232. CIA World Factbook, South Africa.

233. Citizenship and Immigration Canada, "Looking at Health Care, South Africa."

234. Human Development Reports, United Nations Development Programme.

235. UNESCO, "Progress of the World's Women 2002"; "Women in National Parliaments," Inter-Parliamentary Union, 2004, <http://www.ipu.org/wmn-e/classif .htm>; Country Reports on Human Rights Practices, 2003, South Africa, U.S. Department of State.

236. Ibid.

237. Colleen Lowe Morna, "The 'Beginning of Complacency'? Gender and the 2004 Elections," Gender Links, <http://www.genderlinks.org.za/gelections/pressrelease .asp?nid=7> (Sep. 2004).

238. UN Statistics Division, "Statistics and Indicators on Women and Men."

239. Country Reports on Human Rights Practices, 2003, South Africa, U.S. Department of State.

240. Human Development Reports, United Nations Development Programme.

241. The U.S. Library of Congress, Country Studies, South Africa, 1988, <http:// countrystudies.us/south-africa/> (Sep. 2004).

Chapter Six

Asia

CHINA

China is located in eastern Asia. It is bordered by the East China Sea, Korea Bay, Yellow Sea, and South China Sea, and is between North Korea and Vietnam. The other bordering countries are Afghanistan, Bhutan, Burma, India, Kazakhstan, Kyrgyzstan, Laos, Macau, Mongolia, Nepal, Pakistan, Russia, and Tajikistan.[1]

China has a population of 1,298,847,624 (July 2004 est.). The chief ethnicity is Han Chinese at 91.9 percent. The remaining 8.1 percent are Zhuang, Uygur, Hui, Yi, Tibetan, Miao, Manchu, Mongol, Buyi, Korean, and other nationalities. The major religions are Daoism (Taoism) and Buddhism. Islam is represented by 1 to 2 percent and Christianity by 3 to 4 percent (2002 est.). The official languages are Mandarin (Putonghua, based on the Beijing dialect), Yue (Cantonese), Wu (Shanghaiese), Minbei (Fuzhou), Minnan (Hokkien-Taiwanese), Xiang, Gan, and Hakka dialects. Sixty-seven percent of China's population lives in rural areas.[2]

Life expectancy at birth for women is 73.2 years compared to 68.8 for men.[3] There are 120 men for every 100 women.[4]

Constitution

The Qing or Ch'ing Dynasty (in power since 221 B.C.) was replaced by the Republic on February 12, 1912.[5] The present government, the People's Republic, was established on October 1, 1949.[6] China, since 1949, has been a communist state.[7] All citizens of China (men and women) have the right to vote at eighteen years of age.[8]

The Constitution guarantees equal rights to women and men "in all spheres of life." In addition, the Constitution added that the state protects the rights and interests of women. Article 48 further mentions the protection of women through equal pay for equal work for men and women.[9] Yet, women continue to face discrimination.[10] Women are not economic or political equals of men. Women are more negatively affected than men by violence, poverty, and illiteracy.[11]

There is a lack of due process in the death penalty procedure. Pregnant women and minors are explicitly excused from death sentences.[12]

Rape is illegal, and while some men accused of rape were executed, spousal rape is not explicitly recognized in the Criminal Code.[13]

There is a high female suicide rate, five times greater than the global average.[14]

Work Force and Economy

The purchasing power parity is $6.449 trillion (2003 est.). Ten percent of the population lives below the poverty line (2001 est.). The labor force is made up of 778.1 million (2003 est.). Unemployment is 10.1 percent (2003 est.).[15]

Employees belong to a work unit, for which they usually work for their entire career. Work units usually supply their employees with wages, housing, child care, and health care (see section on health care). People can be born into their work unit or assigned to a work unit upon employment.[16]

Women are rapidly entering professional fields such as law and medicine. Women make up 19 percent of the judiciary and 30 percent of the professors at Universities.[17] But, women are still more often in the lesser-paid positions of the work force. They are often office clerks or retail sales assistants.[18]

Since 1988, labor regulations promote gender equality at work. In fact, women are granted special provisions during menstrual periods, pregnancy, and breastfeeding.[19] For example, women obtain ninety days of maternity leave, all of which is paid by their employer.[20] But, these provisions are only granted when the pregnancy is not in violation of the family planning regulations. Employers who do not implement the special provisions for women are subject to administrative punishment by the labor department.[21] Some women are wrongfully terminated during their pregnancy or when they are on maternity leave. In addition, many employers prefer to employ men over women so they can avoid the costs of maternity, childcare and pregnancy.[22]

The retirement age of women is lower (age fifty-five) than for men (age sixty). Some employers set the retirement age for women at forty. Women's lower retirement age adversely affects their pension.[23]

Sexual harassment is not addressed in any statute and is not expressly prohibited. In fact, the first sexual harassment case brought before a court was in
March 2003. Most cases of sexual harassment are not reported as it is not
clearly addressed or defined in the law.[24]

While the law states that women and men will earn equal pay for equal
work, women earn 70.1 percent of what men earn in urban areas and 59.6
percent of what men earn in rural areas. Females in executive or high level
positions earn 57.9 to 68.3 percent of what their male counterparts earn.[25] The
estimated earned annual income is $3,571 for women compared to $5,435 for
men.[26]

Women are more likely to be laid off or demoted.[27] Forty-seven percent of
persons laid off work are women while women make up only 45 percent of
the work force.[28] The majority of employed women are in low paying positions.[29]

Education

Under the Constitution, Article 46, all persons have the right and obligation
to receive education.[30] There are nine years of compulsory education.[31]

Although public schools were not allowed to charge fees, the government
lowered their financial assistance to primary education and schools began
to charge a fee. Many families cannot afford the fee. Consequently, many
children are unable to go to school.[32] In 2001, the High Court of China ruled
that the system of a separate ranking of boys and girls for secondary school
admission resulted in preferential treatment towards boys.[33] The ratio of female to male secondary level enrollment was 98 women for every 100 men
for the 1999 to 2000 school year.[34] In the age group eligible for secondary
education, only 48 percent of girls were enrolled.[35] In 2000, the female to
male ratio of student enrollment in tertiary school was 52 women for every
100 men.[36] In 2003, women made up 46.7 of high school student and 44
percent of university students. Women and girls in rural areas have a lower
attendance rate at school.[37]

The ratio of female youth literacy rate compared to male youth literacy rate
in 2002 was 98 women for every 100 men.[38] In 2003, illiteracy among women
fifteen to forty was 4.2 percent.[39]

Marriage

Under the Constitution, Article 49, "Marriage, the family and mother and
child," are protected by the state. In fact, mistreatment of women, children, or
the elderly is prohibited under the same article.[40]

The minimum age that a woman can marry in China is twenty years old.[41] Males can be no younger than twenty-two years old.[42] The average age for a man to marry is 23.8 and 22.1 for women.[43]

The law gives married couples the right to have a single child.[44] But in some regions, couples must get governmental authority before a women is permitted to get pregnant with their first child. If the couple is not granted permission they must wait a whole year before reapplying for a birth permit to have their first child. Eligible couples are allowed to apply for permission to have a second child. If the couple is not granted approval they must wait until the next year to apply. Many regional regulations require that a woman wait four years or more after the birth of her first child before being able to apply to have a second child. Couples who follow the regional birth laws receive superior treatment and rights. Contrarily, those couples that have a child without approval have to pay a social compensation fee. Coercion of an abortion or sterilization is considered illegal, but the government does not consider compensation fees to be duress despite the fact that fees are very high. In fact, the fee can be equal to several years of wages for an average worker. In addition, the law creates harsh penalties for officials who help people have an unapproved child. Women who are pregnant without approval can lose social services, pay higher tuition for the unapproved child, and may lose their job. This leaves some women with no option but to undergo abortion or sterilization.[45]

Ten percent of Chinese urban marriages end in divorce. Divorce is governed by the civil authorities in China. Either spouse may seek divorce. But, 70 percent of the country's divorce actions are initiated by wives. Since 1998 it has been more difficult to get a divorce. The couple must provide proof of the marriages failure. The courts require full investigations of the marriage's circumstances. This includes family and neighbor statements to prove that a divorce is justified.[46]

Property of a married couple is allotted to men. Consequently, many women lose their housing upon divorce.[47] This leaves women in an adverse position in which many women may stay in a marriage because they are dependant upon their husband for housing and support.

Alimony is determined by the couple. The court may only intervene if the couple cannot agree. Women are usually granted custody, but children have the right to request that changes be made to any agreements. Women also retain the property they owned *before* the marriage. A man may be exempt from providing alimony if the property the woman obtained in the divorce is sufficient to provide for her and any child(ren). Debts incurred during the marriage are paid by both spouses, if the wife has the ability to do so. If she cannot pay for the debt, the husband is wholly responsible. Individual debts are paid by each person.[48]

Abortion and Contraceptives

Abortion is legal in China.[49] The government permits it upon request.[50] In fact, abortion services are provided by the government.[51] Early abortions are performed in a clinic using the vacuum aspiration technique. Second trimester abortions are performed in a hospital by a physician. A woman receives fourteen days paid sick leave for a first-trimester abortion and thirty days paid sick leave for a second trimester abortion. In some parts of the country, women are given extended paid sick leave if they have an IUD inserted or are sterilized after the abortion. The government allows abortions to be performed up to six months after conception.[52]

The one child policy of 1979 was put into effect by the government in order to control the population and ensure that China could feed all of its population.[53]

The one child policy of 1979 has contributed to a drop in fertility rate from 4.8 (births per woman) between the years 1970 and 1975 to 2.2 between the years 1990 and 1995 to 1.9 in 1997.[54] In 2004, the fertility rate was 1.69 births per woman (2004 est.).[55] The government provides direct support for contraceptive use.[56] And although illegal, in some regions there are occurrences of forced abortions and sterilizations. In a number of provinces women are forced to use an IUD or implant and/or must have regular pregnancy tests.[57]

Since 1979, after the one child policy went into effect, sterilization was required for couples with two or more children, abortion for unplanned pregnancies, and IUDs for women who have one child.[58] The law requires that couples use birth control.[59] In 1992, 83 percent of married women of procreating age used contraceptives.[60] In 2003, 84 percent of married women (aged fifteen to forty-nine) used contraceptives (modern or traditional methods). In addition, it is illegal in most regions for a woman who is single to have a child. [61]

Most women use either sterilization or IUD as their contraceptives.[62] There is no other contraceptive method usually used when an IUD fails because it has been expelled by the woman and she may not even know. Consequently, 70 percent of abortions are a result of contraceptive failure. There were 10.6 million abortions in 1989, which was a decline from the 14.4 million abortions in 1983.[63] Today, the abortion rate is 28 percent.[64]

Laws and regulation in China have made it illegal to abort a child based on its sex.[65] This law was made in response to the frequent cases of female infanticide. Traditionally, males are favored. The one child policy has resulted in an increase in female infanticide. It is the common practice, especially in rural areas, to terminate a female fetus.[66] In addition, there is a persistence of female infanticide and abandonment of female infants. There are a much greater number of females in orphanages than males. There are fewer women than men due to infanticide of women.[67] In fact, there are 120 boys for every 100 girls.[68]

Health Care

The public health expenditure is 2 percent of the GDP while the private health expenditure is 3.4 percent of the GDP.[69] Both western and eastern forms of medicine are practiced and available to citizens.[70]

Health care is the responsibility of work units (*danwei*).[71] Employees usually work for the same work unit for their entire employment career.[72] Large work units often have clinics for employees on their premises. Contrarily, employees of smaller work units may have co-payments for medical bills. In rural areas many persons have to pay for their own health care.[73]

Federal and local governments continue to play a large role in the allocation and regulation of services. The government provides insurance, subsidized care, and increasing access to health care to most of its citizens. But, persons in rural areas have less access to health care and health care rates are rising.[74] AIDS awareness and safe sex classes are taught solely at the university level.[75]

Women in Public Office

Women obtained the right to vote and stand for election in 1949. The first woman was elected to parliament in 1954.[76]

Although there are no legal restrictions on the participation of women and minorities in the political arena, women and minorities hold few positions in the government, and even fewer senior post positions.[77] Women hold 20.2 percent of parliamentary seats and minorities hold 14 percent of parliamentary seats.[78] Women make up 5.1 percent of employees at the ministerial level.[79] Women hold fourteen vice-minister or higher ministerial positions out of twenty-eight ministries.[80]

Women in the Military

China's armed forces are the largest in the world.[81] All citizens between eighteen and twenty-two, regardless of sex, nationality, profession, family background, religion, or level of education, are obligated to perform military service. However, only 10 percent of eligible men and only a very small number of women are actually chosen to participate in service.[82]

Officers are drawn from military academy graduates. Few officers and specialized technicians in the military are women. Women serve primarily in scientific research, communications, medical, and cultural units.[83]

JAPAN

Japan, an island chain between the North Pacific Ocean and the Sea of Japan, is located in eastern Asia, east of the Korean Peninsula. Japan has a population of 127,333,002 (July 2004 est.). The majority ethnicity is Japanese at 99 percent. The remaining 1 percent is made up of Korean (511,262), Chinese (244,241), Brazilian (182,232), Filipino (89,851), and other (237,914).[84] The religions commonly observed are Shinto (49.9) and Buddhism (44.2).[85] The official language is Japanese.[86]

The life expectancy of women at birth is 84.51 years compared to 77.74 years for men.[87] There are 129 women for every 100 men.[88]

Constitution

The legal system in Japan is modeled after European civil law system with English-American influences. The Supreme Court conducts judicial review of legislative acts.[89]

In 1947, the revised Constitution and Civil Code granted equal rights to women.[90] Article Fourteen of the Constitution grants equal rights to all citizens regardless of race, creed, sex, social status, or family origin. Yet, women still face discrimination in the areas of education, work, marriage, and divorce.[91]

Until 1983, when the National Law was revised, women who were not married to Japanese citizens were unable to pass on their citizenship to their children.[92]

Rape is prohibited; this includes spousal rape. Unlike many nations, men are prosecuted for spousal rape.[93]

Sexual harassment is widespread. In fact, anti-groping ordinances have been tightened in order to respond to the frequent sexual harassment of female train commuters. First-time offenders can face prison time. In addition, many transportation companies now have female only designated train cars.[94]

All citizens are granted the right to vote at twenty years of age.[95]

Work Force and Economy

Today, Japan is ranked as the second most technologically powerful economy in the world after the United States. In addition, Japan has the third largest economy in the world after the United States and China. Japan has the purchasing power parity of $3.582 trillion (2003 est.). The labor force is made up of 66.66 million people (2003). Japan has a low unemployment rate of 5.3% (2003).[96] Unemployment is 5.1 percent for women and 5.5 percent for men.[97]

Under Article 27 of the Constitution, all persons have the right and obligation to work.[98] Sexual discrimination is expressly prohibited under the labor code.[99] In 1985, the Equal Opportunity Law was passed granting women equal opportunities to employment.[100] However, discrimination still occurs.[101]

Sexual harassment is a wide-spread issue, despite the labor laws that exist to prevent it. There are no punitive measures for violators of the sexual harassment labor laws. But, companies who do not comply with the laws face public scrutiny because companies found to not be compliant are publicized.[102]

Women are entitled to fourteen weeks of maternity leave, 60 percent of which is covered by health insurance and social security.[103] Companies offer little in the way of childcare.[104]

While wage discrimination is legally prohibited,[105] women earn only 46 percent of what their male counterparts earn.[106]

Women make up 46 percent of professionals and technical workers and over 60 percent of clerical and related positions.[107] Less than 10 percent of managers are women. Many women are employed in part-time low paying positions.[108] This offers women fewer opportunities for advancement and long-term security.[109]

Education

Under Article 26 of the Constitution, all persons have the right to receive equal education, correspondent to their ability.[110] Education is free and compulsory through the secondary level (i.e., age fourteen, ninth grade). Education is free until eighteen for children who meet the minimum academic standards.[111] The expenditure on education is 3.6 percent of the GDP.[112]

Japan's adult literacy is among the highest in the world at 99 percent for both men and women. Enrollment in primary school is the same for women as men. There are 101 females enrolled in secondary school for every 100 males. For every 100 males enrolled in tertiary school there are 86 women enrolled.[113] More women than men attend junior colleges as opposed to going to university. But, the trend of women going to a four-year university over junior college is increasing.[114]

Although the numbers are not equal to men yet, the number of women majoring in the sciences and engineering is increasing.[115]

Marriage

Under Article 24 of the Constitution, marriage is based on the mutual consent of both sexes. Marriage is "maintained through mutual cooperation with the equal rights of husband and wife as a basis." Article 24 also states, "with regard to choice of spouse, property rights, inheritance, choice of domicile, divorce and other matters pertaining to marriage and the family, laws shall be enacted from the standpoint of individual dignity and the essential equality of the sexes."[116]

The minimum legal age for men to marry is eighteen and sixteen for women.[117] The average age for men to marry is 30.3 and 26.9 for women.[118] Men and women under the age of twenty must obtain consent from their mother and father in order to marry.[119] Forty-one percent of men are married compared to 35.2 percent of women. Religious ceremonies are not legal marriages.[120] Marriages must be registered at a local municipal government office.[121]

While women may choose their own spouse, arranged marriages are common. In fact, in 1992, 25 percent of all marriages were arranged.[122] Single mother households make up 1 percent of Japan's households.[123]

The divorce rate (2.6 per 1,000 total population) is low.[124] Although many couples do not divorce, an increasing number of married couples live in the same house but are no longer living as man and wife.[125]

There are four different types of divorce: divorce by agreement, divorce by mediation in a family court, divorce by decision of the family court, and divorce by judgment of a district court.[126] Divorce by mutual consent is the most common type of divorce. Grounds for a contested divorce are infidelity, severe mental illness, malicious abandonment, cruelty, severe insult, incompatibility, and loss of love.[127]

Family court will determine custody, child support, and alimony if a couple is unable to arrive at an agreement. In 75 percent of mutual divorce cases child custody is granted to the mother.[128]

Under Article 733 of the Civil Code, a woman cannot re-marry within six months of dissolving a marriage while men can remarry immediately proceeding divorce.[129]

Abortion and Contraceptives

As of 1949 abortions are legal within the first twenty-four weeks to save the life of the mother, to preserve the mother's physical health, or for social and economic reasons.[130] While impairment of the fetus or preservation the mental health of the mother are not considered legitimate criterion,[131] they still would be covered under the social or economic categories.[132] All legal abortions must be performed in a medical facility by a certified physician. The woman or her spouse must give their consent to the abortion. Consent for a mentally challenged person must be given by her guardian. If the pregnancy has resulted from rape or incest the woman's consent does not need to be obtained. A woman who performs an abortion on herself through the use of drugs or other method may be imprisoned for up to one year.[133]

The abortion law is made up of the Criminal Code and the Eugenic Protection Law. The Criminal Code of 1880 and 1908 prohibits all abortions. The Eugenic Protection Law designed to increase the Japanese population and to prevent the birth of genetically inferior offspring permitted sterilization of women who had hereditary diseases and allowed abortions only to save the life of the mother. The Eugenic Protection Law was amended in 1948. During World War II the country was facing economic troubles and had a booming population. The abortion law was broadened. Abortions were allowed to be performed if the mother suffered from hereditary or mental illness, if a relative to the fourth degree of either parent had a hereditary or mental illness, if either spouse suffered from leprosy, if the pregnancy would adversely affect the mother physically or economically, or if the pregnancy resulted from rape or incest. In addition, there was a list of medical conditions that were sufficient grounds for abortion. Consequently, abortions became essentially available on request. But, the consent of the mother and her spouse was needed unless the spouse had died, the father could not be determined, was unable to express his will, or had died after conception. The law states that an abortion cannot be performed after viability. The abortion law does not define when a fetus becomes viable. But the Ministry of Health and Welfare determined that date to be 22 weeks. In 1996, the Eugenic Protection Law was renamed the Maternal Protection Law. It also took out the term eugenic throughout the text. In addition, it deleted statements indicating that its purpose was to prevent genetically inferior offspring. The law no longer authorizes the sterilization of mental patients or those who are considered mentally challenged. The law narrowed the grounds for abortion to save the life of the mother, to preserve the mother's physical health, or for social and economic reasons.[134] In 1990, it was estimated that 22 out of 1,000 pregnant women were adolescents. The majority of these pregnancies ended in abortion.[135] In 2000, the abortion rate was 22.3 percent.[136]

Unintended pregnancy is common. In one recent study 46.2 percent of female participants had an unintended pregnancy, 36.5 percent of which were aborted. The most popular form of birth control is condoms. [137]

The birth control pill, which was legalized in 1999, is not easily accessible.[138] Some are concerned that the HIV rate would increase if more women went on the pill.[139] The IUD was legalized in 1974.[140] Today, 59 percent of married women aged fifteen to forty-nine use contraceptives [both traditional and modern methods].[141] The fertility rate in Japan from 1970 to 1975 was 2.1 births per woman; from 1990 to 1995 it was 1.7 births per woman.[142] The present fertility rate is 1.38 births per woman.[143] The number of births out of 1000 women between the ages of fifteen to nineteen between the years 1990 and 1995 was 4.[144]

Health Care

The public health expenditure is 6.2 percent of the GDP while the private health expenditure is 1.8 percent of the GDP.[145] Boys and girls have equal access to health care.[146]

All citizens are provided health care. The system is funded by employers, individuals, local and national governments. Some people have private health care in order to have access to additional services.[147]

Some companies provide a hospital for their employees.[148]

Alternative medicine is also practiced.[149]

Women in Public Office

Women were given the right to vote in 1945 with restrictions and in 1947 without restrictions. The first woman was elected to Parliament in 1946.[150]

Under Article 44 of the Constitution, the qualifications of members of Parliament may not discriminate against race or sex.[151] While the number of women participating in the government has been increasing, there still is not adequate representation. Women hold thirty-four (out of 480) seats in the house and thirty-eight seats (out of 247) in the upper house of Parliament. They make up 16.67 percent of cabinet members, and 8.5 percent of governors.[152] Women make up 10.8 percent of those persons in elected municipal positions and are 5.7 percent of employees at a ministerial level. Women hold 10 percent of the positions as legislators, senior officials, and managers.[153] Lastly, women make up 4.9 percent of elected members in city and town assemblies.[154]

Women in the Military

The expenditure on the military is 1 percent of the GDP.[155]

When the Self-Defense Forces (SDF) was originally formed, women were recruited only for nursing services. Opportunities for women have expanded since that time. By 1991, more than 6,000 women were in the SDF, 80 percent of whom were in service areas. The National Defense Medical College graduated its first class with women in March 1991, and the National Defense Academy began admitting women in 1992. Women are not allowed in direct combat positions.[156]

INDIA

India is located in Southern Asia, bordering the Arabian Sea and the Bay of Bengal, between Burma and Pakistan.[157] India has the second largest population in the world, 1,065,070,607 (July 2004 est.). While English is an official language, Hindi is the national language and primary tongue of 30 percent of the people. But, there are 14 other official languages: Bengali, Telugu, Marathi, Tamil, Urdu, Gujarati, Malayalam, Kannada, Oriya, Punjabi, Assamese, Kashmiri, Sindhi, and Sanskrit. The major ethnicities are Indo-Aryan (72 percent), and Dravidian (25 percent) (2000).[158] Eighty percent of the population is Hindu. Islam is the second largest religion, at 14 percent. Three percent are Christian and the remaining two percent are Jains, Buddists, and Sikhs.[159]

The life expectancy at birth is 64.4 years for women and 63.1 years for men.[160]

The number of women for 100 men is 94.[161]

Constitution

India gained its independence from Great Britain in 1947 and became a federal republic in 1950.[162] The present Constitution was adopted on January 26, 1950.[163] Due to an overburdened and under funded court system, there is much corruption within the judicial system.[164]

Under the Constitution, discrimination on the basis of race, sex, disability, social status or language is prohibited.[165] Article 15 of the Indian Constitution grants equal rights to men and women in the areas of marriage, divorce, and inheritance.[166] Yet, social and legal discrimination against women continues to exist.[167]

Each religion has its own set of laws called person status laws that relate to marriage, divorce, child custody, and inheritance.[168] Some personal status laws inherently discriminate against women.[169]

Although the government does not restrict a citizen's personal appearance, militant groups have attempted to announce and enforce dress codes for women. Some militant groups threaten punishment by death for women who do not abide by their dress code.[170] In fact, some women have been murdered for not obeying such illegal laws.[171]

Under the Constitution, Article 17, untouchability was abolished.[172] The caste system was made up of different classes of citizens and corresponding rights. There was little mobility for persons to move beyond the boundaries of their class, with untouchables (not even given a caste) as outcasts. The caste system was abolished in the 1960's.[173] While discrimination or mistreatment arising out of untouchability is punishable by law,[174] tension still exists.[175] Dalit (untouchable) women in particular face a great deal of discrimination and harassment.[176]

Under section 375 of the Penal Code, marital rape is specifically exempt and not considered rape by essence that it happens within a marriage.[177]

The Hindu Succession Act of 1956, which applies to Hindus, Buddhists, Jainas, and Sikhs, allows both married and unmarried women to inherit simultaneously and equally to male class I heirs if the propertied individual dies without leaving a will or a similar provision.[178] Women can also be absolute owners of their property and may pass property on to named heirs. If a Hindu woman dies without having made provisions for heirs, any property that is hers will pass on to her heirs, and not to her husband. But if a woman dies while in possession of chattels she inherited from her husband or father-in-law, the chattels will go to her husband's heirs.[179]

Under the Muslim inheritance law, female heirs are only granted half the share that their male counterparts are awarded.[180]

According to the Constitution both men and women have the right to vote at eighteen years of age.[181]

Work Force and Economy

India has the purchasing power parity of $3.033 trillion (2003 est.). Twenty-five percent of the population lives below the poverty line (2002 est.). The labor force is made up of 472 million (2003). The unemployment rate is 9.5 percent (2003).[182]

Under Article 16 of the Constitution, women are granted equality of public employment or appointment to any position or office under the State. Employment discrimination on the basis of gender is prohibited.[183]

In 2001, women made up 25 percent of the paid work force.[184] In the early 1980s and mid-1990s, women earned 12 and 15 percent, respectively, of the wages in non-agricultural employment. In 2002, women earned 16 percent of the wages in non-agricultural employment and 86 percent of employed women were in informal employment.[185] Fifty-seven percent of those women were self-employed but made only 43 percent of the wages.[186] Under the

Equal Remuneration Act [1976], there is equal pay for equal work.[187] But, today women's estimated income is $1,442 compared to $3,820 for men (37.7
percent).[188] This places India in the lowest 20 percent for female share of
wage employment in the non-agricultural sector.[189]

In 1990, women made up 19 percent of professors at universities.[190]

Social security fully covers twelve weeks of maternity leave.[191] Maternity
leave is granted to women after eighty days of employment.[192]

Sexual harassment is prohibited. Employers must take appropriate steps to
prevent harassment. Once an employer obtains knowledge of an incident of
sexual harassment he/she must report the incident to the appropriate authority. Victims have the option of having the assailant or themselves trans-
ferred.[193]

Education

Under Article 45 of the Constitution, "the State shall endeavour to provide,
within a period of ten years from the commencement of the Constitution, for
free and compulsory education for all children until they reach the age of
fourteen years."[194] School is free and compulsory for children ages six to
fourteen.[195]

Public expenditure on education is 4.1 percent of the GDP.[196]

In 2001, the ratio of enrollment of girls to boys in primary school was 71
to 100.[197] In 2000, the ratio of female to male enrollment in secondary school
was 83 women to every 100 men. Thirty-one percent of eligible girls were enrolled in secondary schools.[198] In 2001, there were 37 women to 100 men
enrolled in post-secondary school.[199] The female to male ratio of student enrollment in tertiary school was 66 women to every 100 men.[200]

The ratio of female to male youth literacy in 2002 was 83 women to every
100 men.[201] In 2002, 66.8 percent of female youth (ages fifteen to twenty-
four) were literate compared to 59.5 percent in 1995. In 1990, the literacy of
women twenty-five and older was 19.4 percent compared to 49.8 percent for
men.[202] In 2002, the adult literacy rate for women is 46.4 percent (for women
fifteen and older) compared to 69 percent of adult men.[203]

Marriage

Marriage and divorce in India is governed by the personal laws of the country's religious groups. The four main religious groups in India are Hindu,
Muslim, Christian, and Parsi. Each religion has its own set of personal laws.
The Constitution does not interfere in the personal laws of its religious communities. The Constitution states that it guarantees the "freedom of religion"

to all citizens and groups.[204] The consequence is that the equality defined in the Constitution does not apply to the personal laws that govern marriage, divorce, inheritance, and maintenance.[205]

The minimum age of consent, regardless of religion, is twenty-one for males and eighteen for females.[206] But the median marriage age for Hindu women is 17.3; for Muslim women it is 18.1 years. Among women of other religions, the median marriage age is 20.1 years.[207]

Hindu males who marry a minor are subject to penal consequences. Females who marry a minor are not. In addition, the Hindu Marriage Act of 1976 allows women who marry before the age of fifteen to annul the marriage prior to turning eighteen years of age.[208]

In 1947, widows were given the right to inherit their husbands' property. Widow re-marriage was illegal until the Widow Remarriage Act was passed in 1856.[209]

The Dowry Prohibition Act in 1961 declared the dowry system illegal because of the negative impact it had on female Indian citizens.[210] The act was amended in 1984 and 1986 to widen the definition of dowry and make provisions more stringent.[211] Nevertheless, the dowry system has not been eliminated; it is practiced by all religious groups, particularly in rural areas.[212] Presently, a dowry is often made up of material goods such as a car, refrigerator, or even an apartment.[213] The dowry has had an effect on the practice of female infanticide as females are viewed as a major liability to a family's resources.[214] Dowry disputes still continue to adversely affect women. Often women who are perceived to have not provided a sufficient dowry are harassed by their husband's family. There are roughly six thousand women killed a year over dowry disputes. Under the Penal Code, a court must presume that a woman's husband or in-laws are responsible in the case of unnatural death of a woman in her first seven years of marriage. The woman must have faced harassment by her husband or in-laws for the presumption to exist.[215]

The Hindu Marriage Act of 1955 adopted modern definitions of matrimony. The Act abolished polygamy, marriage of individuals from different casts was legalized, and grounds for divorce were established.[216]

Polygamy is allowed under the Muslim marriage laws. Husbands are allowed to have up to four wives. There are general prohibitions regarding marriage. For example a man cannot marry a fifth wife, marry a woman who is undergoing *iddat* (a period of time in seclusion), marry a pregnant woman, or marry one's own divorced wife.[217]

Christian marriage law also requires that two parties enter into the marriage voluntarily.[218] Minors must obtain permission from their fathers or living guardians.[219]

Parsi marriages are regulated by the Parsi Marriage and Divorce Act of 1936.[220] The groom must be twenty-one years old and the bride must be at least eighteen years old. Polygamy is not permitted.[221]

Hindu divorce is regulated by the Hindu Marriage Act of 1955. Christian divorce is regulated by the Indian Divorce Act of 1869.[222] Parsi divorce is regulated by the Parsi Marriage and Divorce Act of 1936 and Muslims are regulated by the Dissolution of Muslim Marriage Act of 1956.[223] Civil and interfaith marriages are regulated by the Special Marriage Act of 1955.[224]

The Hindu Marriage Act of 1976 allows divorce under the grounds of adultery, cruelty, desertion, conversion to a non-Hindu religion, incurable insanity or mental disorder, virulent or incurable leprosy, venereal disease in a communicable form, renunciation of the world by entering a holy order, and presumption of death.[225] In addition, women can sue for divorce if the husband commits premarital bigamy, rape, sodomy, or bestiality.[226] A woman may also sue for divorce if she has filed for an order of maintenance against her husband and does not re-cohabitate with him afterwards or if she married at fifteen and is under eighteen years old. A couple may divorce on the ground of mutual consent if they can prove that they have been separated for at least one year.[227] They must prove that they cannot reconcile and agree that they should divorce.[228] Once the divorce is final either person can marry.[229]

The Hindu father is considered the "natural guardian" of his children. Consequently, mothers do not automatically gain custody of children after a marriage is dissolved.[230] Under section 25 of the Hindu Marriage Act, the court may order the respondent in a divorce proceeding to pay the petitioner a sum of money. The court takes into consideration the assets of the respondent and the specific circumstance of each case.[231]

Under Muslim law, a man can divorce his wife without grounds.[232] He can do so by saying "I divorce thee" three times (this ritual is called talaq), which may or may not be performed in the wife's presence. Contrarily, a woman must obtain her husband's consent. A woman has four ways to seek a divorce: delegated divorce, *khula*, *mubaraat*, and divorce under judicial decree. In a delegated divorce the husband gives the right to divorce to a third party or to the wife usually through a pre-nuptial agreement. In *khula*, the wife strikes a bargain with her husband. In the agreement, the marriage is dissolved when she compensates her husband for the divorce. Compensation usually comes in the form of the woman's dowry. *Mubaraat* is divorce by mutual consent. Either spouse may proceed. Lastly, women have the right to seek divorce by judicial decree if their husband has been absent for four years, if he has not provided maintenance for two years, if he has been imprisoned for seven or more years, if he has failed to perform marital obligations for three years, if he is impotent, if he has been insane for two or more years or has acquired leprosy or a virulent sexually transmitted disease. A woman may also divorce her husband if she was married when she was fifteen and has not yet reached the age of eighteen and the marriage has not yet been consummated. A woman may also seek divorce if her husband is cruel or if he no longer believes in Islam. After a woman is divorced she must spend a certain amount of time in seclusion. This is called *iddat*.[233]

If a woman petitions for divorce she will lose her right to maintenance. If a man seeks divorce the former wife is entitled to three months of maintenance.[234] If the woman is pregnant, as a result of the marriage, she will be maintained until her pregnancy is complete.[235]

Muslim mothers are granted custody until her son reaches age seven and her daughter hits puberty.[236]

Christian divorce policy is regulated by the Indian Divorce Act of 1869 and the Indian Marriage Act of 1982. Under the Divorce Act either partner may seek a divorce. In order to obtain a divorce a woman must prove her husband's guilt on two grounds. A wife may seek maintenance.[237] But a court cannot grant her more than one-fifth of her former husband's property. If a woman has committed adultery, her husband may seek payment from her adulterer. In addition, the court may award all property and children to her husband.[238]

Parsi divorce law is based on the Parsi Marriage and Divorce Act of 1936. Under Parsi law either spouse may seek divorce. Women alone may ask for maintenance. This is regarded as an inherent right. But it cannot exceed one-fifth of the husband's property.[239]

Since 1997, widows and women who have been abandoned by their husbands are granted ration cards, housing plots, and access to waste lands that can be cultivated. However, women are often not granted land in areas that are highly cultivated. In addition, in some areas local villagers have taken over the land of these women making it impossible for them to cultivate it.[240]

Abortion and Contraceptives

As of 1972, India permits abortion on request during the first twenty weeks of gestation. They may be performed to save the life of the woman, to preserve her physical or mental health, on account of rape or incest, because of fetal impairment, or because of economic reasons. Contraceptive failure is a valid ground for a legal abortion. But an abortion may only be performed after twenty weeks if there is a medical emergency. Women younger than eighteen and mentally challenged women need the consent of their guardian. Abortions are permitted free of charge in government hospitals as of 1991. Out of 189 nations in the world India had the lowest abortion rate of 3.3 percent.[241]

There is a preference for sons in India. Although, since 1994, it is illegal to use amniocentesis in order to determine the sex for sex-selective abortion purposes, infanticide of female infants and also sex-selective abortions of females still occur.[242]

In 1990, 43 percent of married women of procreating age used contraceptives.[243] The number of births per 1000 women between the ages of fifteen and nineteen was 57 between the years of 1990 to 1995.[244] Today the contraceptive use is 48 percent for both traditional and modern form of contraceptives.[245] The fertility rate in India between 1970 and 1975 was 5.4 and between the years 1990 and 1995 it was 3.9 births per woman.[246] In 2004, the fertility rate was 2.85 births per woman.[247]

Health Care

Along with western medicine, traditional forms of medicine such as yoga and herbal medicine play an important role in health care.[248]

The public health expenditure is 0.9 percent of the GDP compared to the private health expenditure that is 4.2 percent of the GDP.[249]

While medical care is free for all citizens, persons in rural areas have little access to it.[250]

Women in Public Office

Women gained the right to vote in 1950, the same year that India became a democratic republic after gaining independence from Great Britain.[251] The first woman to be elected to parliament was in 1952.[252]

In 1966, a woman, Indira Gandhi, became Prime Minister. She was in power for a total of five years.[253] She was assassinated in 1984.[254] Women make up 9.3 percent of the legislature. There are seven women in the cabinet of ministers. Women make up 10.1 percent of the persons in government at a ministerial level of employment. A Constitutional Amendment, Pachayati Raj, reserves 30 percent of elected village council positions for women. Over one million women have entered into the political arena under this amendment.[255]

Women in the Military

The expenditure on the military is 2.3 percent of the GDP.[256] In 1991, the government approved the induction of women into non-technical officer positions in the air force. In 1992, opportunities for women were opened in the areas of transportation, helicopters, and navigation and the first group of thirteen women cadets entered the Air Force Academy. In the army, which employs women as physicians and nurses, the participation of women is small but growing. A small but increasing number of women are officers assigned to non-medical services.[257] Women were inducted into the navy for the first time in 1992, when twenty-two were trained as education, logistics, and law cadres. In 1993, additional women were recruited for air traffic control duties. By 1994 there were thirty-five women naval officers.[258]

NOTES

1. CIA World Factbook, China, <http://www.cia.gov/cia/publications/factbook/geos/ch.html>.

2. Ibid.

3. Human Development Reports, United Nations Development Programme, 2003, <http://www.undp.org/hdr2003/indicator/cty_f_CHN.html> (Jan. 2005).

4. Eric Baculinao, "China grapples with legacy of its 'missing girls'," MSNBC, 14 September 2004, <http://www.msnbc.msn.com/id/5953508/> (Oct. 2004).

5. CIA World Factbook, China.

6. Ibid.

7. Sharon K. Hom, "China: First the Problem of Rights and Law," in *Women's Rights A Global View*, edited by Lynn Walters (Westport, CT: Greenwood Press, 2000).

8. CIA World Factbook, China.

9. Constitution of the People's Republic of China, The U.S. Constitution Online <http://www.usconstitution.net/china.html> (Oct. 2004).

10. Country Reports on Human Rights Practices, 2003, China, U.S. Department of State, released by the Bureau of Democracy, Human Rights, and Labor, Feb. 25, 2004, <http://www.state.gov/g/drl/rls/hrrpt/2003/27768.htm> (Aug. 2004).

11. Hom, "China: First the Problem of Rights and Law."

12. Country Reports on Human Rights Practices, 2003, China, U.S. Department of State.

13. Ibid.

14. Ibid.

15. CIA World Factbook, China.

16. The U.S. Library of Congress, Country Studies, China, 1988, <http://countrystudies.us/china/> (Nov. 2003).

17. Progress of the World's Women, UNESCO Institute of Statistics, 2002, <http://portal.unesco.org/uis> (June 2003).

18. Hom, "China: First the Problem of Rights and Law."

19. Ibid.

20. UN Statistics Division, "Statistics and Indicators on Women and Men," 8 Mar. 2005, <http://unstats.un.org/unsd/demographic/products/indwm/indwm2.htm> (May 2005).

21. Hom, "China: First the Problem of Rights and Law."

22 Country Reports on Human Rights Practices, 2003, China, U.S. Department of State.

23. Ibid.

24. Ibid.

25. Ibid.

26. Human Development Reports, United Nations Development Programme.

27. Country Reports on Human Rights Practices, 2003, China, U.S. Department of State.

28. Ibid.; UN Statistics Division, "Statistics and Indicators on Women and Men."

29. Country Reports on Human Rights Practices, 2003, China, U.S. Department of State.

30. Constitution of the People's Republic of China.

31. Country Reports on Human Rights Practices, 2003, China, U.S. Department of State.

32. Ibid.

33. Ibid.

34. UNESCO, Education, <http://portal.unesco.org/education/> (Sep. 2003).

35. Ibid.

36. UNESCO, Education, <http://portal.unesco.org/education/> (Sep. 2003).

37. Country Reports on Human Rights Practices, 2003, China, U.S. Department of State.

38. Millennium Indicators Database, <http://millenniumindicators.un.org>.

39. Country Reports on Human Rights Practices, 2003, China, U.S. Department of State.

40. Constitution of the People's Republic of China.

41. Ibid.

42. Ibid.

43. Rita J. Simon and Howard Altstein, *Global Perspectives on Social Issues: Marriage and Divorce* (Lanham: Rowman & Littlefield Publishing Group, Inc., 2003).

44. Country Reports on Human Rights Practices, 2003, China, U.S. Department of State.

45. Country Reports on Human Rights Practices, 2003, China, U.S. Department of State.

46. Simon and Altstein, *Global Perspectives on Social Issues*; David Buxbaum, ed., *Chinese Family Law and Social Change in Historical and Comparative Perspective* (Seattle: University of Washington Press, 1978), 482.

47. Country Reports on Human Rights Practices, 2003, China, U.S. Department of State.

48. Simon and Altstein, *Global Perspectives on Social Issues: Marriage and Divorce*; David Buxbaum, ed., *Chinese Family Law and Social Change in Historical and Comparative Perspective.*

49. Rita J. Simon, *Abortion: Statutes, Policies, and Public Attitudes the World Over* (Westport, CT: Greenwood Publishing Group, 1998).

50. Ibid.; "Abortion Policies, A Global Review, China," United Nations, <http://www.un.org/esa/population/publications/abortion/profiles.htm> (Aug. 2003).

51. Simon, *Abortion: Statutes, Policies, and Public Attitudes the World Over.*

52. "Abortion Policies, A Global Review, China," United Nations.

53. "China Steps up 'One Child' Policy," BBC, <http://news.bbc.co.uk/2/hi/asia-pacific/941511.stm>.

54. Women in Development Network (WIDNET), Statistics—Asia & Pacific, Focus International, <http://www.focusintl.statangl.htm> (April 2004); Hom, "China," ed. Lynn Walter, *Women's Rights A Global View* (World Bank, 2000).

55. CIA World Factbook, China.

56. "Abortion Policies, A Global Review, China," United Nations.

57. Country Reports on Human Rights Practices, 2003, China, U.S. Department of State.

58. "Abortion Policies, A Global Review, China," United Nations.

59. State Department Country Report on China.

60. Women in Development Network (WIDNET), Statistics—Asia & Pacific, Focus International, <http://www.focusintl.statangl.htm> (April 2004); the statistics used here are from the United Nations, *The World's Women 1995—Trends and Statistics*, "Abortion Policies, A Global Review, China," United Nations.

61. Globalis—China, 2003, <http://globalis.gvu.unu.edu/indicator_detail.cfm?country=CN&indicatorid=128> (Oct. 2004).

62. Simon, *Abortion: Statutes, Policies, and Public Attitudes the World Over;* "Abortion Policies, A Global Review, China," United Nations.

63. "Abortion Policies, A Global Review, China," United Nations.

64. Zhang Fenga, "Meeting Challenges of a Huge Population," *China Daily*, 16 July 2004, <http://www.chinadaily.com.cn/english/doc/2004-07/16/content_348824.htm> (Aug. 2004).

65. Ibid.

66. "China Steps up 'One Child' Policy,"

67. Hom, "China: First the Problem of Rights and Law."

68. Baculinao, "China grapples with legacy of its 'missing girls'."

69. Human Development Reports, United Nations Development Programme.

70. Citizenship and Immigration Canada, "Looking at Health Care, China," Cultural Profiles Project, <http://www.cp-pc.ca/english/china/index.html> (Jan. 2005).

71. The U.S. Library of Congress, Country Studies, China.

72. The U.S. Library of Congress, Country Studies, China.

73. Citizenship and Immigration Canada, "Looking at Health Care, China.

74. "Medicare System to Cover Rural Residents," *People's Daily*, 3 July 2001, <http://english.peopledaily.com.cn/200107/03/eng20010703_74059.html> (accessed 24 April 2002).

75. Melinda Liu and Mahlon Meyer, "Facing a Demon: Once indifferent about AIDS, China starts to confront a looming crisis," *Newsweek*, 4 Dec. 2000.

76. Human Development Reports, United Nations Development Programme.

77. Country Reports on Human Rights Practices, 2003, China, U.S. Department of State.

78. "Women in National Parliaments," Inter-Parliamentary Union, 2004, <http://www.ipu.org/wmn-e/classif.htm>.

79. Human Development Reports, United Nations Development Programme.

80. Country Reports on Human Rights Practices, 2003, China, U.S. Department of State.

81. The Federation of American Scientists (FAS), "Armed Forces," Arms Sales Monitoring Project (ASMP), <http://fas.org/asmp/profiles/wmeat/WMEAT99-00/03-hl-ArmedForces.pdf> (Oct. 2004).

82. The U.S. Library of Congress, Country Studies, China.

83. The U.S. Library of Congress, Country Studies, China.

84. CIA World Factbook, Japan, <http://www.cia.gov/cia/publications/factbook/geos/ja.html>.

85. Ibid.; U.S. Department of State, "International Religious Freedom Report, 2004, Japan," <http://www.state.gov/g/drl/rls/irf/2004/35400.htm>.

86. CIA World Factbook, Japan.

87. Ibid.

88. UN Statistics Division, "Statistics and Indicators on Women and Men," 8 Mar. 2005, <http://unstats.un.org/unsd/demographic/products/indwm/indwm2.htm> (May 2005).

89. CIA World Factbook, Japan.

90. Ibid.

91. Linda White, "Japan: Democracy in a Confucian-Based Society," in *Women's Rights A Global View*, edited by Lynn Walter (Westport, CT: Greenwood Press, 2000).

92. Ibid.

93. Country Reports on Human Rights Practices, 2003, Japan, U.S. Department of State, released by the Bureau of Democracy, Human Rights, and Labor, Feb. 25, 2004, <http://www.state.gov/g/drl/rls/hrrpt/2004/41644.htm> (Aug. 2004).

94. Ibid.

95. CIA World Factbook, Japan.

96. Ibid.

97. UN Statistics Division, "Statistics and Indicators on Women and Men."

98. The Constitution of Japan, Universität Bern, International Constitutional Law, 2004, <http://www.oefre.unibe.ch/law/icl/ja00000_.html> (Nov. 2005).

99. Country Reports on Human Rights Practices, 2003, Japan, U.S. Department of State.

100. White, "Japan: Democracy in a Confucian-Based Society."

101. Country Reports on Human Rights Practices, 2003, Japan, U.S. Department of State.

102. Ibid.

103. UN Statistics Division, "Statistics and Indicators on Women and Men."

104. "Diminishing Career Tracks for Japanese Women," Employment Practical Solutions, <http://www.epexperts.com/news_index527.html> (Oct. 2004).

105. Country Reports on Human Rights Practices, 2003, Japan, U.S. Department of State.

106. Human Development Reports, United Nations Development Programme, 2003, <http://www.undp.org/hdr2003/indicator/cty_f_JPN.html> (Jan. 2005).

107. "Statistics Bureau & Statistical Research and Training Institute," Chapter 12, *Statistical Handbook of Japan*, <http://www.stat.go.jp/english/data/handbook/c12cont.htm> (Oct. 2004).

108. Tony McNicol, "Barely Managing: The dream of working in an international environment can become a nightmare for Japanese women," *The Japanese Times*, 6 July 2004, <http://202.221.217.59/print/features/life2004/fl20040706zg.htm> (Aug. 2004).

109. "Diminishing Career Tracks for Japanese Women," Employment Practical Solutions.

110. The Constitution of Japan, Universität Bern, International Constitutional Law.

111. Country Reports on Human Rights Practices, 2003, Japan, U.S. Department of State.

112. Human Development Reports, United Nations Development Programme.

113. Ibid.

114. Gender Equality Bureau, the Cabinet Office, "Present Status of Japanese Women, Basic Data on Gender Equality in Japan," Women in Japan Today, 2004, <http://www.gender.go.jp/english_contents/women2004/statistics/s02.html> (Oct. 2004).

115. Ibid.

116. The Constitution of Japan, Universität Bern, International Constitutional Law.

117. Simon and Altstein, *Global Perspectives on Social Issues*; *Population Today* (Washington, D.C.: Population Reference Bureau, Inc., May 1993), 4–5; Angela Melchiorre, "At What Age? . . . Are school children employed, married and taken to court?"; Japan, Right to Education Project, 2004, Second Edition, <http://www.right-to-education.org/content/age/japan.html> (Jan. 2005).

118. Simon and Altstein, *Global Perspectives on Social Issues*; *Population Today*.

119. Ibid.; Angela Melchiorre,"At What Age are school children employed, married and taken to court."

120. Simon and Altstein, *Global Perspectives on Social Issues*; *Population Today*.

121. Ibid.; U.S. Department of State, "Marriage in Japan," Embassy of the United States, Japan <http://japan.usembassy.gov/e/acs/tacs-7114a.html> (Nov. 2004).

122. Simon and Altstein, *Global Perspectives on Social Issues*; *Population Today*.

123. White, "Japan: Democracy in a Confucian-Based Society."

124. Ibid.

125. Ibid.; K. Fujimura-Fanselow and A. Kameda, (eds.), *Japanese Women: New Feminist Perspectives on the Past, Present and Future* (New York: The Feminist Press, 1995).

126. U.S. Department of State, "Marriage in Japan."

127. Simon and Altstein, *Global Perspectives on Social Issues*; *Population Today*.

128. Ibid.

129. U.S. Department of State, "Marriage in Japan;" J. Sean Curtin, "Inequality in Japanese Marriage and Divorce Laws in 2002," Social Trends: Series #12, United Nations Online Network in Public Administration and Finance (UNPAN), <http://unpan1.un.org/intradoc/groups/public/documents/APCITY/UNPAN016633.pdf> (Nov. 2004).

130. "Abortion Policies, A Global Review, Japan," United Nations, <http://www.un.org/esa/population/publications/abortion/profiles.htm> (Aug. 2003).

131. Women in Development Network (WIDNET), Statistics—Asia & Pacific; United Nations, "Abortion Policies, A Global Review."

132. "Abortion Policies, A Global Review, Japan," United Nations.

133. Ibid.

134. "Abortion Policies, A Global Review, Japan," United Nations.

135. Ibid.

136. Wm. Robert Johnson, "Historical Abortion Statistics, Japan, 1947–2004," (Nov. 2004). <http://www.johnstonsarchive.net/policy/abortion/ab-japan.html> (Nov. 2004).

137. Kazuya Kitamura, et al., "Contraceptive Care by Family Physicians and General Practitioners in Japan: Attitudes and Practices," Society of Teachers of Family Medicine, *International Family Medicine Education* 36, no. 4, <http://www.stfm.org/fmhub/fm2004/April/Kazuya279.pdf> (Nov. 2004).

138. White, "Japan: Democracy in a Confucian-Based Society"; "Abortion Policies, A Global Review, Japan," United Nations.

139. Quote of the day, *Japan Today*, 19 Aug. 2004, <http://www.japantoday.com/e/?content=quote&id=1149> (Sept. 2004).

140. "Abortion Policies, A Global Review, Japan," United Nations.

141. Human Development Reports, United Nations Development Programme.

142. Women in Development Network (WIDNET), Statistics—Asia & Pacific.

143. CIA World Factbook, Japan.

144. Women in Development Network (WIDNET), Statistics—Asia & Pacific.

145. Human Development Reports, United Nations Development Programme.

146. Country Reports on Human Rights Practices, 2003, Japan, U.S. Department of State.

147. Citizenship and Immigration Canada, "Looking at Health Care, Japan," Cultural Profiles Project, <http://www.settlement.org/cp/english/japan/health.html> (Jan. 2005).

148. Ibid.

149. Ibid.

150. Human Development Reports, United Nations Development Programme.

151. The Constitution of Japan, Universität Bern, International Constitutional Law.

152. Country Reports on Human Rights Practices, 2003, Japan, U.S. Department of State.

153. Human Development Reports, United Nations Development Programme.

154. Country Reports on Human Rights Practices, 2003, Japan, U.S. Department of State.

155. Human Development Reports, United Nations Development Programme.

156. The U.S. Library of Congress, Country Studies, Japan, 1988, <http://countrystudies.us/japan/> (Nov. 2003).

157. Manisha Desai, "India: Women's Movements from Nationalism to Sustainable Development," in *Women's Rights: A Global View* edited by Lynn Walters (Westport, CT: Greenwood Press, 2000); CIA World Factbook, India, <http://www.cia.gov/cia/publications/factbook/geos/in.html>.

158. CIA World Factbook, India.

159. Desai, "India: Women's Movements from Nationalism to Sustainable Development."

160. Human Development Reports, United Nations Development Programme, 2003, <http://www.undp.org/hdr2003/indicator/cty_f_IND.html> (Jan. 2005).

161. Women in Development Network (WIDNET), Statistics—Asia & Pacific.

162. Desai, "India: Women's Movements from Nationalism to Sustainable Development."

163. CIA World Factbook, India.

164 Country Reports on Human Rights Practices, 2003, India, U.S. Department of State, released by the Bureau of Democracy, Human Rights, and Labor, Feb. 25, 2004, <http://www.state.gov/g/drl/rls/hrrpt/2003/27947.htm> (Aug. 2004).

165. Country Reports on Human Rights Practices, 2003, India, U.S. Department of State.

166. Desai, "India: Women's Movements from Nationalism to Sustainable Development."

167. Country Reports on Human Rights Practices, 2003, India, U.S. Department of State.

168. Desai, "India: Women's Movements from Nationalism to Sustainable Development."

169. Country Reports on Human Rights Practices, 2003, India, U.S. Department of State.

170. Ibid.

171. Ibid.; Constitution of India, Universität Bern, International Constitutional Law, 2004, <http://www.oefre.unibe.ch/law/icl/in00000_.html> (Dec. 2004).

172. Constitution of India, Universität Bern, International Constitutional Law.

173. "The Caste System of India," <http://www.raceandhistory.com/historicalviews/casteindia.htm>.

174. Constitution of India, Universität Bern, International Constitutional Law.

175. "Country Profile, India," *BBC News*, <http://news.bbc.co.uk/1/hi/world/south_asia/country_profiles/1154019.stm> (Dec. 2004).

176. Country Reports on Human Rights Practices, 2003, India, U.S. Department of State.

177. "Trauma of Marital Rape," Women Excel, Law, <http://www.womenexcel.com/law/maritalrape.htm> (Dec. 2004).

178. Simon and Altstein, *Global Perspectives on Social Issues*; Sudhir Shah & Associates, The Hindu Succession Act, 1956, <http://www.sudhirlaw.com/HSA56F.htm> (Dec. 2001).

179. Simon and Altstein, *Global Perspectives on Social Issues*.

180. Ibid.

181. CIA World Factbook, India.

182. Ibid.

183. Constitution of India, Universität Bern, International Constitutional Law.

184. Desai, "India: Women's Movements from Nationalism to Sustainable Development."

185. United Nations Educational, Scientific and Cultural Organization (UNESCO), "Progress of the World's Women 2002: Volume 2: Gender Equality and the Millennium Development Goals," United Nations Development Fund for Women (UNIFEM), 2002, <http://www.unifem.org/www/resources/progressv2/index.html> (July 2004).

186. Ibid.

187. "Employment of Women," Indian Export Import Portal: A Complete EXIM Guide for Businesses, <http://exim.indiamart.com/ssi-regulations/employment-women .html> (Dec. 2004).

188. Human Development Reports, United Nations Development Programme.

189. UNESCO, "Progress of the World's Women 2002."

190. Women in Development Network (WIDNET), Statistics—Asia & Pacific.

191. UN Statistics Division, "Statistics and Indicators on Women and Men," 8 Mar. 2005, <http://unstats.un.org/unsd/demographic/products/indwm/indwm2.htm> (May 2005).

192. "Employment of Women," Indian Export Import Portal.

193. Dhruv Desai, "Sexual Harassment and Rape Laws in India," <http://legalservice india.com/articles/rape_laws.htm> (Dec. 2004).

194. Angela Melchiorre,"At What Age are school children employed, married and taken to court," India, Right to Education Project, 2004, Second Edition, <http://www .right-to-education.org/content/age/australia.html> (Jan. 2005).

195. Country Reports on Human Rights Practices, 2003, India, U.S. Department of State.

196. Human Development Reports, United Nations Development Programme.

197. Desai, "India: Women's Movements from Nationalism to Sustainable Development."

198. UNESCO, "Progress of the World's Women 2002."

199. Desai, "India: Women's Movements from Nationalism to Sustainable Development."

200. UNESCO, Education, <http://portal.unesco.org/education/> (Sep. 2003).

201. UNESCO, "Progress of the World's Women 2002."

202. Women in Development Network (WIDNET), Statistics—Asia & Pacific.

203. Human Development Reports, United Nations Development Programme.

204. Simon and Altstein, *Global Perspectives on Social Issues.*

205. Ibid.; Nidhi Gupta, supervised by Marie Claire Foblets, "Success of Feminist Jurisprudence in India: A critical analysis from the point of view of implementation," European Academy of Legal Theory, <http://www.sos-net.eu.org/red&s/dhdi>, 8 (Dec. 2004).

206. Angela Melchiorre,"At What Age are school children employed, married and taken to court."

207. Simon and Altstein, *Global Perspectives on Social Issues*; Gupta, "Success of Feminist Jurisprudence in India," 45.

208. Simon and Altstein, *Global Perspectives on Social Issues.*

209. Desai, "India: Women's Movements from Nationalism to Sustainable Development."

210. Country Reports on Human Rights Practices, 2003, India, U.S. Department of State.

211. Ibid.

212. Simon and Altstein, *Global Perspectives on Social Issues*.

213. Desai, "India: Women's Movements from Nationalism to Sustainable Development."

214. Simon and Altstein, *Global Perspectives on Social Issues*.

215. Country Reports on Human Rights Practices, 2003, India, U.S. Department of State.

216. Simon and Altstein, *Global Perspectives on Social Issues*.

217. Ibid.; Bharat Matrimony, Telugu Matrimony, Law <http://www.telugumatrimony.com/law.shtml> (Dec. 2005).

218. Ibid.

219. Simon and Altstein, *Global Perspectives on Social Issues*.

220. Ibid.; Bharat Matrimony, Telugu Matrimony, Law.

221. Simon and Altstein, *Global Perspectives on Social Issues*.

222. Ibid.

223. Ibid.; The Hindu Marriage Act, 1955, India Info, <http://law.indiainfo.com/personal/divorce_law.html> (Dec. 2004).

224. Simon and Altstein, *Global Perspectives on Social Issues*.

225. Ibid.

226. Hindu Marriage Laws, Krislon, <http://www.krislon.net/matrimonial/law/law_hindu.htm> (Dec. 2004).

227. Simon and Altstein, *Global Perspectives on Social Issues*.

228. Ibid.

229. Hindu Marriage Laws.

230. Simon and Altstein, *Global Perspectives on Social Issues*.

231. Gupta, "Success of Feminist Jurisprudence in India," 50.

232. Republic of India, Emory University, Islamic Family Law, <http://www.law.emory.edu/IFL/legal/india.htm> (Dec. 2004).

233. Simon and Altstein, *Global Perspectives on Social Issues*.

234. Ibid.

235. Gupta, "Success of Feminist Jurisprudence in India," 52.

236. Hindu Marriage Laws.

237. Simon and Altstein, *Global Perspectives on Social Issues*.

238. Gupta, "Success of Feminist Jurisprudence in India," 56.

239. Ibid.

240. Desai, "India: Women's Movements from Nationalism to Sustainable Development."

241. "Abortion Policies, A Global Review, India," United Nations, <http://www.un.org/esa/population/publications/abortion/profiles.htm> (Aug. 2003).

242. Desai, "India: Women's Movements from Nationalism to Sustainable Development."

243. Women in Development Network (WIDNET), Statistics—Asia & Pacific.

244. Ibid.

245. Globalis—India, <http://globalis.gvu.unu.edu/indicator_detail.cfm?country=IN&indicatorid=128>.

246. Women in Development Network (WIDNET), Statistics—Asia & Pacific.

247. CIA World Factbook, India.

248. Citizenship and Immigration Canada, "Looking at Health Care, India," Cultural Profiles Project, <http://www.cp-pc.ca/english/india/index.html> (Jan. 2005).

249. Human Development Reports, United Nations Development Programme.

250. Country Reports on Human Rights Practices, 2003, India, U.S. Department of State.

251. Desai, "India: Women's Movements from Nationalism to Sustainable Development."

252. Human Development Reports, United Nations Development Programme.

253. Desai, "India: Women's Movements from Nationalism to Sustainable Development."

254. Manas, History Politics, Indira Gandhi, University of California at Los Angeles, Social Sciences, <http://www.sscnet.ucla.edu/southasia/history/independent/Indira .html> (Dec. 2004).

255. Country Reports on Human Rights Practices, 2003, India, U.S. Department of State.

256. Human Development Reports, United Nations Development Programme.

257. The U.S. Library of Congress, Country Studies, India, 1988, <http:// countrystudies.us/india/> (Nov. 2003).

258. Ibid.

Chapter Seven

Australia

Australia is a country on a continent of the same name located between the Indian Ocean and the South Pacific Ocean. Australia has a population of 19,913,144 (July 2004 est.). Ninety-two percent of the population is Caucasian, 7 percent is Asian, and the remaining 1 percent is aboriginal ethnicities. The majority of people are Christian (Anglican 26.1 percent, Roman Catholic 26 percent, and other Christian 24.3 percent); other religions make up the remaining 23.6 percent of the population. English and native languages are spoken.[1]

Life expectancy at birth is 82 years for women and 76.4 years for men.[2] There are 101 women for every 100 men.[3]

Constitution

In 1901, Australia became a commonwealth of the British Empire. A referendum to change Australia's status, from a commonwealth headed by the British monarch to a republic, was defeated in 1999. Australia today is a democratic, federal-state system that recognizes the British monarch as sovereign. The Constitution was adopted on July 9, 1900 and became effective on January 1, 1901. The legal system is based on English common law.[4]

Discrimination based on race, sex, disability, language, or social status is prohibited.[5] Rape, including spousal rape is prohibited. Nevertheless it remains a problem.[6]

In 1989, the government passed the Human Rights and Equal Opportunity Commission Regulations. The regulations expand the definition of discrimination. Discrimination was broadened to make it illegal to make distinctions, exclusions, or preferences based on age, marital status, nationality, or sexual preferences.[7]

The voting age for men and women is eighteen.[8]

Work Force and Economy

The purchasing power parity in Australia is $571.4 billion (2003 est.). There are 10.19 million people in the labor force.[9] The unemployment rate is 6 percent.[10]

Women have equal status to men under the law. Wages, by law, are to be equal between men and women.[11] However, women only earn 72 percent of what their male counterparts earn.[12] The estimated annual income for women is $24,827 (U.S.) compared to $34,446 (U.S.) for men.[13]

Women make up 55 percent of professional and technical workers and 36 percent of administrative and managerial workers.[14]

Sexual harassment is prohibited under the Sex Discrimination Act. Yet, sexual harassment still occurs.[15]

Seventeen percent of childcare is paid for a family's first child. A lesser percentage is paid by the government for additional children. Lower income families receive up to 100 percent childcare coverage.[16]

Women are granted fifty-two weeks of maternity leave, none of which is covered by employers or social security.[17]

Education

The public expenditure on education is 4.6 percent of the GDP.[18]

Education is compulsory, free, and universal for nine to ten years for children between ages six to fifteen.[19]

In 2000, the ratio of females to males enrolled in secondary schools was 101 women for every 100 men. Female enrollment in secondary schools was 88 percent.[20] In 2000, the female to male ratio of student enrollment in tertiary schools was 124 women to every 100 men.[21]

Today, female enrollment in primary, secondary, and tertiary education surpasses that of men.[22]

Marriage

The Federal Government alone has the authority to make laws regulating marriage. Marriage is regulated by the Marriage Amendment Act of 1985. The minimum legal age for marriage for both men and women is eighteen.[23] A person can marry at sixteen if they obtain guardian consent and court approval.[24] The average age for men to marry is 29.2 years and 27 years for women. Fifty percent of men are married compared to 47.2 of women.[25]

A marriage is void if either person is already married to another person or the parties are in a prohibited relationship. Under section 48, a marriage is not valid if one of the parties cannot consent. Consent is not valid if it is obtained by duress or fraud; for example, if one party is mistaken as to the identity of the other party, or if that person is mentally incapable of understanding the nature and effect of the marriage ceremony, or if either party is under the legal marriage age. Marriages are not legal if the marriage is between a person and an ancestor or descendant of that person, or between siblings, regardless if they are whole or half-siblings. A marriage between an adopted child and their parent is illegal. Polygamy is illegal.[26]

Informal marriages are recognized by Australian law. An informal marriage exists if cohabitation has been continuous, or aggregate, for five years, or if sexual relations result in the birth of a child. Children born out of wedlock are given equal protection under the law. Cohabitation before marriage has increased to 67 percent.[27]

Divorce is regulated by the Family Law Act of 1975. The Act established no-fault divorce. The sole ground for divorce is irretrievable break down of the marriage. A couple may be granted a divorce after a one-year separation. The current divorce rate is 5.5 per 1,000 total population.[28]

Child support is determined using a formula in the Child Support Act of 1989.[29] The formula includes the number of children whom the payer is liable for and the amount of the adjusted income.[30] The Family Law Act requires that the Family Court use the "best interest of the child" principle when determining custody. Custody is usually granted to the mother.[31]

Division of marital property is regulated by the Family Law Reform Bill of 1994. Under the Bill, couples construct their own settlements. The standard division of property grants half of the marital property to both spouses. The Bill increases the options for mediation. Many women's rights groups state that mediation is detrimental to the woman's position in divorce proceedings because it limits their access to court-mandated support and bargaining power for post-marital support.[32]

Abortion and Contraceptives

Abortions are legal in Australia. They can be performed in order to save the life of the mother, to preserve the physical or mental health of the mother, if the pregnancy is a result of rape or incest, if there is fetal impairment, or for economic or social reasons. Abortions are available upon request. Government health insurance pays for all legal abortions. Restrictions on abortions depend on the jurisdiction. All abortion law is based on the Offenses Against the Person Act of 1861 (United Kingdom) that allows abortions to save the life of the mother.[33]

In Queensland and Victoria, abortions can also be performed to preserve the woman's mental or physical health or to save her from serious danger to her life. In New South Wales and the Australian Capital Territory socio-economic reasons may be a legitimate ground for abortion. It is unclear whether Tasmania only allows abortions to be performed to save the life of the mother.[34]

The abortion law of the South Australia and the Northern Territory is based on a different Act than the other Territories. The abortion law is based on the 1967 Abortion Act (United Kingdom). Abortions under this law are legal in order to save the life of the mother, to preserve a woman's mental or physical health, or if the child is at risk of being severely mentally or physically handicapped. Under the Northern Territory law, the abortion must take place within the first fourteen weeks and parental consent must be obtained if the woman is under sixteen. The abortion must be approved by two physicians and be performed in a hospital.[35]

Western Australia had fewer restrictions. Since 1998, abortions can be performed upon request up to the twentieth week under certain circumstances. Abortions can be performed after the twentieth week if the woman suffers from a severe medical condition, which is certified by two physicians. The penalty for an illegal abortion in Western Australia is $50,000.[36]

The maximum sentence in all territories for performing illegal abortions ranges from seven years to life imprisonment. Since the 1970s there have been almost no prosecutions for the performance of abortions throughout all of Australia. In the mid-1990s, 92,000 abortions were performed in Australia, resulting in a ratio of one abortion for every live birth.[37]

The fertility rate is 1.76 births per woman.[38] Seventy-six percent of married women ages fifteen to forty-nine use contraceptives [both modern and traditional methods].[39]

Health Care

The public health expenditure is 6.2 percent of the GDP compared to the private health expenditure that is 3.0 percent of the GDP.[40]

The health care system, Medicare, is universal to all citizens from birth.[41] However, citizens have to co-pay their health costs.[42]

The leading cause of death in Australia is cancer. The Australian Bureau of Statistics estimated that in 2001, roughly 128,544 people died of cancer. For men, the top three cancers are prostate, lung, and melanoma. For women, the top three cancers are breast, colon, and melanoma. Consequently, much funding has gone toward cancer research.[43]

Women in Public Office

Women received the right to vote and stand for election with restrictions in 1902 and without restrictions in 1962.[44] The first woman was elected to Parliament in 1943.[45]

Today women make up 27 percent of the seats in Parliament, 12 percent of the members of cabinet, and 17 percent of the members in the Federal Government Ministry.[46] Women make up 35 percent of female legislators, senior officials and technical workers.[47]

Women in the Military

Women are able to join the military. In 2002, the Defense Minister, Robert Hill stated that women should be allowed to fight on the front lines. This is the first time that an Australian defense minister has supported placing women in direct combat roles. Women are excluded from many military job categories involving direct combat. Nevertheless, women do serve on surface ships, submarines, can fly combat aircrafts, and helicopters, and women have served with distinction in army operational roles under war-like conditions.[48]

NOTES

1. CIA World Factbook, Australia, <http://www.cia.gov/cia/publications/factbook/geos/as.html>.

2. Human Development Reports, United Nations Development Programme, 2003, <http://www.undp.org/hdr2003/indicator/cty_f_AUS.html> (Jan. 2005).

3. UN Statistics Division, "Statistics and Indicators on Women and Men," 8 Mar. 2005, <http://unstats.un.org/unsd/demographic/products/indwm/indwm2.htm> (May 2005).

4. CIA World Factbook, Australia.

5. Country Reports on Human Rights Practices, 2003, Australia, U.S. Department of State, released by the Bureau of Democracy, Human Rights, and Labor, February 25, 2004, <http://www.state.gov/g/drl/rls/hrrpt/2003/27763.htm> (Jan. 2005).

6. Ibid.

7. Rita J. Simon and Howard Altstein, *Global Perspectives on Social Issues: Marriage and Divorce* (Lanham: Rowman & Littlefield Publishing Group, Inc., 2003).

8. CIA World Factbook, Australia.

9. Ibid.

10. Ibid.

11. Country Reports on Human Rights Practices, 2003, Australia, U.S. Department of State.

12. Human Development Reports, United Nations Development Programme.

13. Ibid.

14. UN Statistics Division, "Statistics and Indicators on Women and Men," Human Development Reports, United Nations Development Programme.

15. Country Reports on Human Rights Practices, 2003, Australia, U.S. Department of State.

16. Country Reports on Human Rights Practices, 2003, Australia, U.S. Department of State.

17. UN Statistics Division, "Statistics and Indicators on Women and Men."

18. Human Development Reports, United Nations Development Programme.

19. Country Reports on Human Rights Practices, 2003, Australia, U.S. Department of State.

20. United Nations Educational, Scientific and Cultural Organization (UNESCO), "Progress of the World's Women 2002: Vol. 2: Gender Equality and the Millennium Development Goals," United Nations Development Fund for Women (UNIFEM), 2002, <http://www.unifem.org/www/resources/progressv2/index.html> (Jan. 2005).

21. UNESCO, Education, <http://portal.unesco.org/education/> (Jan. 2005).

22. Human Development Reports, United Nations Development Programme.

23. Simon and Altstein, *Global Perspectives on Social Issues*.

24. Ibid.; Angela Melchiorre, "At What Age? . . . Are school children employed, married and taken to court," Australia, Right to Education Project, 2004, Second Edition, <http://www.right-to-education.org/content/age/australia.html> (Jan. 2005).

25. Simon and Altstein, *Global Perspectives on Social Issues*.

26. Ibid.

27. Ibid.

28. Ibid.

29. Ibid.

30. Australian Government, "2.4.1: The Basic Formula," Child Support Agency (CSA), 2003, <http://www.csa.gov.au/guide/2_4_1.htm> (Jan. 2005).

31. Simon and Altstein, *Global Perspectives on Social Issues*.

32. Ibid.

33. "Abortion Policies, A Global Review, Australia," United Nations, <http://www.un.org/esa/population/publications/abortion/profiles.htm> (Aug. 2003).

34. Ibid.

35. Ibid.

36. Ibid.

37. Ibid.

38. CIA World Factbook, Australia.

39. Globalis, "Australia—Contraceptive prevalence, any method," 2002, <http://globalis.gvu.unu.edu/indicator_detail.cfm?country=AU&indicatorid=128> (Jan. 2005).

40. Human Development Reports, United Nations Development Programme.

41. Country Reports on Human Rights Practices, 2003, Australia, U.S. Department of State; Citizenship and Immigration Canada, "Looking at Health Care, Australia," Cultural Profiles Project, <http://www.settlement.org/cp/english/australia/health.html> (Jan. 2005).

42. Country Reports on Human Rights Practices, 2003, Australia, U.S. Department of State.

43. "Leading Causes of Death," Australian Bureau of Statistics, 2002, <www.abs.gov.au/ausstats> (Jan. 2005).

44. Human Development Reports, United Nations Development Programme.

45. Ibid.

46. Country Reports on Human Rights Practices, 2003, Australia, U.S. Department of State.

47. Country Reports on Human Rights Practices, 2003, Australia, U.S. Department of State.

48. Mark Forbes, "Fighting on the Frontline," *The Age*, 20 Sept. 2002, <http://www.theage.com.au>.

Summary and Concluding Remarks

In this explicitly comparative chapter we examine the statuses women occupy, the roles they play, and the successes they have achieved. Women's participation in the work force, in the military, and in public life are compared along with years of education and literacy rates against those of men. Women's rights and responsibilities vis-à-vis marriage and divorce are compared across societies as well as the laws pertaining to the legality and grounds for abortion.

Labor Force Participation and Education

In the Western industrial democracies (the United States, Canada, Australia, and the countries of Western Europe) women make up about 50 percent of the labor force. But in none of those countries are their earnings comparable to that of men. At best they earn about 75 percent of their male counterparts. They work primarily in clerical, sales, teaching, and health care occupations. In the Eastern European countries women make up about 45 percent of the labor force and earn between 58 and 71 percent of their male counterparts.

In the three Latin American countries women make up between one-third and 48 percent of the labor force and earn between 42 and 66 percent of their male counterparts.

In the Muslim countries of the Middle East a much smaller percentage of women are employed outside their homes and they earn less than 40 percent of their male counterparts. In Israel, women make up about half of the labor force, working mostly as teachers, nurses, and social workers and earn 80 percent of male earnings.

In the four African countries, Kenya stands out as having a much higher percentage of women in the labor force, 75 percent, compared to 50 percent and less in Ghana, Nigeria, and South Africa; and in their earnings compared to men 84 percent as opposed to 50 percent and less in the other nations.

Among the Asian nations, Indian women make up only 25 percent of the labor force and earn less than 40 percent of their male counterparts. In Japan and China women earn about 50 percent of their male counterparts.

Turning next to education, nearly 80 percent of the world's population aged 15 years and over is now literate. It is estimated that global illiteracy, 20.3 percent, will drop to 16.5 percent by 2010. But out of the estimated 862 million (20.3 percent) illiterate adults in the world, 75 percent are women. Nevertheless, the number of illiterate women is shrinking. It has shrunk from 44.6 percent in 1970 to 25.8 percent in 2000. In Africa the rate of illiterate women dropped from 82.9 (1970) to 49.9 percent (2000). Men in Africa have an illiteracy rate of 30.9 compared to 61.5 in 1970. The current illiteracy rate in North America is 7.5 for women compared to 6.3 for men, compared to 17.1 and 12.5 in 1970 respectively. In Asia the illiteracy rate of women is 32.1 compared to 17 percent of men. In 1970 the rate was 61 and 36.5 percent respectively. The illiteracy rate in Europe is 2.4 percent for women and 1.1 percent for men. The rate in 1970 was 9 and 3.6 percent respectively. The rate of illiteracy in Australia is 7 percent for women and 5.2 percent for men. In 1970 the rate was 13.2 and 9 respectively. The illiteracy rate in Latin America and the Caribbean is 12.1 for women and 10.1 for men. In 1970 the illiteracy rate was 30.3 and 22.3 respectively. Illiteracy in South and West Asia, and the Arab States and North Africa are now 56.4 and 52.2 percents respectively.

From 1990 to 2000, the number of girls in primary school increased faster than that of boys. The global Gender Parity Index (GPI) rose from 0.89 to 0.93. A GPI of 1 indicates equal enrollment of the sexes. But 57% of the estimated 104 million primary-age children not enrolled in school worldwide are girls. Of the 128 countries for which data for 2000 are available, 52 have already achieved gender parity or will have done so by 2005 at the primary and secondary levels.

In the Western Industrial democracies, women have completed more years of schooling than men and a higher percentage of women are currently attending colleges and universities than men. Of the Eastern European countries, Poland and Russia follow the Western European countries in having a higher percentage of women as opposed to men who have graduated from or are currently students in universities. In Romania and Hungary the percentage of men and women in higher education is about the same.

Among the Muslim countries in the Middle East, literacy rates are lower for women than men, but younger women are enrolled in secondary schools at about the same rate as men. Israel follows the pattern of the Western democracies in that a higher percentage of women (55.9 percent) are enrolled in colleges and universities.

The African countries are similar to the Islamic Middle East in their lower literacy rates for women as opposed to men. Only in South Africa are a higher percentage of girls as opposed to boys enrolled in secondary schools.

India compared to China and Japan has lower literacy rates for women as opposed to men and overall lower rates (46 percent for women and 69 percent for men) as opposed to 96 and 99 percent for China and Japan. In China 44 percent of the university students are women.

Marriage and Divorce

Iran stands out as having the youngest minimum age, nine years old, for girls to marry. The countries that follow with the youngest minimum age (twelve) are the United States, Canada, Chile, Colombia, Ireland, Spain, and South Africa. In most countries the minimum ages for women are between sixteen and eighteen. In countries where there are differences between men and women, it is always the women who have the younger minimum age. In China the minimum age for women is twenty and twenty-two for men. In all of the countries, the average age that men marry is higher than that of women by about three years. The oldest average age among the twenty-six countries is Sweden with 33.3 years for men and 31 years for women. The average age for men in the other countries is about twenty-seven years and twenty-four years for women. In some Muslim countries a Muslim woman cannot marry a non-Muslim man but a Muslim man can marry a non-Muslim woman. In Iran only marriage between Muslim men and women are legal.

All countries have restrictions on who may marry on the basis of blood ties. For instance marriage between parent and child or among siblings is illegal in all countries.

Most countries have civil law as the exclusive form of marriage. Other countries, such as Great Britain and Ireland, allow for civil or religious marriage. In Poland, a couple can marry in a religious ceremony, but they must officially register the marriage within a year. In Romania, a religious ceremony may follow the civil ceremony and formal registration of the marriage.

In Iran and Israel, marriage is governed solely by religious law. Egypt applies a combination of both civil and religious law. Civil law may be used exclusively for mixed-religious couples. But, like India, Egypt applies the religious marriage laws for the different religious communities, Hindus, Muslims, Christians, and Parsis.

Polygamous marriages are legal in Kenya, Nigeria, and Ghana, and only for men in Iran, Syria, Egypt, and the Muslim males in India.

The United States has the highest divorce rates in the world: 10.8 percent for women and 8.6 percent for men. As of March 2003, divorce became legal in Chile! In 1996 divorce was legalized in Ireland and in 1992 in Colombia.

No fault divorce is the divorce law in Britain, Ireland, France, Sweden, the United States, Canada, Hungary, Australia, South Africa, and Colombia. Most of these countries require a twelve-month separation period before the divorce is granted. Germany requires three years. British law requires that the couple agree on the division of assets and child custody before the divorce can be granted. A combination of no-fault and fault divorce exists in Russia, Poland, and the Hindu community in India. Fault must be established in Iran, Egypt, Israel, and Japan. This law is more likely to favor the man than the woman. Countries where the fault law treats men and women equally are China, Romania, and the Christian and Parsi communities in India. There are no countries where the fault criteria favor women.

In the Muslim countries, men may divorce without citing any reason. In Egypt in 2000 a divorce law was passed that allows women to obtain a divorce without proof of abuse. In Syria men may have four wives simultaneously, and in Iran, a man may have as many "temporary marriages at the same time as he wishes." In Israel a woman cannot get a divorce without the consent of her husband but a husband does not need his wife's consent to obtain a divorce.

In China and Japan a form of no fault divorce is most common. In India, in the Muslim community men can divorce without citing any grounds.

The traditional practice whereby mothers in the Western World are automatically granted child custody has undergone slight changes. Joint custody is widely used in the United States and Sweden and the children's wishes (if a teenager) are often taken into account. The legal standard of best interest of the child is still applied in most of the world. In the Muslim countries mothers are usually granted custody of their sons until they are between seven and ten years old and of their daughters until they are between nine and twelve years old. After that they are returned to their fathers. In India among the Hindu community, the father is considered the "natural guardian" of his children.

Women have the same rights as men in owning, inheriting, and passing on property in their own names in the United States, Canada, Australia, Colombia, Britain, Ireland, France, Sweden, Germany, Russia, Poland, Hungary, Romania, Israel, South Africa, Japan, and China and in the Hindu, Christian, and Parsi communities in India. In Egypt, married women have the right to inherit and pass on property. But men receive twice the inheritance of women. In India, Muslim wives and daughters are permitted half the inheritance of male heirs. In Iran, Kenya, and Chile the property rights of women are almost non-existent. Married women in Iran must have their husband's written consent to work outside the home and to leave the country. Husbands in Kenya hold rights over their wives' inheritance and their productive and reproductive capacities. Wives in Chile require their husband's permission to engage in any type of contract.

Abortion, Contraceptives, Health Care

In the United States, Canada, Australia, and the Western European countries (except for the United Kingdom and Ireland), Poland, Russia, South Africa, China, and India, abortions are available upon request. In Chile there are no grounds for legal abortions. In Ireland, abortions are legal only to save the life of the mother. In all of the other countries, additional grounds for which abortions are legal are to preserve the physical and mental health of the mother, if the pregnancy was the result of rape or incest, if there are fetal impairments, or for economic or social reasons.

Concerning the extent to which contraceptives are used, except for Ghana, Nigeria, and Kenya, well over 50 percent of married women use contraceptives, in all of the European countries (Eastern and Western). In Canada, the United States, and Australia, the percentage is in the 70s.

France is ranked first among 191 countries examined in 2000 as providing the best health care to its citizens. Poland has universal health insurance but is one of the lowest spending nations on health care. Of the other twenty-six countries included in this study only Chile's health care is completely privatized. In Russia, Romania, Israel, India, and Australia the health care system is universal to all citizens from birth. In the United Kingdom as of 1948 health care for all citizens is based on need, not on the ability to pay. About 10 percent use private health insurance.

Women in the Military

Of the twenty-six countries included in this study in only two, Israel and China, are women required to serve in the military. In Israel when women reach the age of eighteen they serve for two years. Women who are married or religiously observant are exempt. About 55 percent of Israeli women serve in the military compared to 95 percent of men. In China all citizens between eighteen and twenty-two are obligated to serve in the armed forces. In all of the other countries, they may volunteer; usually when they reach the age of seventeen or eighteen. Only in Canada and France may they, and have they served in combat units, i.e. infantry, artillery, field engineering and as fighter pilots. In most of the countries, women make up less than ten percent of the military. In the United States 15 percent of the active duty troops are women.

Women in Public Life

In four of the twenty-six countries included in this study women have been elected as heads of state. In 1966 Indira Gandhi was elected Prime Minister of India and remained in office for five years. She was assassinated in 1984. In 1969 Golden Meir was elected Prime Minister of Israel and remained in office until 1974. Margaret Thatcher was elected Prime Minister of the United Kingdom in 1979 and resigned from office in 1990. In 1990 Mary Robinson was elected President of Ireland, and in 1997 May McAlesse was elected President. As of 2002 Sweden has the greatest number of women in the Parliament. Forty-five percent of the seats of the Swedish parliament are held by women. Women have gained the right to vote in all of the countries included in this study.

Based on this comprehensive examination of women's statuses the world over, we have seen that they have come a long way in their right to control their reproductive functions through abortion and contraceptives, toward gaining first class citizenship in their active and extensive participation in the work force, in their years of schooling, in their eligibility to serve in their country's armed forces, and in their right to represent their country as President and Prime Minister.

Do women still have a ways to go to gaining full equality with men? In many countries the answer is an unequivocal yes.

Index

About the Authors

Stephanie Hepburn is a graduate of the Washington College of Law at American University. She is a recipient of an Equal Justice America fellowship and the winner of two Columbia Scholastic Press Association (CSPA) Gold Circle Awards.

Rita J. Simon is a University Professor in the School of Public Affairs and the Washington College of Law at American University. She is the author and editor of numerous books, including *Global Perspectives on Social Issues: Juvenile Justice Systems* (with Paola Zalkind, Lexington Books, 2004), and *Adoption across Borders* (with Howard Altstein, Rowman & Littlefield, 2000).